Fear to Freedom

Stories of Triumph After Leaving a High Control Religion

JACK GREY
AND
16 AUTHORS

www.feartofreedom.ca

Tellwell Talent
www.tellwell.ca

ISBN
978-0-2288-2566-1 (Hardcover)
978-0-2288-2565-4 (Paperback)
978-0-2288-2567-8 (eBook)

Dedication

I would like to dedicate this book to my mother who, although remained as a Jehovah's Witness, gave me unconditional love. Her dedication to her children always was the best example of unconditional love I've ever seen.

Acknowledgements

I want to acknowledge my wife, who shows me a lot of patience in order for me to be able to help others many times at the expanse of precious family time.

I would like to acknowledge Rodney Allgood for the incredible vision he created by providing support to ex-Jehovah's Witnesses who want to move forward in life. I want to thank Tamara Larisa Tyrbouslu who helped Rodney create this vision by supporting him every step of the way.

Table of Contents

Foreword

Courage. That is the word that I would use to describe the people who find the strength to walk away from everything and everyone that they know to create a life that is an authentic one. This is exactly what people who leave high-control religions must do if they desire to leave the religion. They must walk away from family, they must walk away from friendships that have lasted since childhood and, lastly, they must walk away from the very identity that they have carried most, if not all, of their lives.

They face shunning, ridicule and a cutting off from anything having to do with their previous life as a member. Life as an ex-member is a challenging one as they were not prepared for the real world. For the most part, they were only trained how to be a good follower of religious rules. As an example, Jehovah's Witnesses typically were discouraged from higher education, and they were kept from the social activities that others participate in growing up. They lived a life that called for limited association with non-members. Hence, once they leave the religion, they have a terribly difficult time fitting in with the rest of society.

Many people feel like an absolute misfit, neither here nor there, after leaving the religion—but not the people in this book. In this book, you will find story after story of victory, triumph and courage. You will read authentic stories from the people who actually lived it. Today they do not merely survive, they thrive. They made it to the other side, and they re-invented themselves. This is more challenging than it would appear as Jehovah's Witnesses or Mormons are not encouraged to think for themselves but are accustomed to following the guidelines of the religion.

The beauty of this book is that the contributors are sharing real life experiences firsthand. This is not researched information. It's the real deal—their stories. With each story, you will come to admire just how strong these people are. You will also come to see the lengths that people will go through to create a truly authentic life. Whether you were once a part of a controlling religion or not, you will come away inspired to overcome whatever you may be going through at the moment. There is no rewind button to life. We cannot change the past, but what we can do is to live with courage from this point forward. As you will see from the 19 stories in this book, with courage, persistence and determination, we can all create the lives that we ultimately desire and deserve!

Rodney Allgood ~ International Speaker/Performance Coach

Introduction

There is one question that everyone who wants to leave a religion, marriage, institution, country or even place of employment must answer for themselves. Am I going to be better off? We all have to face these decisions in one moment or another. Ending a marriage can be very nerve-racking. Immigrating to another country is definitely a life-changing decision. Quitting a job, not knowing when we will find a new one, can be extremely stressful.

How about leaving a religion? Millions of people leave their churches with very little or no consequences to themselves. Others face major criticism, ostracism, shunning, broken families or in some extreme cases even death. Unfortunately, it is very difficult to recognize a high-control organization mainly because people do not know what to look for. One of the biggest signs of a high-control religion is what happens to a person who wishes to quit.

Unfortunately, many people have to deal with a very cruel reality when they realize that leaving religion means losing everyone they ever loved. They are facing a very unfair dilemma: stay in the organization with all family and friends, pretending they are still believers, or walk away, knowing everyone who remains in the institution will never acknowledge their existence. Many who left or got removed end up losing everything and everyone they ever cared for, and as a result they became very angry and bitter.

To make things worse, a majority of people leaving such institutions have enormous amounts of fear of the outside world that was programmed into their minds. Remaining inside the organization meant being safe with God's blessing and hope for everlasting life. Yes, it meant life without death. Leaving meant joining Satan and becoming part of the wicked world ruled by demons that will eventually lead to destruction.

Can life be better without the religion? How can someone overcome the enormous obstacles of being afraid of everything and everyone? Can they be happy? Successful? Can they have a meaningful life with purpose and happiness? These stories answer these questions. This book includes stories of ex-Jehovah's Witnesses, ex-Mormons and one Muslim. They are not super-humans, but rather normal people who experienced lots of fear but found a way to break free from it. As a result, they live a life on their terms. Does that mean they are completely fearless now? Not at all. These stories are not about people without fear, but rather each one describes how they felt fear but did what was right regardless of the fear. That's what courage is all about.

This book includes the story of Eric Wilson from Canada, who was serving in Columbia as a Jehovah's Witness elder for many years. Despite old age, he decided to walk away from the organization, not knowing if he would ever be able to rebuild any type of social network. Dealing with his wife's death and shunning from religion were not easy tasks, but if you ask Eric today, he will tell you that he is happier today than ever before. Why? Read his story to find out the answer.

The story of Terina Maldonado will help you understand how simple things in life can be terrifying for others. As an ex-Mormon, she was shaking at the idea of drinking tea, coffee or alcohol. Showing her shoulders uncovered in a public place would create anxiety as she would have to face some very uncomfortable questions if another Mormon would see her. How did she go from being so afraid to a woman teaching others how to thrive after leaving The Church of Jesus Christ of Latter Day Saints? She will explain in her chapter.

Nesly Brule puts our problems in a totally different perspective. Growing up in Turkey she witnessed stories of refugees who due to war lost their families, homes and everything they knew as normal life. She shares stories of a woman who due to wrong belief accidently killed her 5 children trying to save them. Another woman after losing her children and husband due to bombing she delivered a dead baby that she had to bury herself. Her chapter will put our problems into a different category.

All the stories, although different, have one thing in common. Every single person who paid the price for their freedom will say this: it was worth it.

What was worth it? What can be more precious than living with your family in unity and having hope of everlasting life in paradise and soon be welcoming dead loved ones during a resurrection?

I hope this book will provide you with the answers you are looking for.

About the Authors

Jack Grey
Speaker, Award Winning Author,
Life and Business Coach.

Jack was born in religiously divided household. His father was a Catholic and his mother a Jehovah's Witness. He followed his mother's faith for 36 years. In 2013 he started questioning his faith which lead to his exit few years later. Due to large family being Jehovah's Witnesses and his position as an elder it was extremely difficult to leave. Today he is a proud father of two daughters and a happy husband. He owns businesses and real-estate at the same time teaches people how to become financially free. However, he found passion in helping ex Jehovah's Witnesses rebuilding their life after they exit. If you wish to contact him please write to empoweredmindstm@gmail.com

Cyndi Markey
Mother, Grandmother, Author, Speaker,
Corporate Real Estate Professional

Cyndi was raised a Jehovah's Witness from the age of 2. At age 20, disassociated from the Organization. Even though life proved challenging as a single mother of two small children, Cyndi was able to

successfully deal with that challenge, as well as finding a way to carve out a successful secular career. Currently working as a Corporate Real Estate Professional managing a 2 million sq. ft. Iconic financial property in Chicago for a global real estate management firm, she has also found a real passion for helping others, especially former Jehovah's Witnesses navigate their own transition successfully. Cyndi currently lives in the fabulous "Windy City", Chicago, IL.

Alex Chenarides
Author, Speaker, Self-made survivor

Alex Chenarides rose through the ranks of Jehovah's witnesses at an early age and was able to wake up and break free from the group in his mid 20's. Since then his story has been one of complete self-exploration followed by a well thought out and introspective journey into healing based on proven science and great personal effort. He has been able to heal not only from the anxiety and depression brought about from his childhood but also from his membership in the high-control group. In his chapter he shares his success story as well as the specific steps he took to gain access to his true, authentic self. Spoiler alert: it's a happy ending! If you wish to contact him please write to alexchenarides@gmail.com

Abigail Ramos
Head of Marketing – Student

Abigail was born and raised as a Jehovah's Witness and grew up as one for nearly 30 years until she was disfellowshipped. Prior to returning to the religious group, she woke up, decided to never go back and has returned to school while she works professionally as the head of marketing. She enjoys traveling with her husband and living life on her terms.

Shane Hubening
Father of three, Entrepreneur, Firefighter

Shane Hubenig is a former Jehovah's Witness. He is an entrepreneur and a firefighter. He is married and raising three strong boys to think for themselves and to freely grow to be what they want to be.

Connie Hamilton
Wife, Mother, Grandma & Entrepreneur

Connie grew up as a Jehovah's Witness in a small town in British Columbia, Canada. After years of trying to live as a perfect Jehovah's Witness she turned to sex and drugs as a way to be accepted by others around her. With the help of a great man who became her husband she was able to break those habits.
Connie has been married for over 30 years, is a mother of 2 and grandmother. Connie runs a home daycare in Lethbridge Alberta, Canada. She also makes homemade perogies which she has turned into a business called Perfectly Imperfect Perogies. She enjoys spending her free time with family, reading and traveling. Connie is planning on writing her full memoirs and was thrilled to be a part of this book to share a small glimpse of her past experiences. If you would like to follow Connie you can find her on Facebook, twitter and Instagram. If you would like to contact Connie you can email her at perfectlyimperfectbook@gmail.com

Monika Niezgoda
Explorer, Traveler, Spiritual Artist

Monika was born in Poland and emigrated with her mother and brother to Canada through Germany in 1990, where she got involved in the cult of The Watchtower as a teenager. For almost three decades she was heavily involved in it, spending over fifteen years in full-time service in various aspects of the organization. Around 2016 she started to discover the true identity of the organization and not long after left. She never felt the need to announce her exit in any way. In 2017 Monika graduated with Honors from Humber College in Toronto, Canada and is now a professional language interpreter. She is planning to publish collection of her poetry and organize an art exhibition of her and her father's paintings. Monika loves to make everyone around her laugh and feel happiness. She makes occasional funny videos on YouTube, you are welcome to find her there. She is dedicating this chapter and a future full length story of her life and adventures, to her loving parents and her brother Dominik.

Gary Alt
Financial Advisor, Musician,
Songwriter, and Author

Gary was a Jehovah's Witness for just over forty years, finally leaving the religion in early 2016. He served at JW Brooklyn Headquarters in the 1980s, and also served as a congregation elder during the 1980s and 1990s. He is a prolific songwriter, musician, and indie recording artist. Gary has also written two books, *Force of Will* and *Song of Gil*, as well as short stories, based on his JW-related experiences. He currently resides in the Poconos of Pennsylvania, USA.

Eric Wilson
Meleti Vivlon - Beroean Pickets
YouTube Channel

Eric AKA Meleti Vivlon was born in 1949 and raised as one of Jehovah's Witnesses. He served for a time as a regular and special pioneer, was appointed as an elder at 24, and served as one until 2012 when he was removed for affirming that he would obey God over the Governing Body. In his youth, Eric served in Colombia for 7 years where he became fluent in Spanish. He and his late wife, Reta, served in Spanish congregations in Canada from 1976 to 1990 and then preached in Ecuador for two more years, before returning to Canada where he switched to English congregations. He now publishes articles (beroeans.net) and YouTube videos (Beroean Pickets Channel) to help Jehovah's Witnesses understand the unscriptural nature of most of their teachings.

Sarah Lund
Artist, mother of three

Sarah was raised a Jehovah's Witness and remained one for 37 years until she woke up to discover a whole new world. She has since been discovering all the beauty that surrounds her. For most of her life she lived for what others might think. When she broke away from the mind control of Watchtower, she began discovering her many passions. She loves camping, hiking, climbing mountains, philosophy, non-fiction and documentaries. Sarah's love for painting has been her main source of therapy and expression. Her other passions include self healing, through meditation, music and art. She is a free spirit, open for new adventures and is absolutely in love with life. Her life experiences have made her the strong, passionate and grateful person that she is today.

Kimberly Sherry

Int'l Energy Healer, Money Energy Expert, #1 Best Selling Author, Inspirational Speaker and Frequency Alchemist.

Kimberly was born and raised as a Jehovah's Witness. Kimberly left at 38 when she became suicidal, ran a support group for former members for nine years, deprogrammed through weekly education and practice at Aesclepion Intuitive Training in San Rafael, CA for twelve years, healed with plant medicines while working with shamans in Peru, and after twenty-five ayahuasca journeys broke Dr. David Hawkins' scale of human consciousness to create a new scale that goes to infinity.

Kimberly outlines her new Infinity Scale and the Infinity System in her book, Access YOUR Ultimate Power: The Blueprint to Infinite Intelligence. The system outlines what infinite possibilities are available when you access hidden powers to heal yourself mentally, emotionally, and spiritually.

Today, Kimberly travels the world working remotely with clients wherever there is Wifi. She continues to educate and empower others through group programs, one-to-one sessions, live events, and retreats while continuing to write.

Bess Kristie
Professional Photographer

Bess is a Professional Photographer living in South Carolina where she was born and raised. She studied Photography at Greenville Technical College, Maine Media Workshop and Santa Fe Photographic Workshop. She currently works for Magnolia-Studios.com.

Libby Pease
HBA ACC - Author, Speaker, Certified Life Coach

Libby is an Internationally Certified Life Coach, Trauma Recovery Coach, Author and crisis response expert. She brings many skills to the table including 20 years of experience helping people in crisis, training & facilitation skills, coaching and her natural clairvoyant gifts. She specializes in cult recovery through her practice at Listening Tree Studio & Coaching and supports her clients to create a meaningful life. She was a Jehovah's Witness for 10 years and is now dedicated to helping others with their recovery. Libby is very connected to nature and is an avid gardener, enjoys fiber arts and is a stained glass artisan.

www.clairvoyantcoach.ca
libby@listeningtreestudio.ca

Meandy Bishop
Health, Wellness, Life Coach and Bloggers

Meandy Bishop grew up as a Jehovah's Witness. Devoted for many years, and left at age 42. The years spent within the religion required a total change in mindset. Because of how she was able to overcome, and push through, she is now a motivational speaker, guiding others to overcome similar things. She is a health and life coach, and together with her husband, they are now business owners, bloggers and podcasters. Teaching others to create solid and lasting change in their life. Check out more information about them at KoolKatHealth.com

Rose Smith
Certified Grief Coach, Life Coach, Author, Speaker

Rose was raised as a Jehovah's Witness. She shares her healing journey of transformation and self-discovery after leaving the highly controlled religion. She is passionate about sharing her journey in the hopes of helping others break chains that have kept them stuck. She journeys alongside her clients in the healing process and helps in creating a roadmap to start over. Her message is one of compassion, unconditional love and forgiveness. Befreewithrose.com

Terina Maldonado
Public Speaker, Author

Terina has left behind a life of Mormonism and the shame that accompanied it and is loving her new life of freedom and joy. She loves to share her story through public speaking, knowing as we share our stories we heal together. She also loves writing and plans for this to be the first of her published works as an author, watch for a memoir in the future. Terina's greatest joy is found in her family with her husband and three children. If you wish to contact Terina please email terina@terinamaldonado.com. www.terinamaldonado.com

Nesly Ann Brule
Lawyer – Entrepreneur

I was born in Diyarbakir, a city in southeast of Turkey. I had my law degree in Istanbul, Human Rights Law in Salzburg /Austria and International Criminal Law in Norwich/ UK. I started my career in our family business in hospitality industry and restaurant management. Due to the content of our company and my infinitive desire of cooking I went to Paris to study at Le Cordon Bleu, the oldest culinary arts and cuisine school in the world. I did not recognize how my life was great until I started to work as a human rights lawyer, mostly voluntarily to support children and women. Great experience! It was a revolution for my transformation. I stopped to complain and suffer from small things because I discovered what the other people's life with real challenges.

I want to share some of those people's stories who made me feel very lucky and grateful.

Chapter 1

What's Better Out There?

How loss of identity became the biggest gain of freedom

by Jack Grey

"The strongest force in human psychology is to stay consistent with how we define ourselves."
~Tony Robbins

I locked the front door and checked it twice. I went downstairs to my basement and I locked the door to my office and covered all the windows. My heart was pounding as sweat covered my body. I looked at my hand and it was shaking uncontrollably. Fear was controlling me, and I didn't know how to calm myself down. Why? Most people might think that someone was going to attack me or break into my house. Was I doing something illegal? Did the fear of being caught kick in? No, not at all. I was planning to read a book.

What? Read a book? How can anyone be that afraid to read a book? That sounds insane. Yes, it does. It definitely is insane. I just didn't know that yet. What could possibly drive a grown man with a wife, children, multiple businesses, many real-estate properties, a man who has travelled the world and goes rock or ice climbing for fun to be afraid of reading a book? Allow me to explain.

Persecution Builds Faith

I grew up in a religiously divided household. My mother was a Jehovah's Witness (JW) and my father was a Catholic. Growing up in that environment, I only knew those two religions, and to be honest, following my mother's footsteps felt like the right choice. What I saw in the Catholic Church in comparison with what I experienced in the Kingdom Hall led me to become a Jehovah's Witness. I honestly have to say I never regretted my decision.

Why? Mostly because it taught me how to stand up for my beliefs even if my friends and family disagreed with me. My father tolerated us going to the meetings but he couldn't stand us going door to door preaching. His strong opposition did not push us away from the religion. The opposite took place—it strengthened it. My mother couldn't take my father's abuse so she left when I was nine years old. She immigrated to Canada, hoping one day she would be able to bring her children there. Before that was possible, I was growing up under the supervision of my three older sisters.

All four of us grew very close together. At home, it was us versus my father. We knew that we had to stay strong and stay united in order to keep our faith. So, we did. Right before my mother left, she sat down with all her children.

"Break it," my mother said, after giving us each one match.

We all did. Then she gave us four matches.

"Break those now," she said.

This time it was much harder to do so.

"Do you feel the difference?" she asked.

"Yes, of course," we all replied.

"If you stand alone, your father will break your faith one by one," she said. "If you stand together, you have a chance to keep it."

As most siblings, we were arguing and fighting, but that day it all stopped. We had a common enemy to fight against, and he was not going anywhere. He was in our home. That fight against my own father lasted for many years, and as a result I was living in fear every single day. We had to hide our religious books; all studying was done in secrecy. We would pretend to go to our friends and sneak out to go preaching instead. Because I lived in a small town, most people knew each other, so often neighbors or family would tell my father about our preaching work.

Every single day when we heard his footsteps coming home from work and throwing his keys down, we waited in fear. If he said nothing in the first 30 seconds, we were fine. If he found out about us being in service, there was no end to yelling. We all practiced how to lie to him in case he would ask what we did today, making sure our stories lined up. This anxiety was happening every single day.

We knew this persecution was clearly Satan's attack on God's people. Our faith became so strong that all four of us became leading examples in our congregation. My three sisters became pioneers, which means they were doing 90 hours of preaching work per month. One of them served in Bethel (the headquarters of Jehovah's Witnesses) for many years. I became an elder, fully believing that I was in "The Truth." Religion was not part of my life—it was all my life.

I had many Jehovah's Witnesses friends who were leading double lives. Not me. I believed that Jehovah was watching me all the time. I could lie to my earthly father but not the heavenly one, I told myself. Therefore, before I made any decision in life, I always thought, "What would Jehovah say if he saw me doing this?"

Decisions: Were They Made for Me?

At one point I wanted to get baptized. My oldest sister who was studying with me at that time, said, "No, you are not ready."

I accepted her opinion as a fact and postponed my dedication. Every convention I would ask if I could get baptized, and she kept telling me the same thing.

One day I walked into her room and I said, "I'm getting baptized and neither you, or our father or anyone else will stop me."

She smiled and said, "Now you are ready."

"What?" I replied. "Nothing changed. Why are you OK with me now getting baptized and before you weren't?"

"If I was able to change your mind with one sentence, then you were not ready. Were you?"

"I guess not," I replied.

It was my decision and I did have a choice. Some may say that it was indoctrination, peer pressure, need for acceptance or all of it. Yet in my case, I take full ownership of that decision. I just had one more thing to do: tell my father that I would no longer go to church with him. I wasn't going to worship there.

My father had a photography business, and I was taking pictures at weddings and First Communions. After discussing this matter with my elders, I was told that in order to get baptized I had to quit helping my dad. So, I did. My father was furious. There was a war at home for a very long time. He stopped bringing food home, and if we asked for it, he would say: "Not on bread alone man must live. No work, no money, no food." I had to go to my grandmother's place each day to eat, and we had milk from neighbors, plus vegetables we grew in our land. That's how I survived. But all this was not the worst part.

After about a month of yelling and arguing, my father eventually stopped talking to me. This was the first time I experienced shunning. It was worse than getting a beating or being yelled at. I felt completely worthless. I remember destroying my neighbor's garden just so I would get in trouble, hoping to get punished, but my father simply stopped caring. My family was destroyed because I believed everything was for the glory of God's name. I had to obey Jehovah and his organization.

There was not any black-and-white rule written anywhere that would prohibit me from working for my dad. After all, going to church to take photographs is not considered a sin. As a matter of fact, many issues of *The Watchtower* (the magazine printed by Jehovah's Witnesses) have photographs of churches inside and outside. Why was I told to quit working for my father at the age of 15? It's all based on the rule "what will people say?" This one question is more powerful than the Bible or God himself. What would people say if they saw me entering church on Sunday morning while all Jehovah's Witnesses are entering Kingdom Hall? Based on that reasoning, the decision was made for me. I had to quit helping my dad or they would not allow me to get baptized.

I remember being very confused because I was told that baptism is a personal decision and nobody else's. All of a sudden, one day before my baptism, the elders gave me the ultimatum. "If you want to get baptized, you have to tell your father to find someone else to work for him." Obeying Jehovah's directions was of utmost importance, so I obeyed. It wasn't easy, but I stood up for what I believed in and felt proud of it.

Canada: First Step Towards Freedom

After seven very long years, my mother managed to get me into Canada. I felt free. I had no more fear of going to meetings, of preaching or of having bible studies. The fridge was always full, and my mother would cook every day. I was in heaven. It's true we had nothing. My mother's second marriage had just fallen apart, and we ended up in a small studio apartment with no furniture or money to buy anything. We slept on the floor and kept looking for any decent furniture we could find in a dumpster. After school I would deliver flyers or sell flowers on the street. Some days were so cold I built myself an igloo out of snow in order to make it through the day. I didn't care. I was happy because my father was not around anymore. I felt free, and when you feel free to be yourself, you are happy.

I fell in love with Canada almost immediately after arriving. There was abundance everywhere and beautiful houses with no fences around them. People would leave their cars on the street overnight. Nobody was scared to walk on the street when it was dark. Roads were wide and nicely paved. But what was most shocking were the kind people. They were free to be themselves. I saw gay people for the first time. They even held a pride parade every year. People from all over the world with different cultures, religions and skin color were all living in the same city without killing each other. That was shocking to me but in a good way.

Immigration is not easy. You have to change absolutely everything in your life—a new language, culture, friends, family and much more. Every immigrant goes through the process of adaptation. Immigrants make foolish mistakes; they get embarrassed a lot, but they know that eventually they will learn. Immigration means you do whatever it takes. It's not a short visit, it's a life-changing decision. It was for me and I'm happy I made it.

Desire to Fit in.

When I went to visit Niagara Falls, I saw a replica of the tallest man that ever lived. I learned about his life and saw that this poor man had a very hard life. All his clothes and shoes had to be specially made for him. He couldn't fit into cars and many chairs. I concluded that the best life you can have is a life of an average guy. Truthfully, I felt that was the key to happiness. All those who were in my school class outside the circle of average had a miserable life. If you were too "something," chances are you were picked on and bullied. If you were too fat, too short, too slow, too ugly or too good looking, or too dumb or even too smart you would get picked on. Bullies loved those kids that were not average so they could make fun of them for whatever was different about them. Therefore, I concluded that in order to be happy, you had to be average.

With this belief, I became a people pleaser. The indoctrination from religion was perfectly aligned with my logic at that time—just do what you are told and people will like you. It worked very well. I very quickly became whatever my peers or elders expected of me. Now I had many friends who were Jehovah's Witnesses plus I had freedom to practice my religion. Because I was so far away from my father, everything was working great.

I married a beautiful Jehovah's Witness girl and we started a family. I wanted to help out in the congregation, so I reached out for privileges and with time I became an elder. Life was great. Really, it was. I was very happy with my congregation. We had a prosperous business, a large family living close by, many friends in the congregation, parties, trips, respect from others, great children and a beautiful house. People envied us in the congregation. Life was great until one day when everything changed.

Returning Fear

In 2013 the Governing Body of Jehovah's Witnesses changed one of the main doctrines. It had been changed more than once before, but I was too young to see the significance of it. One of the main beliefs is the desire to see this world being destroyed at Armageddon and transformed into paradise. Based on Jesus's "prophesy," people alive in the year 1914 would see the end of the world. Unfortunately, that did not happen and all those people are dead now, so the Governing Body had to come up with a new explanation. The new doctrine is so complex and illogical that I don't want to even try to explain it here.

Thanks to this one change, I had to adopt a new belief that shifted everything. Until now, I believed that those who take the lead in the religion know more than me. Now I realized that might not be true.

I didn't have time to read one *Watchtower* from cover to cover much less checking the authenticity of those writings. We all put trust in the Governing Body, hoping they did the best research available and are giving us the truth.

When I read the new "understanding," as they call it, of what a generation means, I realized that maybe the Governing Body simply have no idea what's truly going on and are simply trying to come up with anything that would keep people believing the end of the world is "just around the corner." How can a generation last over 120 years? I read all scriptures in the Bible that contained the word generation. I realized that I didn't have to be a genius in order to see that what they wrote is simply illogical and contradicts scriptures in the Bible.

I started asking questions and couldn't find anything that would help me. After all, this was a new belief and only one article in *The Watchtower* explained it. So, I turned to the internet for help. I knew that if I had a question, chances are someone else in the world already had the same question. I wanted to see if the answer they got was anything better than what I had so far.

Wow. All of a sudden, I was face to face with ex-Jehovah's Witnesses, also called apostates. Apostates are the worst because they are working in opposition to Jehovah's Witnesses. Spending time with them and listening to their reasoning was portrayed as "eating from the table of demons." I let them in my home via the internet. In my mind, I believed it was a great sin against God. This was nerve racking. I didn't want to look at apostate websites because I strongly believed it was all Satan's tool to get the weak ones out. I turned to YouTube and came across very bitter and angry people at ex-Jehovah's Witnesses. That pushed me away. That's not what I was looking for.

My doubts would not leave me alone. How could I go on the platform as an elder and teach something I didn't believe was true? How could I go door to door and tell people this was the only true religion, knowing something was off? I got hungry—not for food, but for meaning.

I started connecting the dots backward of all the things that didn't make sense to me, but I simply put them aside because obedience was more important. One of my sisters told me that her ex-boyfriend left Jehovah's Witnesses because he read a book written by a Governing Body member. I realized that if anyone could possibly shed some light on what's going on behind the closed doors of the Governing Body, it was him. So, I decided to read his book. I was way too scared to actually buy a physical copy, so I looked for it online.

Turning Point

There it was—*Crisis of Conscience* by Raymond Franz—right in front of me and I was just a click away from downloading it. I was terrified. Reading apostate material is considered one of the worst sins you can do in the eyes of Jehovah's Witnesses. I was still a strong believer, but I just needed to know some answers.

I kept staring at the screen and hiding in my basement, afraid of my own wife. What if she finds out what I was reading? I had to have an excuse, some sort of justification, or I wouldn't be able to sleep. I found one and a good one too. I told myself that I needed to read this book in order to protect the congregation. After all, if people are leaving after reading this book, I had to learn what traps Satan uses in order to defend my faith. This was perfect justification that allowed me to click on the mouse and download the book.

I started reading and I kept on reading, then I read some more. I just couldn't put it down. I was reading it at night from my phone under the covers so my wife would not see me. I was reading it in my car parked a few blocks away from home. I wouldn't go to work—I was just reading page after page. I kept reading it during meetings in the Kingdom Hall including in elders' meetings. I just couldn't put it down.

When I started reading it, I believed Jehovah's Witnesses had about 95% of the truth and in 5% there was room for "new light," which will be explained later. Every chapter of Raymond Franz's book opened my mind more and more. I was 95% convinced that I was in The Truth on the first page, then it dropped to 80%, then to 60%, and as I was about halfway through the book, I was approaching the 50% mark of my conviction. I knew that if I keep on reading, eventually the scale would tip over and I would not be able to go back to my former beliefs. You can always learn new things, but you can't unlearn what you already know. When I finished reading *Crisis of Conscience,* I realized that everything I believed and fought for was one big myth. Now I experienced a crisis of conscience myself. The question was "what should I do now?"

Religious Trauma Syndrome and Emotional Breakdown

I couldn't think. I couldn't sleep. I couldn't get out of bed. I already knew that everything was wrong. Not one or two things, everything. My mind collapsed. I was unable to make simple decisions, unable to hold a conversation or even think straight. If I could compare my mind to a house, then imagine all foundations and structures collapsing all at once. I didn't know what was right or what was wrong, what was good or what was bad, what the future holds, where we come from, where we are going, who we are, or even who I was? There was no end of questions in my head. I had a handful of questions before my research, and I had a mountain of them afterwards.

I lost all my joy. Depression stepped in, combined with anxiety, panic attacks and nightmares. I was scared of everything and everyone. What if people asked me questions? What would I answer? What if I must give a talk and I would not be able to deliver it to the congregation? What if someone in service of going door to door asked me questions, I would not be able to answer? What about my family? Should I keep my mouth shut? Should I say something? I drove myself to insanity. I couldn't find a way out of this, no matter which way I turned. I tried talking to my wife but that did not go very well. We were both very emotional about the subject, and our conversations would end up in pointless arguments.

All of a sudden, I realized I was becoming just like my father. The man I feared and hated so much all of a sudden appeared in the mirror. Is it possible that I was going to have a religiously divided household? I knew if I opposed my wife and kids, they would hate me and turn against me. Eventually, they will lie to me and start living separate lives. It would become them versus me, a scenario very familiar to me. Would my marriage survive this? I didn't know but I had to try at least wake up my wife. My kids were still very young (five and seven years old) so I knew that if I could convince my wife, within a year or two our children would follow. But if they got into their teenaged years and got baptized, things would be much harder.

I tried and this is what my wife said: "I followed you on many of your decisions even when my opinion was different than yours, but this? This—you are on your own. I cannot stop you from reading and doing your research but don't expect me to do the same. And don't you dare say anything to our kids. You are going to mess them up. I married a Jehovah's Witness hoping we will have our children also be Witnesses. I'm telling you the kids will grow fast, they will get baptized and when they leave this house, you will never see them again. If that's what you want, then go ahead and keep going on your path, but don't be surprised if you are alone on it. If you don't stop, you will destroy this family."

I was truly stuck. She was right. I knew the consequences of me being disfellowshipped. It meant being shunned by all Jehovah's Witnesses for life, including my children the moment they move out of home. It would destroy the family bonds. Not only that, but we were surrounded by Witnesses. We had employees, tenants, a bookkeeper and a cleaning lady, and all our close friends and family were Witnesses. So, I kept looking for answers and I got nothing. I also knew I could no longer live like this. My mind was in such a poor state that I started thinking about suicide. We had enough money for my wife to life comfortably without working, plus she would collect $1,000,000 from life insurance if I could make it look like an accident. Everything went through my head. I just needed a way out, and death seemed like a solution.

Coming Out of Despair

A few beliefs kept me going:

> 1. *"If you are going through hell, keep on walking, eventually you will walk out."*
> ~Tony Robbins

I knew that life, just like every year, has seasons and there would be a turning point in my life when things would change. Even if I couldn't see it now, eventually everything changes.

> 2. *"Everything happens for a reason and it's here to serve us."*
> ~Unknown

I had no idea how my experience could possibly serve me in any way. The only thing I could think of is that if I ever found a way out of this mess, I would help others to come out as well.

I gave myself and my wife two years. I said that I would continue going to the meetings and door to door ministry. While doing that, I would try to open her eyes. If after two years she still remained a Witness, I would make a decision whether I would continue or stop all together and deal with the consequences. I also realized that my chances of waking up my sisters were very slim to none. They were very zealous and married to elders who were very dedicated to the religion. But they are separate families. They were not my responsibility when it comes to shaping their minds. However, my kids are. It was up to me to tell my children the truth, but how when my wife would teach them the opposite?

I realized that my wife was my priority. She was my number one and our kids came second. So, I went out looking for ex-Jehovah's Witnesses who had similar experiences that could help me wake up my wife. I couldn't find one. On the contrary, I met a lot of people whose marriage fell apart because one woke up and the other didn't. I asked them, "If you went back in time, what would you do differently in order to save your marriage?"

Without exception, all told me the same thing: "I wouldn't push."

Thus, I tried to go as slowly as I could. First, I had to deal with something called backfire effect, which happens when you challenge people's beliefs they hold as true and holy. Not only would the person not accept logical explanations, but they will attack all your flaws in order to prove that you cannot possibly be right. My wife concluded that we were in this mess because we didn't study enough. We needed to read more *Watchtowers* and prepare for the meetings. I did not oppose. I prepared with her for the meetings, and at the same time it gave me an opportunity to help her see many differences between what the Bible says and how *The Watchtowers* interpret things. Slowly but surely, her eyes began to open. We started reading things together, and when she read one chapter from Raymond Franz's book about blood, she was shocked and from that day she was no longer afraid to do research on her own. Even though her eyes opened, the fight was far from over.

I resigned from being an elder and slowly faded away. I gave up going to service and meetings. I went to my last memorial of Jesus's death; the only holiday Witnesses have and by far the most important day in a year for them. I was glad I went because it gave me closure. It was my dream to give a talk at the memorial. It was considered the greatest honor for an elder. When I was listening to it, I smiled, realizing how limited their minds were and how I couldn't possibly fit into their mindset ever again.

Where are We Going to Go?

"Fine, I do see some doctrines are wrong," my wife said. "But think about it, where are we going to go? Do you think you will find another religion that has everything right? Do you seriously think you will find another church that does not have problem with doctrines, pedophile cases, horrible history and unloving people? Nothing is perfect in this world. We have a good life, a great family, an awesome congregation with many friends and a well-running business. If you decide to change this, then you better show me something better. If you don't have anything better than what we have now, then why destroy it? What we are going to replace it with? Where can we go that we would have a better life? If you don't show me a better alternative, then I'm not going anywhere."

Great! My wife woke up, but she didn't want to give it up. She wanted us to remain PIMOs (Physically In Mentally Out). She had a very valid point. I had nothing better to offer. If we lost all our friends, family and business, we would suffer and there was nothing I could see worth switching for.

I went on a quest. I wanted to know what was better than being a happy Witness in a good congregation with great loving family. What did I find? A whole bunch of angry and bitter people who, after decades of being outside the religion, are still stuck criticizing it every single day. How could I possibly tell my wife this kind of life was better?

I asked a different question in order to get a different answer. After listening to many stories of how *Watchtowers* and their shunning policy turned their life into a living misery, I asked, "If you feel your life is ruined by being disfellowshipped, why don't you go back?"

None would. Many would rather live one day free than many years in the prison of a mindset. They all loved being able to question things and discuss them freely without fear of being rejected for thinking differently.

I realized that even though the price for freedom was very high, it all comes down to one question. Is it worth it? For those who left and paid the price for it, they all said "absolutely." It's not a fair price but it's a price worth paying.

Freedom to think. Freedom to question even the most fundamental beliefs we had. Where did we come from? Is there a God? Was Jesus real? Is the Bible really the word of God? Did we evolve? We can ask those questions freely without fear of being rejected. People who we never knew would share with us the most intimate things from their lives without worry that we will report them to the elders. Our friendships outside the organizations started to grow from one day to the next.

Rebuilding a Community

I spoke with my three sisters, asking them to treat me no differently than family and friends who are not Witnesses. I reassured them that I would never attack their faith, I would always respect what they believed, and I would treat them no differently than ever before. Fear kicked in, and one by one they cut me off. I know they love me; I love them too. But in their mindset, they think shunning could help me return to the organization, and as a result it would save my life at Armageddon. It's truly a shame they were not able to overcome this challenge. At the same time, this experience greatly helped become the man I always wanted to be. Facing my sisters was a moment when I told myself that I would no longer be a people pleaser. I will be me. If I have to pretend in order to keep them in my life, then I will never live my life. I will always live a life of someone else's expectations of me. I was done with that. I was 38 years old but in the past few years I grew more as a man than all my previous years combined. I started to live a life on my terms.

One of the biggest losses we as former Jehovah's Witnesses experience is a loss of community. The feeling of belonging is one of our basic human needs. We all want to feel loved and accepted. I didn't want to give up on some of my friends who were JWs but I knew that if they decided to stay in our friendship, eventually it would die out. I spoke to some of them. Some shunned me immediately, some got angry, some got curious, some woke up. Our circle of friends kept on growing, plus we found out about others who woke up around the same time. I reconnected with my non-Witness family and our connection today is better than ever. We have meetings and parties every month now. Friendships we have are so authentic and pure that I would never switch them for a million fake ones in the Jehovah Witness organization.

About two years ago, I came across a Facebook group called Empowered ex-Jehovah's Witnesses. Using that tool, I was able to connect with truly amazing people. I know that not everyone is bitter and angry—it's just a phase like a season in every year. In that group, I truly felt at home. The positive attitudes and messages were perfectly aligned with my values and beliefs. This was the answer that I was looking for. For years, I had been training to be a coach and mentor, and now I found a community that was hungry for help, just like I was a few years ago. I started helping people get out of the rut they got themselves into while waking up from religion. I dealt with amazing people whose lives sometimes turned around completely with one conversation. Some phone calls were scary, as many depressed people were contemplating suicide after being disfellowshipped. Nothing brings me a greater joy than to see those who turn their life around, those who start seeing hope and rebuild their identity. What is even more joyful is to see the same ones now helping others to get out of the desperate situation they were once in.

Rebuilding an Identity

All my life had revolved around the world of Jehovah's Witnesses. I had all the answers and I was happy there. All my identity as a person was strongly attached to my religious status. Being an elder in a congregation gave me a lot of self-esteem. I was very much liked due to my abilities in public speaking and approachable nature. I felt like I found my purpose.

When I realized the whole JW religion is based on a myth, I didn't just lose my faith. I also lost myself. I lost my identity because without being a Jehovah's Witness, I was nobody. There was no purpose for me to live anymore, or so I thought. Today with the perspective of time, I realized that it was part of my true calling. There is no way I could have become who I am today without having been a Witness. I had to fight against my father to become one and then against my family to get out of it.

Who am I now? I am a husband, father, son, brother, friend, employer, coach, author, speaker, neighbor, uncle, cousin, business owner, entrepreneur, leader, student and the list go on and on.

This whole experience taught me that we have more than one purpose. As a Witness, you only have one purpose on this planet: serve Jehovah by obeying the directions of the organization. That is it. If you are a father, you have to raise your kids to be good Witnesses. If you are an employer, you have to earn just enough to support your family and focus on supporting preaching work. If you are a husband, you have to teach your wife to be in subjection to you in order to be a good reflection of how to reflect on Jehovah's arrangement. If you are a neighbour, you have to give a good witness by being nice to them in order to be able to win them over without preaching to them. One identity was given with a very clear mission. Life is not like that.

If anything, life is the exact opposite to that. When I am with my kids, I act as a father. I want them to grow up learning the best values, principles and beliefs that serve me and hopefully will serve them when they make their own choices. I discipline them and I play with them. But I act completely differently when I'm talking to my wife. For her, I'm her husband, friend and lover. I'm not thinking of how to discipline her as she is not my child. When I'm at work, I know my identity changes again. When I talk to my employees, I know they are not my children so I behave totally differently with them.

Purpose in Life

What is your purpose? Please remember you may have multiple ones. Your purpose constantly changes, and it depends on the person standing in front of you. Your purpose when you were five years old was different than when you were 25. It changes as you get older and it will change in the future. So, forget the idea of having just one purpose in life—that's a lie. You and I are so much more than just the religion we have or the job we do. Don't get stuck to the idea of only one identity.

Are you confused yet? Let me simplify it for you. There is only one purpose, and I believe it is universal for all humans. I believe that our purpose is to improve the quality of life for ourselves and others. That's it. We are happy when we see progress, when we see life getting better. We feel fulfilled when we see that what we do has a positive impact on others. That's what fulfillment is all about—making life better. That's as simple as it gets.

Think about it for moment. Think about all the identities that you attach to yourself. Is there any area of your life that you cannot improve? Personally, as a husband, I constantly think about how to make my marriage better. I take my wife on trips and sometimes I let her go without me because I know spending time with her best friend away from home makes her happy. As a father, I constantly think about what would be best for my kids. As a father, my role is to protect them, provide for them, teach them and play with them. I can improve in all those small things and it will make me feel like I'm living my purpose. Yes, I go to a playground to push my kids on the swing, and I feel like I'm living my purpose in life because I know I'm making their lives better.

Even now as I'm typing this story, I feel alive. It's four in the morning and I started six hours ago. But I simply felt inspired. I kept thinking about all those people who can benefit from this book and how many people out there need to believe that life on their terms is the best life they can have. That is a life of true success. It's a life you will never regret.

Death is a Gift

As Witnesses, many of us believed that we would never die. Even if we did die, that wouldn't matter because we would be resurrected and in paradise. We would never have to face death. Death is something we don't want. At the same time, death is what makes our life truly precious. Think about it for a moment. If life were without end, what would you feel compelled to do? There would always be tomorrow. You could procrastinate for a million years and it wouldn't matter. No moment in life would be precious because almost everything could be repeated indefinitely.

So many times, we see people who upon discovery of a terminal illness start to live extraordinary lives. The reminder that one day you will die can help you appreciate what you have. It makes each moment so much more precious. How many times did people who almost died quit their jobs and change their life completely? Why? They feel like they have a second chance to live the life they want.

That's how I felt after reading *Crisis of Conscience*. I did not regret the years I lost, I rejoiced in having a second chance at life. I know so many extremely talented people with enormous potential are stuck in a high-control religion that does not allow them to pursue their passion. That is not a story of you and me. Some call it being born again, some call it a second chance. For me, realizing that I will eventually die made me appreciate every single day of my life. Wasting time is a slow suicide. Find your passion, live your passion. There are only so many tomorrows.

"As long as there is life there is hope."
~Stephen Hawking

Chapter 2

The Courage Within: Believe in Yourself

by Cyndi Markey

"You are braver than you think, more talented than you know, and capable of more than you imagine."
~ Roy T. Bennett

I remember walking to the train from work that afternoon feeling so broken, so alone in a strange world. Were they right? Would I never make it away from the organization and the structure? I could not and would not go back! But how would I survive? I felt helpless. They weren't listening to me. They could not see what I saw. I just could not go on, but I was not going back! It had to stop. But how?

As I sat in the hospital visiting room, speaking with my family after my suicide attempt, I was numb. I should have known, but the reality stung worse than expected. The truth hurts sometimes.

Instead of the comfort, love and support that I was hoping I would receive, I heard, "Are you ready to come back to the organization now? This is what happens when you leave Jehovah's organization. This is all because of the worldly people you have been hanging around and the ideas they are putting in your head."

They blamed the guy I had been dating and recently broken up with, the people I met and the life I started living when I moved away a couple of years earlier, and the decision I made to disassociate myself. Blame anyone but the organization or their part in what was playing in my head. My thoughts of living a life outside "The Truth" and my belief in myself and that there could be more than what I had been raised to believe were all in question—these were certainly what caused this problem, according to them. But I knew, even at that vulnerable moment, I just knew their reaction in this moment could not be normal. This could not be how a God of love, as he was supposed to be, would want this situation handled. I could not live this way. I had to find a better way for myself, even if at the end they were right. I wanted to live the life I had, in the time I had left, happier and freer than what I had experienced so far in life. I just had to find how.

How it All Began

My parents became Jehovah's Witnesses when I was two years old. My father became an elder and my mother was a loyal servant and the obedient wife. They taught me their version of The Truth, moving the family from time to time "where the need was greater." Their hopes for me were to grow up fully engrained in The Truth. I would marry someone within the organization and become a pioneer, an obedient wife and a loving mother. But that dream was shattered for them when at the age of 20 I disassociated myself.

Up to that point, my life as a Jehovah's Witness was pretty much the same as most in the organization. I spent my days associating with other Jehovah's Witnesses, attending meetings twice a week and Bible Study nights as well as going from door to door to "spread the good news." In addition to the usual structure and associated constraints of this lifestyle, I had the added stress of having my dad employed as the janitor and maintenance man for the school I attended. Living in a small rural Midwest town of approximately 400 people presented enough challenges. This definitely added to it!

The Doubt Began

As I started high school, I began to question some things I had been taught. I started having more in-depth conversations with some of my teachers at school during study hall. A couple of classmates who rode the bus with me started asking me questions about why we believed what we did; their responses to what I told them planted seeds of curiosity and eventually doubt in my mind. There were more opportunities for me to find time to have conversations and hang out with individuals outside the organization once I bought a car and started a part-time job at a local grocery store. These conversations and experiences opened my mind to the fact that there was a real life outside the organization that may not be as bad as I was hearing.

I started to do more and more activities with people outside the organization without my parents' knowledge. I pretended to be at work, shopping or any other excuse I could think of. Eventually, at 18 I met a man that I became attracted to. I started sneaking away to spend time with him. As we spent more and more time together, our relationship became physical. Of course, I started to feel very guilty, ashamed and afraid of what might happen to me because of the sin I was committing. According to Jehovah Witness doctrine, we were very close to "the end" and I did not want to die at Armageddon. Because of this guilt and fear, I went to my parents and the elders to confess.

The Judicial Committee

As a very young woman, the judicial meeting with the elders was very uncomfortable, embarrassing and disheartening. They seemed more concerned about wanting me to describe my encounters in great detail over and over than they were in providing me guidance on reconciliation or providing comfort for my repentance. I was ultimately publicly reproved for a period of time. At that moment, I knew that I had to get out! There had to be a better life somewhere, and I planned my escape.

A Fresh Start

I moved from a small rural town in Iowa to a town in Tennessee with family friends that were also Jehovah's Witnesses. My excuse was that I needed a fresh start somewhere away from the people I had met and had been spending time with. I explained that I wanted to begin again where nobody knew what happened. This seemed to satisfy my parents, and they assisted me in moving. My way out began!

Once I moved to Tennessee, I found a job. I continued attending meetings and started associating with Jehovah's Witnesses again. I did not know anyone else and I just wanted to believe that maybe, just maybe, the organization there would be different than what I experienced living under my parents' roof and scrutiny. Things were going pretty well. Then I got the news—my parents were now moving to Tennessee! My heart sank.

I moved into an apartment with some girls I had met at work. No, they were not Jehovah's Witnesses; therefore, this decision was not received well by my family or the others in the congregation. I was working as a waitress at that time. It just so happened that a young man from our congregation also worked at the same restaurant. Just my luck. I grew up with my dad working at my school, and now there was a Jehovah's Witness working with me. It felt like I could not get away from the eyes of the organization!

At this point, my mind was set. I was not going to remain a Jehovah's Witness. I just knew there was life outside of what I grew up learning. I started dating outside the organization, hanging out with people I knew from work and stopped attending meetings. All of this, of course, was being reported back to the elders and my parents by my co-worker.

The Judicial Meeting

The day finally came when the elders requested a meeting with me. They advised me that since my behavior was no longer "that becoming of a Jehovah's Witness," they planned to disfellowship me. My stomach dropped, my heart began to pound, my palms became sweaty and I felt like I was going to be sick. I felt panic and anxiety. Although I had made the decision to leave the organization, I did not want to lose my family. After all, they were my parents. I knew they were disappointed in me, but would they really shun me? Would they disown me? How could they? I was their child!

The elders told me that if they disfellowshipped me, my family and the organization would no longer be able to associate with me. I would be shunned. They advised me that they had already spoken to my parents and they understood what my being disfellowshipped would mean. They were fully in support of the decision the elders had made.

Decision Time

I was then presented with an option that both shocked and confused me. There was a new status that I had never heard of: disassociation. As it was explained to me, if I made the decision to disassociate myself instead of having the elders disfellowship me, the organization and its members would still not be able to associate with me, but our family could remain in contact with each other.

Well, this seemed to be the most logical solution to the situation. I felt a sense of relief! I could leave and still keep my family near. Of course, this was what I chose to do. I wrote the letter while they waited. As they were leaving, I was advised they would let my parents know of my decision. As I closed the door, I felt a sense of relief and excitement.

I was out! Leaving was not as hard as I had believed, or so I thought. What came next was nothing like I expected.

Reality Sets in

When I finally heard from my father, who was still an elder, the conversation did not go well. He asked if I realized what leaving meant. How could I do this to our family? My mother was distraught, and it was my fault! I had already embarrassed them at our previous congregation, and now, by choosing to disassociate myself, I was forcing them to no longer be in contact with me, unless of course, I decided to come to my senses and return to Jehovah.

I relayed to my father what I had been told by the elders. I explained that since I disassociated myself, we could stay in contact and still be a family. He told me I should have talked to him first. I must have misunderstood. He explained they would still have to shun me just as if I were disfellowshipped. I tore our family apart and was only thinking of myself. I was selfish just like before. I needed to repent and come back to Jehovah. I needed to think about what I was doing to my mom and the family. That was the last conversation I had with my dad for a very long time. It was also the end of my life, as I knew it or thought it ever would be.

I could not deal with running into my parents and seeing my mom fall apart again and again. The daggers that came from my dad's eyes and words were hurtful, and I felt shame. My mom would call me and cry and beg me to come back. It was emotionally draining me. I once again decided to move away from the situation that was causing me and everyone around me so much hurt.

At first moving with one of my roommates to Alabama was not so bad. I had a decent job. I was making a few friends. I enjoyed going to the clubs and dating some guys from the local military base. But then I started to feel like something was missing. I no longer believed in the teachings of the Jehovah's Witnesses, but I did believe in a God, a higher being, but I just did not know what. And then began my search for my truth, my spirituality, my purpose.

Another Move

About a year later, I was involved in a car accident and also part of a downsizing at work in the same week. I contacted my maternal grandparents to see if I could stay with them. My mother's parents and siblings were not Jehovah's Witnesses and they lived in the Chicagoland area. I had not really discussed the details of what happened with them. Oh, I knew they were aware. My mom told them her side of the events that unfolded. I had been afraid to reach out to them in fear of facing the same thing I heard from my parents. While I understood they were not Jehovah's Witnesses, I thought they would tell me to do what I needed to do to bring peace to the family and make my mom happy.

Much to my surprise, I was welcomed with open arms by my grandma, grandpa and two aunts. I lived with my grandparents while I recovered. I eventually found a job, made friends and felt the love and warmth of my extended family that I did not see much of when growing up. I started dating and eventually felt like life was finally moving forward.

While I was able to find work and enjoy my family, I did not seem to be able to connect with anyone on more than a surface level. The way everyone thought was very different from my own. At first, I went along with things I did not feel comfortable with, because I thought that must just be the way things were done outside the organization. I became frustrated easily and started feeling depressed when I realized this world and people in it were much more complicated than I expected. They were not as bad as I had been told, but I certainly did not fit in.

The Darkness Sets in

About a year after moving to Chicago, the man I had been dating for about nine months had just broken up with me, work was overwhelming, and all of the attempts I had made to convince my parents that I had been lied to and they had to believe me had failed.

I was emotionally drained and angry. I spent much time and energy focusing on how wrong the Jehovah's Witnesses were and how I had been wronged! I was confused and hurt by how my own parents could disown me. It was like I was dead to them—nobody was listening or cared. Was I stupid for believing I could make it on my own outside of the organization? Who was I to think I could make something of myself? After all, if my parents could disown me, if they did not love me enough to help me and take my side, who would? I was an outsider in this world. I had no clue how to move forward or which way to go. All I wanted was to belong and feel happy.

I remember walking to the train from work a few days later feeling so broken and alone in a strange world. They were right—I would never make it away from the organization. I could not and would not go back, but how would I survive? I felt helpless. They weren't listening to me. They could not see what I saw. I just could not go on, but I was not going back. It had to stop. But how? That is how I ended up in the hospital, talking to my parents and doctors.

A New Life Began

A couple years later, after some therapy, I found a new job and a fresh start. I dated a man I met through friends. We were married and had two children. After looking into several churches, I found comfort and belonging as a Catholic. I began attending a very vibrant parish with a lot of young families. I studied Catholicism in their RCIA (Rite of Christian Initiation for Adults) program. For some reason, this faith and their traditions spoke to me. I started to feel whole again. I was making my way in this new world.

However, things do not always go as planned. After a few years of marriage, we divorced. I was very angry and hurt. All the feelings of not being good enough came back. How could yet another person I loved so much and had children with not stay with me? How could we not work things out? My self-worth and self-doubt set in. After my parents had left me, there was no way I could fathom leaving or giving up my children. After what seemed to be a very long and painful divorce, I was alone again with custody of my two children. While my faith was strong, I was very much hurt and afraid. I could not let my kids down—I had to be a good mom. I was determined they would not grow up feeling unloved, unworthy or unwanted.

At this point, I heard from my parents. Was I finally ready to come back to Jehovah now? After all, I had my kids to think about. Did I want them to die in Armageddon because of my stubbornness? If I went back, the whole organization would help me.

This brought back all the anger and resentment toward the Jehovah's Witnesses. I had learned about God in a different way than I had been taught growing up. I found comfort and strength in my faith. I knew a God of love and I could feel His presence in my life. I put all my focus on my kids and in my faith. My kids attended the Catholic school at our parish. They were involved in Cub Scouts, Daisy Scouts and sports. We volunteered together at parish events and homeless shelters, and we spent time with our friends.

I met a man who started attending our parish. We dated and married three years later. I landed a great job at a global financial institute. Life was good ... for a while. But I had much more to learn and did not even know it!

More Life Struggles

My son became addicted to drugs, my daughter faced several years of health issues, and my marriage to my second husband ended after 10 years. Once again, all the self-doubt, self-worth and self-blaming returned. I believed I must have messed it all up! Like most ex-Jehovah's Witnesses, when things went wrong, I blamed myself for everything.

With my marriage now ended, my son addicted to drugs and my daughter away at college, I was left to put the pieces together for myself. No longer regularly attending Mass at my parish, I began to wonder where to look to get help for my son and how to build a life as a single empty nester.

I began counselling and struggled to understand addiction and the pain it causes the addict and those closest to them. Watching someone so close to me suffer from addiction was very painful. There were many nights I spent not sleeping, just wondering if I would see him again. Would that night be the night I would get "the call" I was dreading? I began to mentally plan for that call and the steps that would follow. I would have done anything to make it better. Life was a struggle surviving one day to the next.

I finally found the strength to move my life forward during his addition. I learned not be co-dependent and how to show tough love without feeling like I was abandoning my child. This had been hard for me, as I knew how it felt to be abandoned by my parents.

My son went to rehab a few times and found his way to living a life sober from drugs My daughter moved home and had a successful career and a beautiful daughter. I had made new friends. I began to enjoy travelling and was promoted at work. Life seemed to be good again. But there was still something missing, but what?

By going to counselling over the years, I was able to make friends and continue to have a successful career. I enrolled in classes to enhance my skills and advanced at work each time I made a move. After over 30 years of being outside the organization, I felt as if I was navigating pretty well. But little did I know that there was an even better life out there if I added a few more pieces to the puzzle, which always seemed to elude me.

True Healing Begins

In 2019, I connected with a person who had belonged to the congregation I had attended as a child. He told me that he also left and talked to me about some groups out there for ex-JWs. I resisted this at first because I really did not want to get involved in reliving the past. After all, it had been so many years and I made it, right? But I searched out of curiosity and stumbled upon a Facebook group called Empowered ex-Jehovah's Witnesses (Empowered Minds).

The mission of this group is to provide former Jehovah's Witnesses with the knowledge and tools they need to not only survive, but thrive, in the "real world." I contacted the organizer of this group, Rodney Allgood. He actually took the time to speak with me on the phone. He explained to me that many ex-JWs struggle making new friends, feel like they don't fit in and experience resentment about years we felt we lost. We talked about the common feelings of negative self-judgement, low self-esteem, anger, regret and limiting beliefs that come from years spent in a highly controlled environment.

The harm that has been done to our thinking requires healing and reprogramming. I then decided to sign up for the online JW Deprogramming Bootcamp that Rodney developed. This program illustrates how your conscious and subconscious mind operates and gives us tools to override the years of previous wiring done by the JW organization. It has helped me take my life to the next level. I was able to identify those things that felt missing.

In addition to taking this class, I attended one of the Empowered Minds conferences, which includes speakers who are ex-JWs who have found the way to navigate outside the organization successfully. They share their stories and the tools they used to find their true self and best life. After listening to these individuals, I started looking into the things they suggested, and in a very short time, I noticed a whole new vision of life and the opportunities for me.

My Blueprint for Growth

I believe there are four important steps to achieving what you want and creating your best life.

1. Know Yourself

- Truly take the time to get to know yourself. This is something we were never allowed to do. The organization told us who we were. It defined us. Many of us rush into relationships to feel a sense of love and belonging. But since we have not taken the time to get to know ourselves, we are not able to fully engage in a successful relationship with someone else. This generally results in a short-lived "high" from the relationship. We also do not understand why we feel the way we do when issues arise and, therefore, respond negatively. We are also missing some of the tools needed to navigate rough waters in our relationships.
- Truly learning who we are takes time, reflection and awareness. This clarity comes with the help of step two.

2. Teach Yourself

- As JWs, we were never allowed or encouraged to expand our knowledge outside of the organization. We became very narrow-minded and had limiting beliefs. There are so many things we can and should discover, including a path that resonates with us. Be curious about life! Talk to others to find out what they believe. Read a variety of things, investigate, search for answers. Learn new skills, contemplate new beliefs, understand and be curious about other cultures. This enables you to relate to all kinds of people. This also helps us wash away the judgement of others we developed by thinking we were right and we had "The Truth." After all, we experienced that judgement after leaving the organization.
- Do not limit yourself. We were all affected by the constraints and narrow-mindedness of the organization. Learn about the world and how it operates. Understand the Laws of the Universe

31

and how to live in harmony with it. We are all energy forms and vibrate at various frequencies. As we learn to understand this, we learn to navigate life. Learn how our mind works. It is amazing and has the ability to remove old thoughts and patterns taught to us. We can teach it new beliefs by changing our mindset and developing daily habits. This will result in reaching goals we never thought possible.

- The mind directs the orchestra of our life—how we live, react and think. Our mind is made up of both the conscious mind and the subconscious mind. Our life is controlled by the subconscious mind. Ours were programmed with negative files and false beliefs that hold us back. The good news is that our subconscious can be reprogrammed. It is similar to deleting old files from our computer and replacing them with new files.

- Learn and practice gratitude. Until we appreciate what we have, we will not attract or appreciate anything else. Start small by making a list of three things you are grateful for each morning. Truly feel the emotion of gratitude as you write them down. This can be as simple as being grateful for our home, the safety and warmth it provides, our family, clean water, fresh air, our health or our job. As this is practiced, the list gets longer. By starting the day with gratitude, we no longer have the room for negative emotions.

- Meditation helps us center ourselves and find clarity. Learning to quiet our mind and reflect is very calming and aids in reducing anxiety and depression, and increases our ability to focus.

- Learn to build self-confidence, self-worth and a positive mindset by using daily affirmations. Listen to motivational speakers every day. Some that have helped me are Les Brown, Bob Proctor, Sarah Gallaher, Abraham Hicks, Bob Baker and Joel Olsteen. There are many others. Find some that resonate with you and listen to them daily.

- Realize that our mindset is crucial in moving forward with positivity. Changing our life is as simple as changing our thoughts. This is because thoughts become actions, actions become behavior, behavior becomes habits. Habits become rituals. Rituals change the subconscious. It rewrites the program! Create daily rituals that support a positive mindset, and I promise that the results are quick. But it is important that they are practiced daily. As with anything else, we need to invest time to develop anything worthwhile. It is time to invest in yourself.

3. Trust Yourself

- Trusting yourself is one of the keys to finding happiness. This is because if we do not trust ourselves, we will not be able to truly trust anyone or anything else. Trusting ourselves provides a solid foundation for everything else. If we develop self-trust, we create an anchor. We become grounded and will not easily be swayed.

- We were taught to only trust the elders and the organization. For many of us, this created a feeling of self-doubt. We were not allowed to trust what we thought had any value or meaning. This is not true! The more we learn about ourselves, the more confidence we develop. We need to understand that our thoughts are valid and trust that our intuition can lead us in the right direction.

4. Love Yourself

- Until we develop the ability to love ourselves, we are unable to love anyone else fully. When we love ourselves, we no longer look for others to make us happy. When we achieve this, we are now open to the joy other things in life can bring us.

- We must learn to embrace our entire life, including our past. We must become our authentic self. We can't change our past, but the past does not determine our future. One of my favorite passages is this: *"The butterfly does not look back at the caterpillar in shame, just as you should not look back at your past in shame. Your past was part of your own transformation."*

- I love music. One of my favorite singers is Garth Brooks. In one of his famous songs, *The Dance*, he says "I could have missed the pain, but I'd have had to miss the dance." Don't miss your dance by refusing to embrace the whole of your life. Become your authentic self. The pain has taught us many lessons and made us who we are.

- Loving ourselves also means being cautious of who we allow closest to us. It is said that we are the average of the sum of the people closest to us. Are those around you encouraging you to be better and are they moving forward? If they are not moving in the same direction as you, then you may have outgrown them. They may hold you in the past and therefore prevent your further growth.

- Set boundaries. We should not allow others to treat us poorly. Just because someone is family or a friend does not give them the right to mistreat or abuse us. Only give from what overflows from your cup. This means taking care of ourselves first! Yes, this is not being selfish! We must be rested, healthy and mentally fit before we can give of ourselves. This is a new concept for some. We were taught to always put others first, and if we did things for ourselves, we were being selfish. But self-care is necessary.

I read somewhere there are three C's of life:

> Choices, Chances, Changes. You must
> make the Choice to take a Chance, if you
> want anything in life to Change.

But I believe there is a necessary fourth C of life: Courage.

Deciding to leave the organization takes courage. Courage comes from the Latin word "cor," meaning of the heart (as in the seat of emotions) or being your authentic self! Courage does not necessarily mean being brave or heroic in a big way but overcoming the small things in life every day. Deciding to leave the organization takes courage. Many ex-Jehovah's Witnesses do not feel like they have courage.

I *know* you have courage. Without courage, you would not have been able to break free from the organization. Courage allowed you to be strong enough as a child to do many of the things you did as a Jehovah's Witness. As a child, you sat while others stood for the Pledge of Allegiance, and you left the room while other kids celebrated birthdays and had holiday parties. You knocked on doors of people you knew and went to school with as an adolescent. You were brave and courageous then and you are courageous now! Do not let that courage be forgotten or for naught. As you read this book, if one or more of the authors' stories resonates with you, please reach out! We are here to help!

How do you move forward? With courage. Remember your courage within and step into your new life.

Chapter 3

The End, A New Beginning

by Alex Chenarides

"History is just one damn thing after another."
~ Mark Twain

At the tender age of 24, I was given a death sentence. To my highly indoctrinated conscious mind, it was terrifying. However, to my subconscious, wise mind, it was a welcome relief. No one living outside the bubble of religious fanaticism would think my crime was any more serious than jogging. Yet, in the grand design of my controlled universe, I was no longer worthy of living. Surprisingly, my response to this sentence was to sabotage any hope I had for appeals. As Socrates probably once said, "What the hell's going on here!?" If you're wondering the same, I'll explain.

My mother was baptized as a Jehovah's Witness (JW's) in 1975, the glorious year that, according to the religion, marked the end of God's seventh day of creative rest, the time when He was to gift His children a cleansed earthly paradise by simply murdering the four billion people who were alive at the time. This new world would be shaped by just a few million, relatively unskilled people who were lucky enough to be the chosen few. My mother was a goodhearted but lonely and depressed person, burdened by choices she felt she had to make in life. She was deeply attracted to the love-baited message offered to her by a couple of fervent evangelizers who just happened to knock on our door in Lakewood, California, a suburb of Los Angeles.

My early home life mostly involved attending to the emotional needs of my parents while mine remained mostly unseen and stifled. My parents grew up in abusive environments, so it was all they knew. Although I know my parents truly loved me and my sisters, I learned at a tender age that my survival depended on navigating a minefield of chaos and dysregulation. After my mother's 1975 initiation into the JW's, we had a new influence in the house, a "church family" we met with three times a week for over 20 hours a month. I sought refuge from my family in this new "family" contained within the walls of the Kingdom Hall (as our church was called) and the members who attended my congregation. I was eager to please and sought the approval of those around me, so I energetically gravitated to this group as I found the members in this new family willing to engage with me and give me the seeming reassurance I was so desperately devoid of at home. You could say my mother joined willingly, but I joined unwittingly. My father didn't want much to do with it but went along with things to keep the conflict at home to a minimum.

At the age of five, I was giving five-minute speaking parts from the podium to all the congregants, which I wrote myself. I went from door to door "sharing" the literature written and distributed by the JW publishing organization. I felt like I had found a place of belonging where I truly mattered. Yet, I had no idea of the true nature of the team I was gleefully representing: a group bent on feeling superior to any who disagreed with our tenets, a group whose collective conscience felt zero conflict with the early death of billions of people solely for the crime of believing something different than we did.

Without a framework of reference, which I was purposely shielded from by those in religious authority, I grew up in a highly structured climate of shame and judgement. I was taught that people who weren't a part of our group were evil, ruled by Satan and thus by default worthy of capital punishment at the hands of a God, who also conveniently happened to be the personification of love. We were "good-for-nothing slaves" (Luke 17:10), whose entire lives should be filled with activities as determined by the heads of our organization. My tiny mind absorbed this heavily incongruent maxim at the same period in life when I learned that kids don't cross the street by themselves, that stoves are hot, and that you don't get into cars with strangers. Completely absent were any filters to critically analyze these directives. They just went straight in, unquestioned.

For reasons pertaining to both my family life as well as my religious upbringing, I have damn near total amnesia when it comes to most of my childhood. My most relevant memories didn't take shape until I was in my teens. My favorite hobby was skateboarding, and I hung out with all types from skinheads to straight edge nerds. I somehow convinced my parents to let me build a halfpipe in my backyard, but I wasn't allowed to invite any of my "worldly" (non-JW) friends over to skate, which meant that I practiced endlessly in solitude. My closest friend lived five doors down from me on my block, but I wasn't allowed to associate with him because he was Catholic and had long hair. I had to go to galactic lengths to hang out with the people I wanted to hang out with. I smoked weed on occasion and skated my heart out, but still did all my homework, made it home before the streetlights came on and was on time for all of our church meetings.

When I was 15, my dad caught me smoking weed in my best friend's garage and hit me so hard on the side of the head that I felt my spirit leave my body (I have forgiven him for that). At this time, I was also increasingly making my mother upset by not completely bending to the will of our church, and I felt that I was the reason there was so much discord in my family. So, I made the choice to give up all my unholiness and become baptized as a JW. It was 1989 at a large annual convention they used to hold at Dodger Stadium, in front of approximately 35,000 people in attendance. It was extremely uncomfortable, and afterwards I drank a Shasta by myself.

After that, the energetic pleaser inside me manifested again in full force. By the age of 17, I had volunteered to join the ranks of a full-time door-to-door goer, called a Pioneer (which at the time meant doling out 90 hours a month in the preaching work). By the age of 19, I was appointed to the rank of Ministerial Servant (equivalent to a Deacon), and by the age of 20, I was accepted to join the headquarters staff of Jehovah's Witnesses (called Bethel which means "House of God"), located in Brooklyn, New York. My father was dead set against me taking this gig, but to his credit, he didn't hold it against me when I went. And while he was absolutely right path the time. (I should not have gone to see the Wizard). In hindsight this was one of the best decisions in my life.

House of God

I had a great time in New York. I was surrounding by over 3,000 volunteers of all ages from all over the country who were just as naïve and determined as I was. We were compelled to take a vow of poverty which basically made us monks, at least for tax purposes. We were revered by the rest of the JW's who looked at our privilege as being at the height of Godly service, immediately adjacent to Jesus's earthly brothers directing the worldwide work of our organization. Everywhere we went, we got the red carpet. Yet the real gift this opportunity gave me was seeing through the veil of magnificence. What I saw was a bunch of regular men, making regular man-like decisions to maintain rigid obedience.

On one occasion, this hit me on the head as hard as when I got busted for weed. I had missed a monthly, mandatory Monday evening discourse because I was sick. I went out that night to the nearest store for some cold medicine and spent the rest of the night in my room. Three days later, I was pulled into conference with three Bethel elders and was tongue lashed for an hour-long session because I missed this event, and it didn't matter that I was sick. I was told that I fell short of the privilege I had been given, and "who did I think I was" to just discard God's gift of spiritual food. I walked out of that room feeling like donkey shit.

You see, it didn't matter that I worked five and a half days a week with one Saturday off. It didn't matter that I still had to attend meetings three times a week in Brownsville Brooklyn for the same 20+ hours a month, with an added hour-and-a-half round trip. For the record, Brownsville Brooklyn was on the other side of Bedford Stuyvesant, which were both highly dangerous places in the 1990s. It didn't matter that I was expected to spend my one Saturday off a month along with Sundays in the preaching work. It didn't matter that I was paid only $90 a month plus room and board for my services. To these "brothers" of mine, they needed to ensure that I knew I crossed the line. I mean, some people commit genocide, but I missed a talk on a Monday night because I felt like actual garbage. The point was missed on me.

This is what weaponized shame and judgment looks like.

For the first time ever, my self-constructed armor cracked, and I got a peek outside. It wasn't all black like I was told it would be. It was actually kind of bright and shiny. My first thought was "who the hell ratted on me?" Then, "OK, why"? "Was this level of verbal ass whooping really necessary? What was the actual worth of what I was contributing to this cause? Were my feelings that disposable, even though I was at the height of my potential level of servitude at the time?"

The shame they tried to pump me with for this phenomenally benign infraction got me thinking that maybe, just maybe, I might be in the wrong place.

Unbaptized

Imagine that you decided to change your opinion about what color to paint your living room or if you now preferred boxers over briefs, Autobots over Decepticons, days at the beach over literally anything else. Now imagine that the consequence of you changing your mind meant that everyone you valued in life would stop speaking to you and would never speak to you again. This is the reality for any JW who decides they can't follow the program anymore. It's a bone-chilling position to be in and one that every molecule of cognitive horsepower will fight against. I wished so hard that I could stifle the voice in my gut telling me something was wrong. But, I couldn't. I waited a few months after that meeting and turned in my resignation as a member of the Bethel Family.

After I turned in my letter, I remember having to see Daniel Sydlik in his office for something work related. He was an extremely affable member of the Governing Body (the board of directors for *The Watchtower*) and main Bethel Overseer. He was as close to Jesus as you could get on earth, as we were taught. I mentioned to him that I was leaving Bethel in a few months to head back home. "But we need good brothers here at Bethel; why won't you stay?" he asked. He must have thought I had a light stroke right there in his office because it felt like I stared at him for half an hour. It was really just a few seconds, but when I saw the confused look on his face, I just said "because I need to go help my family". That was a lie and I was a big fat liar. Truth is, at that moment I was a mindless grey cloud and couldn't even process enough brain power to spell my own name right. I certainly couldn't tell him what I was feeling. So, I turned around and walked out of his office as if I just saw my parents having sex. I'm sure he thought I was as strange as a football-bat, but I did what I had to do to get out of there.

When I got back home to Los Angeles, I had the added burden of translating everyone's confusion as to why I was home into shame that I let everyone down. It was a big deal that someone from our congregation went to work at the Bethel headquarters, and now that claim was gone. Match this with some major, unbelievable changes in church doctrine, and my subconscious mind kindly took over and decided we needed to find a way out. I noticed serious negative changes in my mood and demeanor. For the absolute very first time in my life, I started asking questions, and I was completely filled with horror over the conclusions I was coming up with. Not because I was ashamed of my thoughts, it was because I knew that those thoughts were going to cost me everything I cared about if I acted on them.

Here are a couple examples of where things started to break down for me:

1. There were still billions of non-JWs alive, and it wasn't 1975 anymore. I discovered the JWs had incorrectly stated that Armageddon (the end of the world) was coming about half a dozen times since 1879. So, by that time, the JWs had been claiming that "the end" was right around the corner for over 120 years. Millions had lived and died being told they would never grow old in this world.

    Being lied to was not OK.

2. Shunning. The JWs affectionately coin this action "disfellowshipping" because I guess shunning sounds too mean. This is a long explanation so stay with me here. If I left, I was going to be shunned. The concept for shunning came from a few choice verses written by the Apostle Paul in his letters included in the New Testament. I'm going to offend a few folks here by saying this, but Paul was kind of a dick. He was a dick when he was Saul of Tarsus, and he stayed a dick after he saw the bright light on the road. It didn't change who he was as a person, it just changed his opinion on who to be a dick to.

I say this because JWs use a few select things Paul said to justify complete shunning of former members of the religion, even their own family. Here's the problem I had with that: in the very same Bible, it plainly states that both God and Jesus had lengthy conversations with Satan. That's right, Satan. We were told to be loyal to God and not to talk to apostates (which are former JWs who leave and/or say negative things about the church). Yet in the Bible book of Job, Satan, the king of all apostates, barges right into a heavenly meeting with all the angels and challenges God to a duel. Twice! Satan wanted to turn Job away from serving God. This was a perfect opportunity to shun Satan, but instead God chose to have nice, cordial conversations with him, even making a wager out of it. God didn't even attempt to stop Satan from interrupting His angelic assembly. There was no cherubic escort out the back door. Like Abraham Lincoln once said, "Dude, that's absolute bullshit." (I can't back that up.)

Then I read Luke 11:1-12. Right after Jesus was baptized and spent 40 days in the wilderness not eating and somehow also not dying, none other than God himself led Jesus into a meeting with none other than Satan himself. They visited the Temple together. Yes, Jesus was seen in public walking into the Temple with Satan, his literal apostate brother. I wondered if Jesus were here on earth today, would he bring Satan to the Kingdom Hall? Then they went on a long hike together up a mountain, and all the while Satan was solely focused on getting Jesus to change his mind on whom to worship. As the story goes, Jesus decided not to change his mind. For the dozens of times we read those verses, Jesus was praised for staying in God's camp despite the overt temptation to leave for something better. He was never praised for shunning Satan, because Jesus didn't shun Satan (again, his brother and the biggest apostate in the galaxy).

This was a huge contradiction in my mind that I couldn't possibly reconcile, especially because shunning does so much psychological damage to a person. It's emotional blackmail. JWs talk about how disfellowshipped people are so sad and depressed that they are out in the "world" alone and how they would be so much better off back in the fold. It's the same thing as taking food away from someone and then judging them for how much they're starving. Being cut out of the group meant death to our ancestors, and our reptilian brains translate it no differently today, especially when the JWs tell you that you are literally going to die when God decides to murder everyone except the people in their group. If a JW associates with a person being shunned, then they are in turned shunned. This is a classic move used by high control groups.

Again, this is weaponized shame and judgement at its finest.

There were a few other thoughts that gave me cognitive trouble. Why did God kill everything during the Flood of Noah's day even though it fixed absolutely nothing at all? Why did Lot's wife need to be killed for looking back at her home when it was on fire, but Lot could get drunk in a cave and have grandkids with his daughters and suffer no consequences? Or, why did it seem like John was on LSD when he wrote the Book of Revelation?

These thoughts left me petrified the same way you would feel if you knew you were going to face a firing squad. Since I was still so indoctrinated at the time, I placed the choice of my exodus in the hands of the overseers/elders in my congregation. So, I got drunk a few times, made out with girls and confessed my sins to the elders in my congregation (working on that NC-17 rating here).

After the 3rd strike, the congregation elders gave me my death sentence. I was going to be disfellowshipped. Oivay. The final nail I put in my coffin was when I was leaving the room after my sentence was delivered. I told them I was relieved. My subconscious mind knew that I was finally going to put myself out of this toxic environment. I can tell you they did not like that one bit.

They were to make the announcement official at next week's service. I had until then to say goodbye to the people I was closest to, and this was another loophole I didn't understand. The only difference between me being good enough to talk to and a pariah on death row was a public announcement, even though I already knew what the verdict was.

Once the shunning kicked in, my survival mode also kicked in full gear. I tried to get back into the fold, going to every meeting, feeling like the eyes of everyone were on the back of my neck. It was awful. I wrote a letter asking to be reinstated (allowed back into the church's good graces) and I never received a reply. After seven months of this torture, I eventually decided to stop going altogether. I lived in literal purgatory for the next seven years, thinking that I was going to be killed by God because I could no longer bring myself to be a part of this group anymore. It wasn't cute.

Act 2

I knew absolutely zilch about healing, meditating, therapy or self-compassion because none of those concepts were ever discussed or encouraged within the JW ranks. So, how did I deal with the pain of being rejected by every friend I had ever made in my entire life? Drugs. Lofty, snowcapped mountains of drugs. I hit it big too. My new friends ranged from attorneys to gang members. One of my closer friends was a drug-dealing Crip whose mother was a JW. We bonded over that, which of course meant I got a great deal on my drugs.

By this time, I was 26 years old and lucky enough to have taken a job as a vice-president/bank manager without having to be in the office much. I lived in Belmont Shore (a town in Long Beach, California) in a huge Spanish-style home built in the 1930s. There were constantly people around. Another good friend (one of the very few friends from that time I'm still friends with today) owned a clothing line, and we would have photo shoots at the house all the time. He just reminded me the other day that the band who always showed up to play in my living room was Avenged Sevenfold, when they were just starting out. I had no idea who they were, I just remember having to take calls in the backyard because they were super noisy. On my 27th birthday, I was up for four days straight. A couple friends and I went to Toys R Us and bought remote control boats so every night we could put fireworks on them and sail them around the bay. There were so many all-nighters that I eventually came to hate seeing the sun come up, and I especially hated joggers and birds chirping.

So, yes, on paper it looked like I was having a great time and was connected with a wide variety of interesting people. The truth was that I was hiding a deep level of misery. I was running just fast enough to stay two steps in front of the pain that was trying so desperately to get my attention and be healed.

I eventually grew wise to the common denominators that existed between me and all my new associates. # 1 was drugs. # 2 was that all of them were trying to hide deep pain just like I was. I developed a nifty cocaine habit. I smoked and drank so much that Marlboro and Jameson sent me Christmas cards. There was an endless supply of everything I needed to kill the pain. The dark side of all this was that my comrades who revolved around drugs weren't really my friends. The fun I was having wasn't happiness. The pain I was numbing from didn't leave; it didn't go away with time. It was an entirely unsustainable course.

I needed a change, or I was going to die emotionally and/or physically. First, I had to get off the drugs. So, at the end of a couple days of unusually hard partying, I wrote a letter to myself about how completely shitty I felt. Then, whenever I felt like diving in again, I would read my letter and be reminded of how I was going to feel the next day. It worked. The pain of keeping up my resistance marathon became greater than the pain of sitting with myself and trying to figure out what was wrong. I stopped using coke, stopped smoking cigarettes and stopped drinking. It felt great. I was a lot fatter, but I was in a much better place. However, I was still pretty deep in the weeds and had a lot of work ahead of me, most of which I had absolutely no concept of. Where would I start?

The Path Thickens

Right around my 32nd birthday, I decided to finally investigate online resources into the JWs, their origins, and opposing viewpoints. For perspective, this is a process that normal people do with nearly every single endeavor in life, but when it comes to the religion I was raised with, this path was entirely forbidden. I gave myself permission to do this because I couldn't understand why such dire threats of exile and punishment were needed to keep people in a place that was supposedly best for them. If the everlasting life on a paradise Earth that God promised was factually real, then it would stand up very well in the face of criticism. Do you ever notice that scientists don't get angry or threaten someone who believes gravity isn't real or the Earth is flat. They just shake their head and go about their business, because, why waste the time? The facts are indisputable, and there is no need to get upset if someone else can't figure it out. There is no fear in the truth. There were heaps of fear laid upon us for investigating anything contrary to our beliefs, and I wasn't going to fall for that any longer.

I read two books: *Crisis of Conscience* and *In Search of Christian Freedom*, both written by Ray Franz who was a former member of the Governing Body of JWs. Those books changed my life forever. Although he has since passed, I am forever indebted to him, as are thousands of others. He wrote in such a non-judgmental, non-aggressive way while at the same time exposing the blatant inconsistencies in JW teachings. All of my doubts were legitimized, and it finally started to click. I was so relieved because I realized I didn't have to believe this stuff anymore. I could finally let it go and stop hating myself because of failing to live up to a completely artificial standard. In full disclosure, while Mr. Franz decided to remain a Christian, I decided it was time to free myself of religion altogether. If the God of the bible existed, I figured he had a lot of explaining to do.

I'd like to say that I took on the task of healing and therapy at that point, but I was still very ignorant to my colossal need for them. I took up smoking weed to numb out, which I did about every half hour for the next 12 years. During this time, I managed my dysfunction brilliantly. I was making money, had real friends and travelled extensively, but I was still racked with anxiety. I thought this was just how life was.

Fast forward to my early 40s. Up until that time, I dated mostly for the sake of dating, and I picked women that I knew would only last a short time. Then I finally met someone that I accidentally fell for. The problem was that she was mired in unresolved pain from her past too, and it triggered every trigger I had to be triggered. I emotionally took on her problems and ruminated to the point of exhaustion because this is what I had been trained to do. The result was that my nervous system exploded, and I broke down for about three years. This was a real awakening for me, and it was not elegant. It was painful, shattering and raw.

What I Wish I knew From the Beginning

I've clearly spent the better part of my life in the practice of avoidance and ignorance. I didn't consciously resist trying to heal myself, I just didn't know it was possible. If I could go back in time to my 24-year-old self and say a few things, they would sound like this:

1. I was institutionalized. For anyone born into the JW organization or anyone who spends any significant amount of time in a similar organization, they are going to become institutionalized just like a person who spends most of their life in prison. In the religion, our activities were monitored, people were encouraged to snitch on each other, our thoughts were dictated to us, our associations were chosen for us, our opportunities for work were curtailed, and our access to the outside world was limited. We were told what we could watch, what we could listen to, what kind of art we could look at and how we were supposed to dress ourselves. Personal style choices were prescribed. Solitary confinement was the punishment for the worst offenders.

That's a prison's playbook. Just like a person who's been institutionalized, folks in high-control groups are convinced they are better off inside the confinement zone. The outside world is too dangerous. It's just like the inmate that would rather stay in prison than venture outside. Think about that; they'd rather stay in prison where people stab other people just so they can join a gang! If someone can believe they're better off in a place like that, then someone can also be convinced they are better off being highly controlled by a religious group. However, here's where the difference between the two pops: people in prison know they're being punished and it's supposed to suck. People in high-control groups think they are in the best place ever.

If you are or were a JW, think about how many choices you were actually able to make for yourself. We had what were called "conscience matters," and these were areas of life where we could decide for ourselves what we wanted to do. But if they offended another person or made them "stumble," then we had to quit. I can't even remember what any of them were, but I know if I said we had five of them that would be too many. How does that equal freedom?

It would have helped to know this back then. Since I didn't know, I couldn't grasp the work I needed to do to get out of it. I also couldn't grasp that it was going to be worth it.

2. Leaving a group like JWs voluntarily or involuntarily is very likely going to be one of hardest things I would ever do in my life. Trying to do it by myself only made it harder. Not only did I have to deprogram myself from years of being improperly shamed into submission, I had to heal from a tremendous loss of both everyone I cared about and the individuality I gave up to be apart of the group. I needed to find a new tribe of real support and learn as much as I could about how to form my own thoughts and, explore my own uniqueness. Basically, I had to learn what life was supposed to be like all along. People who weren't born into a highly controlled environment (from any source) don't experience what it's like getting to learn that being whoever you truly are was not only O.K., but how you actually win at being human.

3. Moving into a new life meant that part of my old life had to die, and I had to let it die. I then had to accept that loss and grieve it. I couldn't bring that life or the people I used to know into my new one. Plus, the new life was going to be a little scary because I had never seen it before. This is all for perspective. By not seeing it this way originally, I got stuck between my past and potential future without the ability to move forward.

4. Going through this process would eventually lead to a life that was authentically mine, and it was going to be absolutely worth

it, even though at the beginning it felt pointless to try. For example, I could now plan for my retirement unlike millions of people in the group before me who died broke because they thought the end of the world was coming and it didn't. I could explore any field of interest I had and take any employment I chose. I could vote, I could volunteer with charities, I could look however I wanted to, I could date whomever I wanted to, and I could feel safe without all my values being dictated to me. I could enjoy my life now instead of thinking I was missing out on some artificial future that no one has ever seen and never will. Most importantly, the relationships I developed would be with people I actually wanted in my life, and they were not going to stop being my friends because I changed my mind about a religion. Once I started creating my own life, the memory of the old one would slowly fade into the background. It would be 100% worth the effort, even though a lot of times I seriously doubted it would be.

The light of Day

I do not view the depression or anxiety I felt as relentless enemies, bent on my demise. I now view them as I would a close, longtime friend. They were at the core of a crisis that represented an appetite for growth that had found no other way of expressing themselves. They were my teachers. They were the protectors that kept me safe during my most vulnerable times in life. They just needed to be reassured now that they could relax and stop trying to keep me safe from a danger that didn't exist. Those threats weren't real and had been dissolved long into my past.

Rather than having panic attacks, I had a fear reflex that was constantly blaring and it caused me great physical pain. Pain is an excellent motivator though, and I was determined to finally tend to my own intrinsic well-being. Here's how I did this:

Therapy: A good therapist is worth their weight in moon rocks, and I found one that had deep insights into resolving trauma and processing grief. I had developed post-traumatic stress disorder (PTSD) from my shunning and years of self-loathing. They say that the cure for the pain is in the pain. I learned how to sit with myself and let all the emotions I was running from finally come to the surface. Instead of focusing on the symptoms, I focused on the reasons for the symptoms. For example, why did I ruminate myself into oblivion? Because I felt it was my responsibility to save the world, and I couldn't stop trying to find a solution to that problem because as that's what I was taught. But I now realized that not only is it not my job, it's an impossible task and also none of my business. I can't solve everyone's problems. It's also personally harmful to seek revenge on those who hurt me or those whom I cared deeply about. One by one I confronted my erroneous thoughts about life that stemmed from my poor training growing up. I sat with all the painful emotions surrounding those beliefs and allowed them a pathway out of me. I let them go.

Medication: While I was only on medication for a little over a year, it helped stabilize me enough to do the deep internal work that I so desperately needed to do. That's the point of medication, it doesn't solve anything, but it allowed me the calm space to find the solutions I needed.

Through my investigation into anxiety, I discovered the organization called MAPS (Multidisciplinary Association for Psychedelic Studies) and their research into curing PTSD through the use of MDMA (methylenedioxymethamphetamine, or Molly for short) and psilocybin (mushrooms). While its usage is currently still considered a felony in the United States, the Food and Drug Administration has approved clinical trials, currently in their third stage. I found a practitioner outside of the country and I'm here to say that it was an enormous game changer. MDMA dulls the amygdala, the brain's fear center, while flooding the brain with serotonin, which allows one to look deep inside at their most frightening thoughts and emotions without being triggered. From there, new pathways of thinking can develop. Psilocybin acts in a way similar to having your brain defragmented, like a reset to the factory default settings. It allows for the removal of a lot of toxic thought buildup. I plan on becoming very involved with this work as it progresses. The results are real and staggering when done properly in a well supervised set and setting.

Meditation: There is so much to unwrap with this one. Our brains physically change in response to persistent stress, fear, shame and other difficult emotions. The amygdala actually grows with prolonged exposure to anxiety and gets stuck on high alert, always looking out for threats despite there being no real threats whatsoever. Meditation calms the mind and allows for the management of thoughts. I compare the mind to the sky. Clouds form in the sky, storms come and go, typhoons rage and hurricanes snarl past. Yet, above all that is a peaceful, calm place that exists and remains even during the worst disruptions. Meditating puts our minds above the storm clouds and enables us to observe them rather than participate in every tempest.

Mindfulness: Fear, anxiety and depression all live in the past and future. In the present, we are safe. "Be where your feet are" is a reliable mantra. This goes hand in hand with meditation.

Exercise: There is a plethora of science to back up the fact that we need to exercise our mind and bodies. The results of mental calm and euphoria are real, and immensely helpful.

Self-Compassion and patience: Overcoming a traumatic past is going to take time. There was absolutely nothing wrong with that, or me. I never got annoyed with myself for feeling the way I did. I grieved heavily and for a period of 9 months I was a sobbing mess. Why? Because that's what I needed to do, and I let it happen. I welcomed it. This was a huge gift to myself, and I didn't care what other people's opinions were of the process. (for the record, people that you will want to be around recognize what growth and healing look like, and they will be very supportive)

Non-judgment: I stopped judging both other people as well as myself. Judging was what we were taught to keep ourselves safe from faux threats and to keep us in submission, but all it does is separate us from our true nature and from each other. Judging is so goddamned exhausting, so I was thrilled when I finally let it go.

Where Do We Go from Here?

This is a huge part of the next step in the process. I had to find out what mattered to me, what my values were and how I wanted to spend my life that gave me meaning outside of the artificial and arbitrary life that had been proscribed to me in the group. This felt scary, because my prior programing kept screaming that I was doing something wrong; something worthy of death. I had to realize that not only was I finally where I was supposed to be, I was where I should have been all along. This is how normal people live their lives and there was absolutely nothing wrong with it.

Today I have a life that I truly enjoy and worked hard to put together. I have amazing friends who don't judge me, I have a career that I can focus on which provides me with fulfillment and comfort. I travel extensively, I work with charities and devote time to helping people in the same situation that I was in. I do things that bring me joy and I spend my time as I wish.

I will always be using my new skills. I kept the good traits I had developed in my life up until that point, but the life I have now is all new. My life is mine now, I own it. It doesn't belong to anyone or anything else. This is where true freedom is, and it is something that everyone, including anyone reading this, completely deserves.

Even though we may have never met, I wish you absolute success in your journey. May all roads you travel lead you back to yourself. We can all do hard things, and the rewards are literally endless.

Chapter 4

Clearing My Conscience Gave Me More Than I Asked For

by Abigail Ramos

"Truth Fears No Questions"
~Unknown

I did it. I found the perfect guy. Jehovah had blessed me with the perfect spouse. John was everything the Society said to look for in a husband. He was a Ministerial Servant and a Regular Pioneer. He came from a strong spiritual family who were regularly involved in Circuit and District level parts. We had been friends since we were teenagers, growing up in the same Circuit so he was no stranger with an unfamiliar past or upbringing. He even caught my eye while he was on stage for a part during a Circuit Assembly. It couldn't have been more perfect.

Many sisters wanted his attention, but he chose me, a simple and relatively unknown girl from a small, quiet family. Sure, there were details of my life he didn't know, but that shouldn't matter. I did my share of stupid things in high school, but I stopped so it should be the same as repenting. Jehovah must've forgiven me by blessing me with a good man. That had to be it. I was forgiven and now I'm being blessed.

Three and a half years after marrying this "perfect" brother, I was filing the divorce papers. But this was my chance to start over. In a short period of time, I will be the best Jehovah's Witness but this time with a clear conscience.

My Upbringing

Born and raised in Los Angeles to second-generation Jehovah's Witnesses and the only child and daughter to immigrant parents, I reached out for the few privileges in the organization that were available to me. I joined the Theocratic Ministry School at age seven and was baptized at 13 so that I could begin high school with "spiritual protection." Every summer break, I Auxiliary Pioneered with a goal to become a Regular Pioneer immediately after graduating. Everything seemed to be going according to the spiritual plan.

For my entire life, my parents' marriage was rocky. In fact, they lived separately throughout my teenage years. They did not have "scriptural grounds" for a divorce even though they were extremely unhappy and incompatible. Each lived in a different city with me being shuffled from one parent to another until I was old enough to have my own car and drive myself between the two houses. I felt like I was living out of my car most instances, as I wasn't sure which parent I'd be staying with each night, so I carried my essential toiletries and extra clothes with me at all times. Even though my parents were living separately, they appeared to be "normal" to the congregation. We attended the same book study group and even sat together at all the weekly meetings at the Kingdom Hall.

The elders didn't seem to know until I brought it to their attention. Looking back on it now, I knew my motives weren't entirely for my parents' spiritual welfare, but for my own convenience and revenge,

revenge for being too strict and not letting me go out with my Witness friends. But life as an only child wasn't always bad.

As a child, they enrolled me in numerous extracurricular activities outside of school. I did it all: dance classes, music classes, sports classes, art classes, talent shows and pageants, even hiring a talent agency and doing a few TV commercials. The ones that stuck the longest were piano (their choice) and figure skating (my choice). Because of these various activities, I befriended my peers and got to know different people outside of my school and the congregation. I would discover as an adult that many of these friendships forged at a young age would become a valuable life-saving asset later in life. My parents probably kept me busy with activities so I wouldn't get bored and to see if I would develop a hidden talent. Even though my parents would remind me not to tell anyone in the congregation about my figure skating competitions (extra-curricular activities were already discouraged, especially if they involved competition), I couldn't help but excitedly tell my Witness friends in the Kingdom Hall when I placed first or second in those competitions, or that I went to a Pepsi commercial audition earlier that day.

My parents didn't entirely forbid or discourage a college education, but they did want me to be self-sufficient with certifications or skills so that I could eventually support myself and Pioneer. But under the influence from the Pioneers in my congregation, I decided to forego a formal college education so I could focus on Regular Pioneering (preaching 70 hours a month). They had me convinced I wouldn't need a college degree since Armageddon (the end of the world) would likely occur before I turned 21.

Once I had attended Pioneer Service School and pioneered for a couple years, I was looking to the next step—dating and getting married. And I already had my eye on who would make the perfect mate.

Teen to Young Adult

I noticed him for the first time when I was a young teenager. He had a part at the Circuit Assembly and I even wrote his name and congregation down in my assembly program. I didn't officially meet John until a couple years later, when the young ones in the circuit started networking and meeting other young ones from neighboring congregations and foreign language groups. As Jehovah's Witness youths, we weren't allowed to cultivate friendships outside the organization. But in my case, I also had friends at school and from the various activities I was involved with. I kept the two social circles from ever meeting the other. I did my best to be the perfect Jehovah's Witness, so I made friends within the organization and eventually my social circle meshed with John and his friends.

We got along instantly, sharing the same interests and humor but also, the same spiritual goals of continuing to Regular Pioneer and eventually serve where the need was great, whether local or abroad. I was 18, barely turning 19, when John and I expressed our feelings to each other. Initially, my parents forbade us from seeing each other since we were too young to get married. Jehovah's Witnesses don't date unless they are ready to get married. We would occasionally see each other from afar at the assemblies or gatherings, but we would sneak in secret phone calls to each other whenever possible.

Once my parents lifted the ban on us seeing each other, we were able to hang out in group settings or he would come to the house when my parents were home. Because a male and female could never be alone together unless in the presence of a chaperone, John and I spent plenty of time in the preaching work, alongside our friends, to get to know each other. The only moments we got to be ourselves and speak what was on our mind were on the phone. John mentioned we should start getting our timeline in order: becoming an "officially dating couple" soon, determining how long until we get engaged and deciding when we would get married. In my mind, I knew once we made it official, everyone would expect us to date for a year, two at most, then be engaged for a short period to be followed with a wedding. Something held me back from jumping right onto that path.

I still lived with my parents, Regular Pioneered, had a part-time job and recently completed trade school with computer certifications in hand. There was a kind of life I wanted to–NEEDED to—experience. I didn't want to go straight from my parents' house to my husband's house. I wanted to experience being on my own and taking care of myself before committing to married life.

My First Taste of Freedom Within Limits

Shortly before turning 21, I moved out of both my parents' houses. I found a place to call my own—one roof, one home. In reality, it was just a bedroom that I rented in a shared house with three other single Jehovah's Witness females. But it was my own space. Everything in my life was now entirely up to me. While I was enjoying this newfound freedom, John patiently waited for me.

Culturally speaking, it was unheard of for a young woman to move out of her parent's house unless it was to get married. As a Jehovah's Witness, it was considered a "spiritual risk," but my reasoning was that living between two parents who were separated was worse for my spiritual health. I also wanted to experience life on my terms, within the rigid standards of being a Jehovah's Witness of course, before committing to a husband.

Life was extremely busy while living on my own. I began working full time to support myself financially, continued to Regular Pioneer and went out with my friends. Most of my friends were Witnesses from the Spanish congregations. My English congregation rarely knew how late I was out most nights, especially weekends, and why I was exhausted and sleep-deprived at Sunday morning meetings. John wasn't a partygoer, so he wasn't at most, if any, of the gatherings or parties I attended. My friends and I, being of legal drinking age, were able to purchase alcohol for house parties or get into nightclubs, bars and lounges. Alcohol usually flowed freely at most of the Witness parties and weddings. Everyone claimed they weren't drunk, just extremely buzzed, which was a popular thing to happen in major metropolitan areas like Southern California, where the Witness parties were getting out of control and rowdy.

John and I started to drift apart since I was spending less time with him, and I was spending more time with my friends and going on trips with them. Naturally, I started to meet other Witness guys and I started to feel John wasn't as fun or exciting. After a few months of living on my own, I decided to end my relationship with John. It wasn't fair to keep him waiting with the possibility we'd become "official" soon. I felt my desire to go out with my friends and meet new people would never end. John and I stayed friends, but we rarely saw each other outside of assemblies and conventions.

Two different times, my friends and I went on week-long cruises, one to the Caribbean and the second to the Mexican Riviera. During both vacations, many of us were straight up drunk throughout the cruise. We used every opportunity to drink, do shots and buy more alcohol to sneak onto the ship at every port we visited. Another time, we grouped into four or five cars to drive down to Ensenada, Mexico. Each night spent there we were a drunken mess, stumbling from one bar to another. Once we returned home, we discovered some of the guys in our group had hickeys from non-JW girls they met at the hotel pool. I remember feeling guilty for keeping that secret within our circle and for being present when such "loose behavior" was happening.

After a close friend got into a car accident the morning after a night of heavy drinking, I realized this was my wake-up call. Although the constant partying with Witness friends was a lot of fun, it felt repetitive and unfulfilling, and I knew sooner or later there would be worse consequences if I continued this way. I also learned that the excitement but unpredictability of the guys I was interested in was scary and they weren't always aligned with my spiritual goals. Nearly a year after "breaking up" with John, I began to crave the safety and stability I had with him.

John didn't welcome me back immediately with open arms. As was expected, we had many serious conversations about my motive for wanting to get back together. I promised him I was done with heavy drinking and partying, and I wanted to focus on being a spiritual-minded girlfriend and future wife to him. We finally began dating, eventually got engaged and then had the big wedding with only our spiritually strong friends in attendance. By this point, I only focused on maintaining friendships with Witnesses who were spiritually minded and had even stopped communicating with relatives and family who weren't Jehovah's Witnesses. I felt there was no purpose in keeping contact with them since they probably wouldn't survive Armageddon for not learning about "The Truth" anyway. But life was back on track.

Life Unhappily Ever After

I had married the perfect brother who was a Ministerial Servant and had a stable full-time job. I was able to work from home and continue Regular Pioneering. When we got married, I moved into his congregation because they had a low publisher count, or low attendance. They needed all the help they could get. For the first time, I felt indispensable, and I was used on nearly a monthly basis for parts in the Theocratic Ministry School and demonstrations in the Service Meeting. Our goal as a couple was to help the congregation thrive spiritually before moving to another local congregation that needed assistance. I joined the Regional Build Committee and was able to count the hours painting the interior and exterior at Kingdom Hall building projects as service time. In reality, I wanted to avoid the preaching work when I could; painting was much more enjoyable than speaking to people who had zero interest in hearing about "The Truth", paradise or Armageddon.

After a year or two of married life, John was appointed an elder, and I felt I had reached the top of the ladder. Being an elder's wife, I was expected to socialize with the other elders' wives in the congregation. I quickly learned I did not enjoy their company much at all, but I endured it because that's what was expected.

The elders' wives of my congregation enjoyed gossiping about others, but the most disturbing part was hearing them speak of confidential and judicial matters that their elder husbands told them. I was proud that John never spoke with me about any confidential matters nor did I ever ask, but it troubled me knowing the elders in our congregation weren't trustworthy. There was a high chance that anything told to the elders in confidence would become pillow talk between them and their wives, and in turn the elders' wives would speak about it amongst each other, usually to compare stories.

This may have been one of the first things to extremely disappoint me in our congregation, and I concluded this could be a problem in other congregations or circuits. I told my father-in-law about my concerns, also an elder in the congregation. Whether or not this issue was truly addressed with the other elders and their wives, I'm not entirely sure. The only change I noticed was the decrease of invitations and the limited topics of conversation when I was present with the elders' wives, which I was perfectly fine with.

Giving My All to God Wasn't Enough

An elder from the Tagalog Congregation did our taxes. One year when I went to drop off our tax documents, he said to me, "You should move to the Tagalog Congregation." I told him that we were already serving in a congregation that not only needed our help but needed John as an elder. What he said next stunned me into silence and then quiet anger. He said, "You would be a better Witness if you served in a Tagalog Congregation." What? That stayed on my mind for weeks after. How could my service and worship not be good enough if I'm already giving and doing everything I possibly can?

John reassured me that we shouldn't worry about such things, and I tried to let it go. But it still bothered me that an appointed elder would ever think someone's worship wasn't enough, especially when they were already serving as a full-time Pioneer, participating in the Regional Build Committee and preparing for an upcoming part at the District Convention. If one elder felt this way, no doubt other elders or publishers felt that way too. On a worldwide scale, was anyone's worship to God considered not enough just because they haven't moved to a foreign language congregation? Was it not enough to worship and serve in a congregation of your native tongue? Until this moment, I had not questioned myself as not being enough or doing enough.

The Unravelling

By the third year of marriage, I began to feel anxiety every time a fellow worshiper in the congregation would complement me, especially after a preaching/teaching demonstration on stage. When they would say "you're such a great example" or "you're such a good wife" or "you're such a faithful Pioneer," I cringed internally from guilt but put on a fake smile. I didn't deserve to be complimented on such things when I had done so much wrong as a teenager and prior to getting married. I felt the anxiety growing whenever I thought of the future. This was going to be the rest of my life until Armageddon arrived: never-ending preaching to people who were not interested in our message; repetitive weekly meetings; and empty, insincere and forced friendships within the congregation.

I found myself wanting to spend more time with my friends doing anything else but preaching or going to meetings. I was spending less time at home, especially with John who was usually too busy preparing his outline for his next part or public talk. I started to appear on the party scene again with friends who still kept up with those activities, even after some of them had also gotten married. I had everything I thought I had always wanted. I was living the life I had planned since I got baptized at the tender age of thirteen.

But I was not happy. I was feeling more and more restless and uneasy. What was I doing wrong? What was I not doing enough of? Why didn't I feel satisfied or fulfilled? Why would I rather stay busy with friends than enjoy a quiet evening at home alone or even with John? When John and I would make plans, I couldn't help but want to invite friends or other couples to join us.

I began attributing the anxiety and guilt to the weight of my secret sins of the past. I never confessed to not being a virgin prior to marrying John. He had no idea. Almost no one knew I drank alcohol in high school, ditched class frequently and smoked weed with my worldly boyfriend on Grad Night at Disneyland. I regularly hung out alone with worldly and Witness guy friends, some even spending the night when I was living on my own, even though nothing sexual happened. In hindsight, this wasn't unusual behavior for teenagers or young adults to experience. But for a baptized Jehovah's Witness and Regular Pioneer, these were major offenses and likely required a judicial committee review and discipline. I felt like a hypocrite. How could I encourage others who were spiritually weak when I was guilty of a past I kept a secret?

I believed this was why I wasn't happy in my marriage. At no fault to John, this had to be the consequence of keeping such things a secret. I believed not only did I need to confess these things to him and the elders, but I needed the highest form of discipline in order to clear my conscience and standing before God. I needed to be disfellowshipped so that I could restart my life as a Jehovah's Witness with a clean slate. I believed my marriage wasn't blessed nor was it ever going to be because I entered into the union with deceit and lies.

I had a serious talk with John and told him everything that was on my mind. As expected, he was heartbroken and stunned when I told him I didn't want this marriage to continue. Internally, I was freaking out, and the only thing I felt sure of was that I needed to be disfellowshipped and we needed to get a divorce. I did not want to end up like my parents, stuck in a miserable marriage for eternity. I felt we were past the point of saving our marriage. He deserved to be free to remarry, and I deserved to be disfellowshipped to pay for my past sins. But we didn't have scriptural grounds to get divorced. Jehovah's Witnesses believe the only grounds for a divorce and to be free to remarry is if one partner commits adultery.

I did not want to sleep with someone else just to be free. That wasn't me—I just couldn't go that far. So, I chose the lesser of two evils. I decided to lie in my judicial committee and say I cheated on my husband. Even though John knew this was what I was doing, he didn't stop me. I sat before three elders, and John sat in silence next to me as I confessed to the things I did in high school, while living on my own and prior to getting married. If anything involved other Witnesses, I left their names out of it; I felt it wasn't my place to confess to someone else's involvement with my own sins. In reality, I didn't want judicial committees formed against my Witness friends.

And then I told the story I had rehearsed in my head. I lied about sleeping with a former friend, someone who wasn't a Witness. I was not prepared for the questions they asked next. They asked me how I met this person, where would we meet up, how many times we hung out, when and where did things get intimate, and how far we went sexually. I remember having to make up fake details on the spot. Through what felt like a humiliating and demeaning interrogation, I kept my goal in mind: get my past sins off my chest but make my confession believable and bad enough for them to decide to disfellowship me. Confessing that I cheated on my husband was enough to give him the freedom to remarry. At this point, I still believed this meeting had God's backing, and ultimately, I was doing the right thing. I cried and sobbed tears of disappointment in myself but also tears of relief for getting everything off my chest. I knew I just had to survive and endure the impending disciplinary period of time to be right with Jehovah.

When they finally gave their decision to disfellowship me, I felt immediate contentment. But I began to stress at the thought of telling my parents and friends that I would be announced as disfellowshipped at the next meeting. You're still allowed to associate with fellow Witnesses right up until the moment they announce from the stage in front of the congregation that you're no longer a Jehovah's Witness. I only had a few days to break the news to my closest friends and family and say our goodbyes. They treat it like a death, which is the point of disfellowshipping. You are completely cut off from associating or being acknowledged by all your Jehovah's Witness friends and family. Only in extreme circumstances can your family members speak to you and only about family matters.

During the phone calls I made to out-of-state friends, there were lots of tears and lots of sadness, but also promises were made that we'd pick right up once I returned to the organization. Some of my friends stayed with me the days and nights before the official announcement to savor our last hours of friendship. I didn't tell them details of why I was getting disfellowshipped, but I know they assumed. When a divorce was about to happen and one spouse was getting disfellowshipped, there was only one obvious reason. I told one, maybe two, of my best friends the truth, that I did not cheat on John. All I said was that I committed enough sins to merit disfellowshipping. Whether they believed me or not, I never knew. It was a very confusing time, but I felt a freedom I had never known before: freedom of being alone, freedom of not having anyone be allowed to ask me any questions, and freedom from fear of anything worse than disfellowshipping happening to me. I finally enjoyed the solace and quiet of being alone with myself.

Unconditional Friendships

I may have lost my Witness friends and family, but this was where my non-Witness friends stepped up and became my new family. They were there for me and kept me busy. At first, they did not understand why I wanted to leave a seemingly perfect marriage, but they never judged me. They wanted to be sure John didn't abuse, neglect or hurt me in any way. The best and most honest explanation I could give was "I wasn't as happy as I knew I should've been, so I had to get out and start over." That was enough for them to support me and keep me from falling into a downward spiral. As I was navigating my newfound freedom with lots of time on my hands, they made sure I was OK. They spent time with me and invited me to many social activities, and I was surprised that I felt no guilt at being out with people who had zero involvement in the organization.

I was expecting to see numerous cases of non-Witnesses lose their livelihood to drugs or alcohol, or deal with unwanted pregnancies and life-threatening sexually transmitted diseases. I was expecting to be targeted by evil people waiting for every opportunity to take advantage of me. I was always taught by the organization that worldly people were unhappy and were searching for the truth, and we were the fortunate ones to know The Truth and offer it to them. I found the complete opposite. My worldly friends were the happiest and most authentic people I had ever known. They didn't judge each other or criticize each other's choices. As long as you weren't a danger to yourself or to others, they supported you wholeheartedly and without ill will. I still believed I had The Truth, but my view of worldly people had definitely shifted. They weren't all bad, and they were nothing like what the Society had led me to believe. Sure, at times you'd come across a few bad apples, but in the grand scheme of people I chose to surround myself with, I was around a very good bunch.

I recall the first few months of attending meetings at a different congregation where no one knew me. To my surprise, I felt relaxed. I was so happy with not talking to anyone, and no one was allowed to approach or speak to me because I was disfellowshipped. I loved arriving right before the meeting began and leaving immediately after the final song and prayer. I felt there must have been something very wrong with me to feel this kind of peace at not having to interact with anyone. I entertained the thought of staying disfellowshipped indefinitely but still attend all the meetings and be completely happy. If Jehovah could read our hearts, he'd know I still loved him and wanted to make him happy. I just didn't want to deal with everyone else. I even planned to continue preaching to worldly people, and if they wanted a Bible Study, I could refer them to someone in the Kingdom Hall.

My best friend, Sarah, was disfellowshipped a week before me. She was a true lifesaver who never left my side through everything we experienced as Jehovah's Witnesses and then on the other side of the organization. As disfellowshipped members, we carpooled and sat together at the meetings. In the beginning, the elders approached us and after giving them the gist of our situation, they said it was nice that we were able to encourage each other not to give up. After a short while of attending the meetings and sitting with other disfellowshipped ones, we were told by the elders that we shouldn't be associating with each other. Obviously, they noticed us talking to each other outside in the parking lot.

I was appalled at this tedious rule that I never heard of before. It didn't make any sense. We were isolated from the rest of the active members, but now they wanted us to stay away from each other too? I spoke to my disfellowshipped friends from other congregations and from the Spanish congregation. I discovered that mixed instructions were given. Some disfellowshipped friends were told not to hang out with other disfellowshipped ones, whereas others weren't told anything was wrong with it. I researched in the Society's publications and couldn't find a definite answer. Was this a rule some elders made up to impose their authority? Why was this enforced in some congregations and not others? Why the difference, not only between one language group to another, but from one congregation to another? Should things like that be happening within God's earthly organization? What if our association with each other was the only good thing happening, an actual positive influence?

My Crossroad

For the first couple of years after getting disfellowshipped, Sarah and I continued to attend some meetings, assemblies, conventions and the Memorial of Jesus Christ's death. I wasn't serious about getting reinstated right away; I knew they'd expect me to be out for a minimum of a year or more before considering my reinstatement. Although I missed my Witness friends so much, I realized life goes on with or without them. They didn't check up on me, and I didn't hear a peep from them. Were they just waiting for me to be a Jehovah's Witness again before they would be my friend? How much of my life outside the organization would they even want to know, or would our friendship be based on gaining titles and privileges back? As each month and year passed, I missed my Witness friends less and less.

I learned to figure out life. Even though my friends from childhood, school and activities remained the best people I ever knew, I came across people who weren't so great. But they didn't scare me, and they didn't hurt me. I felt like a child re-learning to distinguish the "good people" from the "bad people." But I learned to trust my instincts and look at their qualities and character. I let go of the "trust only Jehovah's Witnesses but not worldly people" mindset. I learned to see people for who they truly were, not based on their religion, titles or privileges they had. I started to analyze the friendships I had in the organization. If it weren't for being Jehovah's Witnesses, would we have been friends in the first place? Would we be friends now?

An elder who occasionally checked up on me started to ask if I was ready to turn in a letter to request reinstatement. I told him I was working on it. I began to draft a letter stating how I had repented my past ways and what I've done to regain my good standing in the congregation. Something in my conscience started to eat away at me. I wasn't doing anything bad, but did I really want to go back to the organization? Why wasn't I as eager to go back? Had I been out too long? I decided to even put the matter to prayer. Until I felt absolutely sure this was the truth, I wouldn't hand in my letter.

I spoke to my best friend, Sarah, about it. I love that she never discouraged me from going back to the organization. We only promised that we'd stay friends no matter what, whether one of us was in or out. I could never, and would never, abandon Sarah based on the standing given by any organization. We'd proven our friendship was stronger than a title.

I allowed myself to research and study the one topic that was forbidden my entire life. I gave myself permission to research and prove The Truth to myself. Once I did that research, which to this day hasn't stopped, I am constantly grateful for every hour of every day now and forever, because that has set the tone for the rest of my life. I learned that the truth, and not "The Truth" the organization has defined as the truth, will truly set you free. Finally, this was the freedom and inner peace I had been searching for.

Waking Up When I Didn't Know I was Asleep

Recently I was asked "what would you tell your younger self?" Something obvious like "you're in a cult, this isn't the truth, get out now" seems to be the expected answer but also the most ineffective way to reach young Abby. I was fortunate to have a personality trait that my parents instilled in me: the hunger to research. Whatever sparked my interest, "look it up" is what my parents would constantly tell me. I did not have the internet at my fingertips. I did not have Wikipedia, Reddit or the countless research resources on the worldwide web as a child or even a teenager. I had good old-fashioned book fairs and public libraries. And you know what piqued my curiosity as a child? Rocks, dirt, gemstones, sediments, the various layers of Earth's core and the ancient civilizations that archeologists uncover. I wanted to be the next Indiana Jones! I wanted to find long lost civilizations of hundreds of years ago. I'll never forget what my parents said when I told them I wanted to be an archeologist when I grew up. They said, "There's nothing left to discover. Everything has already been found." Well, damn. That put an immediate end to my hopes and dreams.

Before I revealed that dream to them, I've always had the thirst for knowledge, especially for things I found interesting. I always asked "why?" When those book fairs happened at school, I would circle the books in the flyer that were about rocks, gemstones and crystals. I wanted to learn more. While I was young, this was always my passion— researching, digging deeper and finding the answers to my "whys" and "how's." When the internet started gaining popularity to research and search engines became the method of getting answers to questions, I researched anything and everything that I felt like reading about. I loved this and still do to this day: going down the rabbit hole of research and studying. Once I felt that I had found the answers I was looking for, once I had added 10 more books to my endless wish list or once I had added several more documentaries to my Netflix queue, I'd finally shut things down and know my brain was satisfied for now.

But as a young adult, the two words I never typed into those search engines were "Jehovah's Witnesses." Even though I knew I could get away with reading all sorts of things on the internet without my parents or anyone in the congregation knowing, I still had the fear that God would know. It's funny how with certain actions I almost had no guilt or remorse, but there was that one line I was afraid to cross. I had convinced myself that I had no need to research "Jehovah's Witnesses" on the internet. Because this was the one true religion, I was confident there was nothing but good and positive stories out there, which I should already be aware of since that's what was published by The Watchtower Society. I believed I wouldn't find anything I didn't already know.

We come back to the question "what would I tell my younger self?" I'd tell young Abby this: "Don't ever stop doing the research, especially when they tell you not to." Young Abby was stubborn enough to not believe it if Future Abby tells her she's in a cult. Young Abby wouldn't believe Future Abby that the friends she's made thus far in the organization would one day shun her. Young Abby would've dug her heels in deeper just to prove a point to Future Abby that that is not what would happen in the future. Telling my younger self, the actual truth about the truth would've driven Young Abby deeper into the cult. By telling my younger self to just keep doing what was already her natural strength and passion, which was steering and satisfying her curiosity towards research, I'd encourage Young Abby to just keep going. Listen to the little voice in her head telling her to search those two words because it will open her mind and she'll reach the point where nothing in this world is ever held back from her again. That's all I'd have to tell Young Abby, and I trust that if she listens to that small piece of advice, she'd save herself a lot of wasted time in her youth and set herself up for a bright, truly free and truly happy future.

It's not always easy, and it definitely hurts waking up to the harsh reality that the truth was, in fact, nothing but lies. I've lost communication with a large portion of my family, and my Witness friends are probably wondering why I haven't returned. I've learned to see my friendships and relationships with others for what they are. My former friends within the organization were conditional, based on superficial man-made titles in a man-made religious corporation. But the friends I've made outside the organization have shown me what true unconditional love is, based on mutual respect of each other's free will to choose the best path in life they decide for themselves, because that is their human right. I no longer base my friendships based on religious beliefs or lifestyle choices, and I've experienced a freedom and joy I never experienced as a Jehovah's Witness.

My story may not be shocking and is not one filled with abuse or extreme trauma. It doesn't mean there wasn't grief or pain at losing a long-held and deeply ingrained belief system I used to hold in high regard. To see members of my own family treat me like I don't exist just because I no longer share their religious views is extremely hurtful. But I've found comfort reconnecting and rebuilding relationships with my non-JW family members. There is nothing like unconditional love among family and friends. Losing family and conditional friendships is a small price to pay for the freedom to open my eyes and know true happiness and authenticity.

To all of you reading my story—whatever doubts, questions or seemingly insignificant thoughts you have, I encourage you with my entire being to keep doing the research, but especially when someone, ANYONE, is telling you not to. The worst that can happen is you realize what you wanted to believe so badly as the truth no longer isn't, and you can find your way to heal and then grow from it. The best that can happen is you reaffirm your belief. It's only a win-win scenario. If anything, research and dig deeper and harder when someone is giving you resistance because more than likely, there's something they don't want you to know and you have a right to know why. I believe everyone is entitled to know ALL the facts, the good and bad, behind every major life decision. Know that no choice is permanent. You always have a choice.

At one time, my back was up against the wall and I knew I couldn't continue to pretend on my former path in life. I had no idea what my next steps were going to be, but then I made a difficult choice for myself. I'll be forever grateful to the inner resilience I didn't know I had to just keep going, keep surviving and slowly but surely become more confident in myself. I lied before an organization, but I eventually found the truth. I'll never stop asking why, because truth fears no questions.

Chapter 5

They Clip Our Wings

But We Can Still Learn to Soar

by Shane Hubenig

I'm not a person prone to anger or angry outbursts. It's in my nature to remain calm under most circumstances, even antagonistic ones. Yet here I was, standing up at a table at lunch, my head feeling like it is going to burst from elevated blood pressure. I am shouting down at my seated mother. She appears shocked. I am already embarrassed inside. My children never see me like this. They are confused and a little bit afraid, I think. I am not proud of this momentary loss of control. The conversation leading up to it went something like this. I am trying to repeat it as best I can remember it.

"Do your boys ever go to the Kingdom Hall with their cousins?" my mom asked my wife.

"No, not really," my wife answered.

"Do you teach them about God or the bible?" Mom asked.

"No, we just raise them to be good people, and when they get older, they can explore religions and believe what they want to believe and what makes sense to them," my wife said "We don't want to make them believe anything, or not give them a choice."

My mom gives me a look, like I have disappointed her and am failing my children. It's OK, I'm used to it. I rarely see my mom and she rarely sees her grandchildren. I can ignore this for the sake of a peaceful lunch. Or so I think.

"Well, we Witnesses raise our children to know about God," Mom said. "We don't force them to believe as we do. We just encourage them to make the best choice."

Calmly, I said, "Mom, that is not true. Witness kids are taught one belief system, and they are not allowed to explore other possibilities and are entirely expected to become JWs like their parents."

My mom stares at me for a moment, then turns back towards my wife and repeats herself, as if I said nothing. "We don't force our children to do or believe anything," she said. "We believe our children have free will and free choice to do what they like with their lives. We hope they follow our teachings, but we don't force children to be JWs."

She is saying this very slowly, and with each word I feel myself getting more and more angry. Unbidden images of lonely days at school, boring afternoons at home studying scripture and waiting for the next meeting fill my head. I remember having every dream or aspiration shot down with a reminder that only "God's Kingdom" matters in life. I'm remembering what I escaped from. I picture my little boys being made to dress up in uncomfortable child sized suits, being punished for not sitting still enough or not paying enough attention, and sitting still for hours listening to someone talk about the JW view of God and Bible for hours on end. I visualize driving around in a hot car and knocking on doors on beautiful sunny days when other kids are laughing and playing. I picture my own boys in these situations. I lose it. I start out feeling a bit sad from the memories, but it's slowly turning into anger as I picture my own boys growing up as I did.

"No, you are not being truthful," I said. "JW kids are certainly not given any choice about what they can believe or be as they grow up. I get it. That's what parents do teach children to believe what they believe, but it's not honest to suggest they are given any choice in the matter or that there is no consequence to making the 'wrong' choice."

I'm angry now, but I am speaking calmly.

My mom chooses to be dismissive of what I am saying and insinuate that I am lying.

"Well, that's the way YOU felt, but it's NOT true," she says. My mom turns to my wife again. "We teach our children The Truth and encourage them to follow it, but they have a free choice if they choose to follow it or not," Mom said.

This is when I lose it. I have lost control over my actions and am acting entirely as my emotions are driving me. This is an unfamiliar place for me. I hardly recognize myself. I stand up. My head is pounding and feels like it is going to burst. I shout down at my mom and involuntarily point a finger at her. "YOU ARE LYING," I yell "The words coming out of your mouth ARE NOT TRUE! I can't sit here and let you LIE to my wife about JW children and choice!"

"You raise children to only believe or accept one path. You do not allow them any non-JW association, you isolate them from all critical thought, you don't allow them to have friends or mentors outside the faith, and then as they grow old enough, you tell them they have a choice. That choice is to believe as taught and get baptized, or walk away from everything and everyone they have ever known! They must say goodbye forever to anyone that they ever thought loved or cared about them, off into the world alone with no support in any form. WHAT KIND OF CHOICE IS THAT? Is that what you call "free choice"? I will NOT subject my children to that! I will NOT raise my children telling them that love and support are dependent on them believing what I tell them to believe and tell them they either accept this or go off into the world alone. I will NOT raise my children like that or allow them to be raised like that!"

My usually loud and rambunctious boys are silent, looking at me. My wife is staring down at her plate. My mom looks at me like I slapped her and has nothing to say. I calm down. Lunch is over. I think to myself, "My wings were clipped, but my boys will be free."

Born in

My parents were Jehovah's Witnesses when I was born. My dad was from an Austrian farm family that was several generations JW. My mom was a Jamaican immigrant and a convert to the faith. My dad was following family tradition. I have no idea to this day the true, deeper reasons my mom was drawn to the faith.

My parents were good parents. I have no complaints about their care and love for me. I think I was around four years old when I realized our family was just a little bit different. I realized at some point that not every little boy had to dress up uncomfortably and sit still for hours at meetings. From my car seat, I saw kids playing outside and running around while we drove to meetings. Then there was the field service. Again, I had to dress up in weird, uncomfortable clothes, drive around and knock on doors. Most people were kind but didn't want to see us, and that was clear to me. Holidays were always exciting to a child, but along with my first memories of the exciting holidays came the admonitions of how evil these events were and how we were not part of them. I accepted all this without question.

Meetings were boring, and my mind always wandered. I wished I could bring books, as I always liked books. My mom read to me a lot. From a combination of her reading aloud to me and a natural aptitude I had for reading, I was actually reading simple books even before kindergarten. Not till recent years did I realize how uncommon that actually was. I wish I could bring some of my books to the meetings, but I was only allowed to look at the Bible and *The Watchtower* publications. Some of them had interesting illustrations, but I got tired of looking at the same ones again and again.

As I grew a bit older, my parents expected me to pay closer attention to the speakers. I was often punished with spankings if I fidgeted too much or they didn't think I was paying close enough attention. Sometimes I would be quizzed after a meeting about the subject the speakers talked about. I was good at guessing and paying just enough attention to give a good answer, but if they didn't think I paid enough attention, I would be punished and experience their disappointment in me.

Honestly, punishment generally had less impact then did the feeling that I was always letting them down and that I was a disappointment to them, especially to my Dad. He was a distant figure when I was young. He was an elder, and it was clear to me he was important. People always needed to talk to him. He left most child-raising and discipline to my mom. She was impatient and hard to please. It was important to her that I was the perfect little Witness child. I think I did well in that role, but she always made me feel I was not doing well enough. By the time it was time to attend school, I knew our family was a little bit different from most, but it was at school I started to realize how different.

Our Wings are Clipped

It was in Kindergarten that I started realizing how we didn't really fit in. The first few holidays I did wrong in my parents' eyes. I was shy about expressing myself, but I knew I had to tell the teacher I could not participate in holiday arts and crafts and activities. My Kindergarten teacher tried to respect that and still include me. She gave me activities to do that were still with the class but slightly different. For example, when Valentine's Day came along, I said I could not draw or cut out hearts. I was told by the teacher I could make circles or other shapes and make a non-valentine card. I took this home to my parents, and boy was I in trouble!

I now realize that different Witness parents took different views of this kind of thing. My parents were very extreme; they expected me to take NO part in activities related to "pagan" holidays. I was punished and made to feel extremely bad for "displeasing Jehovah." I was to pray for forgiveness and told I made Jehovah sad. Now looking at my own little boys, I realize that my parents put an unrealistic expectation on me to "stand up for my faith." I viewed my teacher as an authority, and if a teacher said something was OK, well then it was OK. But I soon learned I was to exclude myself and have nothing to do with holidays. Exclusion from holiday events combined with refusal to attend other children's birthday parties meant I stood out as odd and different more and more.

I had some JW friends in my early years, but I didn't see them often, and they were never in my class or school, so I was very much alone. Contact outside of school with non-JW children was forbidden. I found myself with very limited friendships at school, never feeling like I belonged in a group. I accepted it but realize now I spent most of my early childhood in a state of child depression. Only as an adult did I really see it for what it was.

As I grew a little older, I started to realize that as a JW kid, my ideas and dreams of the future were not mine to make. Unless they were "theocratic" goals.

I recall one school day when I was about six or seven years old. Our project was to draw what we wanted to be when we grew up. I thought sailing the seas would be cool. I wanted to be a sailor, so I drew a boat with myself in it. My mom flipped out when she saw it. Why did I not want to be a Pioneer? A Pioneer is a full time JW door knocker. These people tend to work at part-time jobs, only making enough money to support themselves while doing free full-time preaching work for The Watchtower organization.

I remember my mom crying about my career choice. My Dad didn't seem to think it was a big deal, but to my mom, I was not paying enough attention at the meetings, and I did not love God enough. I should proudly tell my teachers and classmates that I intended to be a full-time servant of Jehovah, knocking on doors, selling Bible literature and conducting Bible studies. This would be a theme as I grew up. Any ideas I ever had of things to do when I grew up, would be a choice that would disappoint my mom. I now realize that she placed her identity of being a successful JW parent in the zeal and status her children displayed in the JW organization. My dad, even though he was a JW elder, was a little more pragmatic and secular.

Acceptance and Growth in the Organization

As my school years went on, things never got better socially at school. I have heard of some JW kids that managed to "be cool" and "fit in" even with the JW weird factor. In some cases, it's because their parents were a little more relaxed, others were allowed a few non-JW friends and allowed to play sports and engage in other non-educational activities. I was not one of these, my parents were of the stricter variety. On the rare occasion I was allowed to have a non-Witness friend come over to hang out after school. But it had to be one my parents approved of. Never on weekends because Saturday morning was door-to-door service, and Sunday was meetings in the morning and more door-to-door work in the afternoon. Half our weekends, sometimes more, was entirely taken up with religious JW obligations. I don't know how parents did it. As a child, I found it exhausting.

I was allowed very few non-JW friends. If my parents thought a child might be interested in what JWs taught or if they had parents that occasionally took JW literature, it was deemed OK to have some association with them. But for the most part, the isolation intensified. I'd usually have only one or two friends at school at any given time. Association outside of school with these ones was very restricted. Standing out as different is never a great thing for a kid in school. Being part black, I also stood out racially. The West Coast rural Canadian schools I went to when growing up were mostly filled with white kids. So being part black and being of a weird religion made me a common target to being bullied.

Thus, I grew up hating school even though I was good at it. I was a good reader, and I remembered things well. I generally aced tests with little to no studying. But I didn't really try or apply myself. I was constantly told that "the end was near." My parents told me that Armageddon would likely happen before I graduated, or shortly after, so all "worldly" vocations or goals were pointless. It didn't make me feel inspired to study hard at anything. I knew university was out of the question. At that time, very few Witness kids ever got a higher education. It was not banned, but it was highly discouraged. JW youth were expected to become Pioneers, or do some other form of service to The Watchtower corporation, like Bethel, or be part of the international building projects. Anything else was considered "a waste" of youth.

As I floated through school always feeling like an outsider, I grew to fit in more and more in the congregation. I was good at giving talks on Thursday night. I was well behaved and so was quickly given "privileges" like handing the microphone around for comments at The Watchtower study or giving longer and longer talks at the meetings, helping manage the literature counter, etc. I was a regular in the preaching work, even though I still found it embarrassing and not at all productive or fulfilling. I would go out often with a variety of people in the congregation. I was viewed as an "up and coming" young brother, with lots of potential in the JW world, even as my social life and social skills outside the congregation sucked. I placed more and more of my identity on being a good JW and flowing with the program. Many young JWs coped by living "a double life." I was not one of those. I was always a little bit judgmental and at the same time a little bit envious of those ones.

My Primary Issues Being a JW Kid

I don't want to give the impression I had a terrible life as a child. My dad worked hard, and we always had a decent standard of living. Dad also taught me fishing and hunting, which were great times that meant a lot to me. I felt liked and cared for by the members of the congregation. Many felt like extended family to me.

I never was a victim of the child sexual abuse we hear so much about now. Over the years, I learned that the congregation I grew up in had at least two active, brutal pedophiles, but I was never among the victims.

The issue I have with Jehovah's Witnesses and the raising of their children are as follows.

1. **Very little mental freedom**: Children are expected to become JWs themselves. They are not given any freedom to explore other ideas, thoughts, morality or religion, or to make rational, independent choices for themselves.

2. **The blood doctrine**: If a JW child is injured or sick, JW parents can and will deny blood-based intervention that can save them. In denying these treatments, JW parents may allow a child to die, and the children never have the chance to make a true free will choice on the matter for themselves of accepting or refusing treatment. I'm shocked by the stories we grew up with about children (highly indoctrinated) pulling IVs out of their arms and fighting medical staff to "protect" themselves from the perceived violation of blood based medical treatments. Amazingly, *The Watchtower* never really banned blood transfusions until the 1960s and now even today are relaxing the rules on the use of "blood fractions." To allow a child to die because of a doctrine that's barely 60 years old, based on an extreme interpretation of an ancient document, is insanity to me.

3. **Lack of support or encouragement for secular careers**: Some JW kids have progressive parents who encourage higher education for their children. Other parents tow *The Watchtower* line about the dangers of "worldly" education and do not support or encourage their children to follow their dreams and explore career options. JW children are to "find joy" in menial jobs that can support a life of volunteer work for a religious publishing company.

The First Serious Doubts

There was a Pioneer service moment that stood out among others. I had a return visit with a young Anglican minister. He decided to listen to me explain JW belief. At one point we were talking about "the live forever" book, and he got very interested in the Witness interpretation of 1914 and "this generation." Remember this was before the internet age. I visited him a few times with other Witnesses, thinking what a "score" it would be if I could convert a preacher to the JWs! This pastor was phoning up and talking to other people about the Witnesses. He discovered that previous end-of-time predictions had been made by the JWs, and he brought these to my attention. I was strongly invested in my place in the JW faith. I had my own doubts, but no preacher was going to shake my faith!

But he said to me, "In a few years, if the end doesn't come, your leadership is going to have to move the goal posts. They will do it in a way that doesn't alarm most of the members, but your religion will move forward with a change and "new light" (he had talked to people who made him familiar with the term, I assume). You will be preaching towards a new 'soon to come' end time. This prediction of his would prove to be correct.

He said to me that real "Truth" doesn't need "new light" or "changes of understanding." It just is what it is. True.

Loneliness and Isolation and the Path to Freedom

I had serious doubts about the teachings of the faith. The idea of "living forever in paradise" was becoming more and more unreal and not believable to me. However, I thought that the JW community at least was good, and that kept me in it.

I loved the community I grew up in. I loved the sea and the access to wilderness that was available. But as a young person, I was finding the social situation stifling. Although I was happily well behaved by JW standards, I was resenting what felt like constant scrutiny. Everything one did or said was subject to congregation gossip. Also, I was feeling like I was missing out in the JW youth mad scramble to find a mate. I went through all of high school without dating. I grew up more isolated and with stricter views than the average JW, so although I had a few romantic interests, I was very poor at navigating them. I was awkward socially. Also, my mother was so critical, interfering and controlling I hardly felt comfortable even expressing I truly liked or had an interest in a girl. My mom wanted me to be her virgin sacrifice to Bethel it felt like to me. She was always pushing me in that direction. I needed personal space. I needed to discover who I really was, independent of parents and the congregation I grew up in. I was still loyal to the organization even with my nagging doubts, but I needed to leave my hometown to grow as a person. I had a few good friends and a few older people I liked to spend time with, but I needed to expand my world.

I drifted through a few congregations. I was always warmly welcomed and highly recommended with each new congregation I found myself in. But a part of me was always feeling empty. There had to be more to life than rehashing the same information again and again in hours and hours of meetings. Weekends had to be more fun and fulfilling than service and meetings. I was getting tired. Tired of being broke and poor. Tired of a nonexistent sex life and limited dating options. Tired of repetitive meetings. Tired of being worried that what I might say or do may "stumble" or offend someone in the congregation.

There must me more to life than living this drab existence, waiting for God's Day of Judgment and Armageddon to come and solve all my problems and make life fun and interesting.

To be clear, JWs certainly do some fun things. They travel, go on vacations and buy nice things when they have the means. It's not like JWs are made to live like monks. But in my circumstances in my youth, that's where I was, and I saw no path out of it. In JW lingo, I could have been described as "discouraged," although that is an oversimplification of the cocktail of doubts, needs and lack of sense of self I was dealing with.

I needed to get out, at least for a bit, to save my own soul from this dreary existence.

Fears and Reality

I was concerned about one thing regarding leaving the organization. As a JW youth growing up, you are raised on the whispered stories of the fate of wayward youth. It sounded like all the girls that leave the faith are in abusive relationships or are drug addicted prostitutes. Young men are either criminals or greedy soulless beings, all concerned about making money and living a high-roller lifestyle. Now of course I know this is not all true. Plenty of people leave the JWs and go on to life rich, fulfilling lives. I also realize that for those who do live a fast-burn lifestyle often lack social support when they leave or are kicked out, and they don't have positive examples of life outside the JW organization. They are simply not prepared for the "real world."

When I was about 19, I really enjoyed rollerblading. I spent a lot of time rollerblading around the city of Vancouver. That was like a drug for me. I was never great at making new friends, and no JWs in my circles of friends were into this sport, so I cruised around alone. One day I passed a sign that was advertising for a "roller patrol." These volunteers on rollerblades would have a radio and a first-aid pouch, and would be a first-on-scene responder for the parks of Vancouver. I always had a spirt of community service. The idea of hanging out with other people who loved rollerblading around the city and being a force of positive good was very appealing to me.

For those who are not a JW, understand that it's hard to have an excuse to hang out with non-JW people. JW's don't do the volunteer thing. They feel that the preaching work is the best volunteer work possible. I didn't realize exactly what I was doing, but on a certain level I was creating a justification to expand my association beyond just fellow Jehovah's Witnesses. That was not truly my intention, yet I did like this idea.

This was the best decision I made in my entire life. In some ways, I was lucky. In the roller patrol association, I found healthy friendships and a sense of purpose. I was raised to believe that "Jehovah's people" are the best people, the most honest and, the most truthful. My life experiences to this point had at least taught me that they are no different from anyone else. There are good people, bad people, honest people and dishonest people. JWs are no different from anyone else. I made wonderful new friends and spent time on the thing important to me.

Leaving the JWs did not turn into a life of self-destructive indulgence and debauchery. I was not only going to survive, but I was going to thrive.

The Way Out

One of the many things I am critical about in the JW organization is that it's not easy for a person holding any responsibilities or positions to step down from those in an honorable way. In the organization, you are always supposed to be striving onward and upward, earning ever higher levels of respect and responsibilities. I was a young Ministerial Servant. At first, I was very proud that my Bible knowledge and speaking ability were recognized when I achieved them. However, as a young single guy trying to find my way in life both socially and economically, the added burden of time that being a Ministerial Servant entailed was becoming too much. As I rollerbladed more and did less with the congregation, this got noticed, and the elders decided to remove me from being a Servant on the grounds of "not setting a spiritual lead." I was spending more time in a community volunteer position versus taking a lead in field service, and that was of great concern to them. When they told me I was being removed, they made it clear that I was still "in good standing."

However, when elders announce that a person is no longer a Ministerial Servant, they never tell the congregation what the reason is. People being people, they assume the worst, and the congregation assumes you must have committed some sin. No one considers that emotional exhaustion or stress could be the reason. People still greeted me and smiled, but there was no doubt that my position in the congregation had changed. No one sought out my company, and my presence was merely tolerated. I no longer felt I was truly part of the congregation. The last chain holding me in was broken.

I can remember it like it was yesterday—the first time I intentionally decided I would not go to a meeting. No sickness, no work, no excuse, just the conscious choice that for the first time in my entire life I would choose not to go to a meeting because I just did not want to.

It was a beautiful early summer Sunday. I knew my new friends in the roller patrol would be out cruising. I had an invite to go for drinks and dinner after patrol. There were people who wanted my company, people who had some of the same values as me. I could do something I loved in the beautiful West Coast sun, or I could drag myself to another stuffy meeting, wearing a ridiculous suit on a hot sunny day in the company of people who didn't care if I was there or not. Up to this point in my life, I did not feel that I had a choice to go to meetings. It was just something I always did. The very thought that I had a CHOICE to go to a meeting, or not, was powerful. I made the choice to drive back home, change into comfortable cloths, strap on my rollerblades and do something I actually wanted to do. I felt so free and powerful, like I never had before. And I loved it.

Conclusion

My story is a simple one. There was no powerful force of trauma that drove me to leave the JW organization. There was no moment of spiritual or doctrinal clarity. I was not trapped in an unsatisfying or abusive social or relationship situation that I needed to escape from. I was simply a young guy trying to know what it meant to be free. I wanted to live life on my terms and to make choices for myself, not worrying about what other people thought of it.

I wanted to live my life by intention and to make choices that meant something to me in the moment, not dragging myself through the exhausting JW schedule. Multiple failed prophesies made clear to me that the JWs had no secret knowledge of truth.

A line in a punk song I found inspiring says "I don't run no race where there ain't no prize." Paradise is a pipe dream. I'm here to live this life now. Death is a natural part of life, and the only thing to fear is a life not truly lived.

Since I left, my life has soared. I excelled in my employment, and I started a business and grew it to levels of success I never thought imaginable. I dated freely until finding a wonderful woman to make a beautiful family with.

My life is very rich. In addition to running my business, I serve my community as a firefighter. I am raising three little boys to know they can build a life the way they want to and to explore the world the way they want to. The cycle of oppression is over. My life is my own, and I am happy beyond what I ever dreamed possible.

Chapter 6

Perfectly Imperfect

by Connie Hamilton

"Sometimes we strive so hard for perfection that
we forget that imperfection is happiness"
~ Karen Nave

Sitting in my car, hands sweaty, heart racing and stomach turning, I am about to walk into the Kingdom Hall of Jehovah's Witnesses. It's been 27 years since I've seen any of my dad's side of the family—aunts, uncles, cousins—all will be there for the funeral of my grandfather. My husband is at my side, but even though he supports and loves me, he can't begin to understand the emotions running through my mind. Twenty-seven years ago, I left my hometown as a troubled 18-year-old Jehovah's Witness, having been publicly reproved, labelled a sinner and shunned for my actions. The people in the Kingdom Hall I'm about to enter have all shunned me. Why would I torment myself and go to this funeral? Because my dad and mom want me there, the only people who loved me so much they could not shun their daughter.

At this point in my life, my husband of 25 years and I have made a good life for ourselves and our two children. On the outside, my life looks like a success, but on the inside I'm sad, lonely and lost. Many times, I have wished I could be reinstated as a Jehovah's Witness so I could be reunited with my paternal side of my family.

Six months before my grandfather passed away, a knock on my door brought two Jehovah's Witnesses with *The Watchtower* and *Awake* magazines. I was polite, took the magazines and shut the door. Instead of throwing the magazines out like usual, I sat at my kitchen table and flipped through the *Awake* magazine. I stopped at an article about disfellowshipped people rejoining the religion. I sat and cried while reading the articles, reminiscing of family members I had been so close with at one time. I decided to contact the local elders and ask to be reinstated. I felt that I had proven over 25 years I was a good person and the indiscretions as a teenager should be forgiven. The elders gave me strict guidelines to follow to be considered for reinstatement: I had to attend all meetings, sit in the back and not speak to anyone, and leave immediately after. When they felt I had attended enough meetings continuously, they would consider my request.

I began going to meetings, sitting alone and listening to their messages on stage. I reached out to one of my aunts and told her that I was attending meetings again and would be going to the District Assembly and would love to see her and her family there. She seemed so excited that I was attending meetings, but said until I was fully reinstated, she was not comfortable seeing me or letting the rest of the family know of my intentions to become one of Jehovah's Witnesses again. I went to the assembly, continued going to meetings and wrote a letter requesting my membership be reinstated.

Finally, I was meeting with the elders to discuss my progress. They were happy with my attendance and said the next step would be to start participating in door-to-door service and discontinue any volunteer work I was doing that wasn't related to the organization. The problem was I wasn't asking to go back and be a part of the religion. I wanted to go back to be reunited with family. The steps I needed to take were ones I couldn't do, so I stopped going and gave up this dream of seeing my extended family again. I didn't let my aunt know; I couldn't figure out how to "disappoint" her again.

Two months later my Grandfather dies, and I'm about to walk into his funeral.

Pursuit of the Unachievable: Perfection

I grew up in a small town, always wanting to be perfect—the perfect daughter, student and Witness. I followed rules and I was respectful. Because of that, I was respected by schoolteachers and more importantly by fellow Jehovah's Witnesses.

My parents started studying and attending meetings of the Jehovah's Witnesses around 1972 or 1973, when I was three or four. I didn't know any better when I started school and had to leave the room for the Lord's Prayer, had to sit when *Oh Canada* was sung and had to go to the library to study when people had birthday parties in class. We believed we were better than everyone else because we had the Truth. The real God, Jehovah, was with us, and everyone else were sinners and would die in Armageddon. Instead of going to sleepovers and birthday parties, I spent my weekends going out in service, Sunday meetings and planned outings with other JWs and family. I didn't make many solid friendships with non-JWs as this was not allowed, and with only one girl close to my age in our Kingdom Hall, I didn't get a lot of practice creating and building friendships.

Summers were spent going out in service during the week or going into the city and standing on the street corner handing out *The Watchtower* and *Awake* magazines. I was 14 years old when I dedicated my life to Jehovah and was baptized along with my 13-year-old friend. I decided to get baptized because I didn't want her to get baptized before me since I was older than her. I wanted to be the first of the grandchildren in our family to be baptized. It was all about being the perfect JW child and competing for the attention of the congregation. Did I even know what I was about to do? Thinking back on it, I didn't have a spiritual mindset, I was a robot in the JW religion, I don't know if I believed a lot of the teachings, I just assumed they were right. After my baptism, everything changed.

When I was fifteen, I had my first kiss with a young JW boy from the city. I spent two weeks visiting my grandparents every summer, and their congregation had a lot of young people my age. One afternoon, a bunch of Jehovah's Witness youth were meeting up at a soccer field to socialize and play soccer. I was introduced to a cute boy; we started talking and ended up talking the entire afternoon. When it was time to leave and after checking that no one was looking, he leaned in and kissed me. The kiss was perfect, exactly how I had practiced into my pillow so many times.

That summer we hung out, dating as a Jehovah's Witness meant you must be in groups and chaperoned by older baptized Witnesses. Witnesses could only date if they were looking for a spouse, so this is how I saw our relationship—getting married as soon as we were finished with high school. He had other ideas, and this was my first experience with JWs not being perfect. He was seeing another girl that was fooling around with him. He had his fun, plus he had his perfect JW girl he could marry later. We never really broke up. I didn't have the courage to confront him about the other girl, so I just stopped calling him.

When school started again, I was in Grade 11, and after seeing how the big city JWs acted, I wanted more from my own school experience than just going to class then going home. I decided to join a club. JWs are not allowed to be in clubs or sports teams in school so this was huge for me. I was part of Grad Club, helping to plan graduation for the students in Grade 12. One of the duties I signed up for was working the day of graduation. I told my parents I had to be at the dinner and dance to serve food and to stay till the end of the night to clean up. This was not entirely true; I had been asked to be one of the grad's dates and was attending as a guest. I got ready at my neighbor's house and spent the night as a normal teenager without worrying about anyone catching me being on a date at a school dance. I had not been to a school dance because that was another activity young Jehovah's Witnesses were not allowed to participate in. When the night was over, I went back to the perfect JW life, but I had a taste of what a normal life was like and I wanted more.

The Fall from Perfection

My senior year started out with having my first "worldly" boyfriend (not one of Jehovah's Witnesses). We met during summer break when the family moved into our neighbourhood. He was so cute. We would play basketball with other neighbour kids, ride bikes or just hang out and talk. I wasn't allowed to date him because he was not a JW, but we secretly started meeting up and holding hands. To most, holding hands seems so innocent, but if I had been caught, I would have been in a lot of trouble with the elders.

One day we were hanging out at his house, and he started talking about sex. I didn't know anything about the subject. Sex education was exempted for Jehovah's Witness youth at school because it taught safe sex (not abstinence) and masturbation (which was a sin), so I didn't even have the basics to know what I was talking about. I lied and said I had a sexual relationship with my previous boyfriend. I don't know what possessed me to lie, especially about something so big, but there it was.

Once school started for the year, we started to plan to meet to have sex. Two weeks into the school year, we had sex. I had just turned 17. During lunch, we walked to the end of the school field, down the hill and laid down under a tree by the river. There was no foreplay, no fireworks, just sex. It hurt so much, and I didn't know it was going to hurt. Plus, I bled, and I didn't know you would bleed the first time. My reaction to the blood was to apologize that my period must not have been over. As we walked hand in hand back to school, I realized I was not the perfect JW anymore, as I had just committed a disfellowshipping offense.

All the cards fell: I had lied, committed fornication and had started smoking that summer. I started to get the attention of the boys in my class as word had gotten around that I was no longer a virgin. I was sexually active, and guys were now interested in me. I worked at a local restaurant, and some of the boys from school started paying attention to me at work. One night after work I went for a drive with one of the guys down to the rail tracks where I gave him my first blowjob. He was one of the most popular, good-looking guys in school. I couldn't believe I was there, sitting in his truck by the tracks. How did the perfect JW girl end up on her knees in the popular boy's truck?

It didn't matter—I wanted more. I was willing to do anything for attention. I wanted to feel popular—it was like a drug. My boyfriend broke up with me when he found out I had been with this other guy, but I was O.K. with that. I started sneaking out of my bedroom window every night, meeting up with different guys to have sex. I was the girl that helped guys lose their virginity, I was the girl that gave blowjobs at school, I was the girl that would have threesomes, and I was the girl that would have multiple sexual partners in one night. I was addicted to the attention I got from being that girl.

One day my parents received a call from the elders that I was to meet the judiciary committee to discuss my behaviour at school. My parents went to this meeting completely in the dark, and I did not prepare them for what they were about to find out. I was freaking out. What did the elders know and who had told on me? The meeting was in the basement of the Kingdom Hall, and in attendance were three elders, my parents and me. One of the elders opened the judiciary meeting with a prayer, then they immediately accused me of giving boys blowjobs in school. They wanted me to explain in detail what I had been doing. The room was spinning, and my parents were in shock. Remember, I was still the perfect Jehovah's Witness daughter to them.

I was instructed to come to all meetings but could not talk or visit with anyone, especially the youth of the congregation. I was a bad influence now. I was labelled a sinner and needed to repent through my actions at school, home and the Kingdom Hall. Going to meetings became hard on me as my peers no longer talked to me. I was no longer allowed to participate in the meetings, and I lost the respect of the adults in the congregation. The worst was the loss of my friendship with my cousin who was the same age as me. On the day of graduation, he and I were partnered to walk the Grad March together. He took my arm, and we marched with everyone to the podium and received our certificates. When it was over, he turned and walked away. Not one word was spoken between us.

When you are raised a Witness, you are taught that when you graduate from high school, your goal should be to become a Regular Pioneer. Going to college or university was strictly not allowed. After being publicly reproved, my future as a pioneer was on hold, so my parents decided that for the time being I was going to move and stay with relatives. I was excited about this as the relatives I was staying with were not Jehovah's Witnesses and thus I would not have to go to meetings all the time. I would be spending the weekdays babysitting, and in the evenings and weekends I was free to be me. I made friends with a couple of girls in the neighbourhood right away, and we would hang out at their places or at the beach.

One of the girls lived across the street from me, and she is the person who introduced me to drinking. I started drinking a lot, mostly beer and coolers. I thought I was so cool, drinking and smoking and hooking up with random guys I would meet around town. One of the guys from school that I regularly would hook up with was living in the town over from me, so I went to visit him one day. Two guys were there with him, and I spent the afternoon being passed around to all three guys. I didn't say "no" because I didn't know how to say "no" and I thought they wouldn't like me if I said "no."

The summer continued and I was having a great time with my new girlfriends, meeting guys, getting drunk and going to parties. I felt normal, and I envisioned this is what normal teenagers did on the weekends. I met a guy closer to the end of summer, and we started seeing each other. He was in town for the week, and I spend all my free time with him. One night my friend and I met him at his hotel and started drinking Tequila in the lounge. I had never had a shot before, and I drank way too many. We got in a fight over another girl he was flirting with in the lounge. The fight ended with him hitting me in the parking lot, and I took off running down the street.

A few guys that had seen this caught up to me and took me to their hotel to calm down. I passed out, and when I came to there was a guy on top of me. I was scared. I was being raped and I had no idea what to do, so I just laid there with my eyes closed, wishing for it to be over. When it was over, another guy got on top of me, then another and another. I was frozen in fear—I couldn't think, I couldn't move, and I thought I was going to die. Finally, after I don't know how many guys, they finished and left.

I was now alone in a strange hotel room. I didn't know if they were planning on coming back and raping me again, so I ran. I ran across the street to the hotel I thought my friends were at, but I couldn't find their room. I sat on the stairs between floors and started to cry. A guy came by and asked if I was OK and asked why I was crying. I was sitting on the stairs, and he was standing at the bottom of the stairs. I didn't answer him, and then he said that he could see I wasn't wearing any panties (I hadn't grabbed them when I ran) and that's when he pushed me down on the stairs. I thought I was going to be raped again. I kicked him, pushed him off me and started running down the hall banging on doors.

Finally, a couple opened their door. I told them I had just been raped, and they let me into their room to call my friend. They called the police instead. When the police came, they took me to the hospital to be checked out and then they took me to the police station and questioned me. I told them the guy on the stairs raped me. I did not tell them I had been gang raped at a different hotel, as I was ashamed and embarrassed. The rape kit showed that I had had sex but there was no tearing, so the police decided I had not been raped and they were going to charge me with mischief for giving a false story. How was this happening to me?

It felt like I was being raped all over again. My parents came the next day and took me home. My summer of freedom was over.

I didn't last long at home, my parents arranged for me to move to Alberta to again live with extended family. My parents were trying to protect my two younger sisters from my bad behaviour as I had not repented from my sins. I don't remember much about this time. It was probably about two weeks. I was suffering in silence about the gang rape, feeling like it was all my fault, and I had no one to talk to. The night before I was to leave, I got really drunk with two other Witnesses at a ball tournament we went to watch. I ended up inviting everyone to my house for a party. The party quickly got out of hand. My aunt and uncle came and tried to break it up, but I stood in the front yard yelling and swearing at them. The next day, I left my house without cleaning up and moved to Alberta. Years later, I found out that the damage was in the tens of thousands of dollars.

By the time I moved to Alberta, I was completely out of control and had no respect for anyone. I refused to follow the rules and was asked to leave my new family's house after only a month. I was living on my own for the first time and I took full advantage of my freedom. I started throwing parties every night. This was when I was introduced to marijuana. I started smoking weed everyday as well as drinking, and I was still having sex with many different partners.

On New Year's Eve I travelled to Jasper with a friend to kick off the new year. We found a bar that my 17-year-old friend was able to get into. I spent most of the night at the DJ booth flirting with the cute DJ, and when the night was over, I left my friend and went home with the DJ. I didn't give any thought to my friend, her safety or how she was getting home. I was selfish and only thinking of myself. Two weeks later, I had packed up all my stuff and moved to Jasper to be with the DJ. We lasted about a month before I cheated on him with a one-night stand.

I lived in Jasper for two months before I was introduced to cocaine. The first night I did cocaine, I had more energy than I ever had in my life. I felt on top of the world and like nothing could ever get me down. After that night, I did cocaine every day. My days consisted of smoking weed during the day, a few lines of cocaine at work to get the night going and a shot of tequila. I would then work as a cocktail waitress/bartender at a local bar, high and drunk most of the night. Then I would head to a party and do more lines, party till morning, sleep and then start the routine all over again. When I tried crack cocaine, the high was a thousand times better than the powder, and I was hooked the first time. My life was about getting high. I didn't care who I had to sleep with to get drugs. I was giving away my body and my dignity for a fix.

One day there was a knock on my door, and two Jehovah's Witness elders asked to talk to me. We sat down at the kitchen table, I lit a joint and they talked. I can't tell you what they said, but at the end of the visit I assumed I was disfellowshipped. After all, I had smoked a joint and drank a beer while playing Mega Death on the stereo—what else could I have done to say I wasn't living a perfect JW life and was not interested in ever going back?

Years later when I was looking at getting reinstated, my aunt told me to tell the elders about the letter I had written. Now I'm not saying the elders fabricated a letter or wrote it themselves, but I was taken by complete surprise that there was a letter from me disassociating myself. Either way—disassociated or disfellowshipped—I was shunned by family and friends that I had spent my life with.

I was free to finally just be me, not looking over my shoulder that I would be caught by a Jehovah's Witness doing the things I was doing. The only problem was I knew in my heart what I was doing was not normal, but I had no idea how to quit what I was doing. I had been giving my body away for fear of being rejected if I said no, but I was tired of getting high and so drunk that I would black out. The night things started to change for me, I was at some guys house smoking crack, and there was a young girl who was smoking crack and she looked to be very pregnant. I was horrified. How could someone who was expecting a baby do this? That baby didn't live long after coming into this world before dying. I thought about that a lot, and it was the start of changing my thinking and looking for a way out.

The Start of a New Journey to Perfection

A few months after this experience, I was at the local pool hall and noticed a couple of guys I knew in passing, so I went over and started flirting with one of them. Before I left, I told him I hoped I'd see him later that night at the bar. When he showed up at the bar, I was so excited. He was very attractive with an amazing body, and I hoped he would like me enough for more than a one-night stand. After the bar closed, I took him back to my place, where we were having an after-hours party for everyone that was at the bar. We drank, smoked some pot and went to bed together. In the morning, he left early, saying he had to go to Saskatchewan for a few days.

At that point, I knew it had been a one-night stand. I was devastated as I really liked this guy and wanted to stop sleeping around and have a real relationship. A couple of days later, I was at home on my day off and my phone rang. It was my friend saying the guy from the other night was at the bar asking for me. I couldn't get there fast enough, and that was the day my life changed.

When we started dating, Jim said he knew about my cocaine habit, and if I wanted to date him, I had to stop using. I stopped cold turkey, and it was some of the worst weeks of my life. Jim would hold me as I cried, shook and vomited. Getting clean from any drug is hard. I'm one of the lucky ones that survived because of the support Jim gave me. We officially started living together two months after our first night. Three months later, we moved to Lethbridge, and three weeks later we found out I was pregnant. It had been a whirlwind relationship, and now Jim was asking me to marry him and raise this baby together.

Jim and I married in a small ceremony in Lethbridge, Alberta. We had 125 people at our wedding, seven were there for me. My parents and sisters were not part of that seven, the elders made sure of that. When I shared the news that I was getting married and was expecting the first grandchild in my family, my parents seemed so excited for me. My sisters were going to be my bridesmaids and my dad was going to walk me down the aisle. I was so thankful that they had agreed to come and be a part of my day.

Two weeks before the wedding, my mom called and said that my sisters were not going to be in the wedding. Two nights before the wedding, my mom called again and said that Dad could not walk me down the aisle. They said they were going to come on Friday and drop off the cake that my great aunt had made for me, my presents and my high school friend who was now in my wedding, but they could not stay for the wedding. I think a normal person would be devastated, but I took it for what it was. They were doing what they were told to do in order to continue in good standing in the congregation. To this day, I still do not hold any ill will towards them for not coming to the wedding. It was a tough situation they were in, and at the time they were doing what was right for them.

Married life and motherhood all came crashing down on me at once, and I went from being a drunken, stoned town whore to a church-going mother, wife and volunteer literally overnight. I wish I had learned moderation as a child, I seemed to go to the extreme with everything I did. Three years into our marriage, Jim and I started attending a Baptist Church when our second child was nine months old. There were so many things I did not believe in, and I would have debates with the pastor over them. I still believed that the Jehovah's Witnesses were the actual true religion, but I couldn't be a Witness. Maybe I was too proud or stubborn to return to a religion that had rejected me.

We attended this church for a few years, both our children went to the Christian preschool, and I worked as a teacher's assistant for a bit while our firstborn was attending. When Jim decided to get baptized, I asked the pastor if I could be rebaptized. I still do not know to this day why I decided to get baptized again, as I still didn't believe that this religion was the true religion, but I wanted to be baptized with my husband. We stopped attending the church a few years later. I found that the church was becoming negative and putting down other religions, and this really bothered me. Then they called us up and said we had not been attending much but still needed to be sending in our tithes, and that was it for me.

We did try to find a different church and tried different faiths, but each church taught the same things, had the same fake people and claimed they were the only true religion and put down all others. I found that a lot of the people attending church in the community were clearly hypocrites living a good Christian life on Sundays. So, we continued with our lives, raising our children and volunteering at their school and sporting activities. Life was a struggle for me, though. I had so many issues I was concealing deep inside. I put on a front while everyone thought I was so strong to have gone through the things I'd gone through and be the person I was now. Who was I though? I really had no identity—I was a chameleon that took on the characters of the people I was around, with a smile and a laugh.

Perfection is Not Happiness

My need for perfection finally came crashing down on me. I could no longer keep everything bottled up, and I had a complete breakdown at work and was diagnosed with depression. I had to start dealing with all my demons, and everything that I had hidden deep inside came crashing out. No matter how hard you try to hide your true feelings, they have a way of coming out. Mine came out through my depression. I had to deal with my self-respect. I felt ashamed of my high school past, I felt ashamed of my past drug use and sexual past, I felt ashamed of my paternal family shunning me, and I felt ashamed of being a fraud to everyone.

I started seeing a therapist, finally truly talking about how I felt being shunned and feeling alone with no real identity. We worked on my PTSD from the rape and from my past life as a Jehovah's Witness. I started looking to books, especially memoirs of people who had struggles leaving highly controlled religions—I still was not prepared to say cult. The first book I read was *Beyond Belief: My Secret Life Inside Scientology and My Harrowing Escape* by Jenna Miscavige Hill. I was so deeply moved by her story and had to read more. I read every single book that I could find on people leaving Scientology and other religions.

What I was seeing within all the books were many similarities to my story, to the religions and to the demonizing of people who would leave the religion. I started to see that I was not alone and that ultimately what I had been taught by the Jehovah's Witnesses was extremely damaging to who I was and who I had become. I was in such a sheltered environment that I was not given the skills I needed to live in the real world, to make lasting relationships and to be able to make decisions on my own. Still I was not ready to admit that the Jehovah's Witnesses were in this cult category that I was so enthralled in learning about.

It wasn't until I read Leah Remini's book *Troublemaker* and started watching the *A&E* show *Leah Remini: Scientology and the Aftermath* that I really saw the similarities to the Jehovah's Witnesses and finally admitted out loud that I grew up in a cult. That was life changing for me, and it was the start of my healing process. I was able to see myself in a new light. I was no longer the girl who was shunned but someone who has many great qualities and some not so great but that's OK. I leaned on my family for support, I started telling my story, and I forgave myself for my past. It has been an up-and-down emotionally draining process but I'm coming out as a more confident happy individual.

Loving My Imperfect Perfections

I went to my grandfather's funeral at the Kingdom Hall of Jehovah's Witnesses as a broken, depressed and confused person. I was ignored by some and embraced by others, but the most important part was sitting in the front with my parents and my husband, saying goodbye to the grandfather of my childhood, not the man who shunned me. Today, I am getting stronger every day. My depression, which has at times challenged my husband and children's patience, is part of me, and I'm learning techniques to live with it.

I am no longer seeking to be perfect in everyone's eyes. I know that I am happiest when I am perfectly imperfect, and I am embracing my recovery with the online support of an amazing group of fellow ex-Jehovah's Witnesses. I have learned that I am stronger with a group, and I'm no longer trying to heal on my own. I've stopped being ashamed of my past imperfections. I am proud to have learned from them, and I am proud of the person I am today. Yes, I'm still going to struggle at times but that is life. I'm finally embracing my skills and ready to start a business I have been afraid to start because of a lack of self-confidence.

Today I live a happy life. I am a grandma, and I am excited to watch my grandson grow up happy and healthy. I have learned to speak my truth, and I'm not afraid to put myself out there for all to see. I don't see myself as a broken, shunned ex-Jehovah's Witness anymore. I see my past as what has made me the person I am today. I will never go back to the Jehovah's Witness religion. I'm no longer sad that my paternal family has shunned me, but I feel sorry for them for not being a part of my amazing family life. I know I have more healing to do, but the most important thing is I'm now happy with my life and with who I am as a person. I read a quote today that I feel sums up my life:

"Stop trying to fix yourself, you are NOT broken.
You are perfectly imperfect and powerful beyond measure."
~ Steve Maraboli

Chapter 7

The End of One Journey

by Monika Niezgoda

*"You cannot discover new oceans unless you
have the courage to lose sight of the shore."
~André Gide*

I t was a Sunday afternoon in Toronto. A sunny, warm fall day when I stepped out and closed the door behind me. It was the door to a place I had thought of as the mecca of spiritual guidance, where I received life-saving instructions. Where my whole world resided: my network of friends. In fact, behind that door lay the only people I had ever known—or were allowed to know. Once I closed that door, I knew I would never open again.

My youth, my hopes, my life ... I left them all behind that door. Would I regret it? How would I survive in "Satan's world" now? Would they come after me, interrogate me and try to make me come back? Those questions were storming in my mind while heart beat wildly; my hand on a doorknob was shaking. *Will it be better out there? Where am I going to go?*

What made me take such a step? Before I answer, let me tell you how I became a Jehovah's Witness in the first place.

What Made Me Join the Watchtower.

"Wasn't it easier in your lunchbox days?
… Wasn't it beautiful when you believed in everything?"
– Taylor Swift

I was a God-loving child for as long as I can remember. Even before I started going to school and attending classes in religion, I just knew there was a God. I felt Him as a happy being who wanted me to be happy also. I grew up in Poland. In the picturesque countryside, there was our house surrounded by beautiful fields full of fragrant grass and wildflowers. We had a river close by in which my brother, my cousins, and I spent most of our summertime, swimming and having happy, innocent childhood fun. And on the other side of our house, not even a ten minute walk away, was a forest, a place full of magic and mystery— and the setting for many of the most fantastic stories that we made up.

I loved my childhood: my life, my surroundings, and my friends. I saw it all as an expression of the creator's love for us, for me - little Monika – a girl full of life with happiness in her heart. As I admired flowers in the field and triad to catch butterflies in my jar; as I found myself in awe of those always mesmerizing and magical fireflies and watched the ever-changing shape of the clouds in the blue sky, I thought of that happy God to whom we prayed "Our Father" each night and my little heart wanted to give thanks to that spirit in the sky.. We were addressing the one who gives us food every day, that happy God, and I wanted to serve him when I grew up.

You'd think that I would have become a nun given my Catholic upbringing, but I didn't. Instead, I found myself knocking on people's doors on Saturday mornings offering them copies of *The Watchtower*. So how did that happen?

When I was thirteen years old, mom left the country and went to Germany, and year later I joined her there and a year after that my brother came. Being separated from everything I knew –, all friends and the world I grew up in - I found myself as a teenager in a very vulnerable state of mind and heart. I was, I would learn later, the classic target that Witnesses were trained to search for to approach.

But how did I, a Catholic girl who was raised in a culture that has a negative view of anyone with a different religion to mine, why did I even open the door to those peddlers and their magazines?

A few years before leaving the Poland, around the time of my first communion, a rumor started going around our church that our beloved priest was having an affair with a married woman in a nearby village. This shattered my trust in the church, in priests and in that Catholic faith. I felt that God could not be present in any religion in which such hypocrisy is practiced. It was a blow to my heart. At seven years-old I felt cheated and betrayed by a man of God doing what he was forbidden to do. Sinning. I wanted no part of this religion, but I still wanted to serve God. How could I do that now? And then ... the Witnesses came to the rescue!

Having lost my loyalty to the church I was raised in, and in addition being separated from the environment I knew, when I was handed a *Watchtower* with Bible verses saying how Jehovah's Witnesses are the one true and God-approved religion, I felt that I had found *my* God's true church. For the first time in a long time, I felt that my dream of serving him would become a reality after all. At the age of seventeen (after moving now from Germany to Canada) I got baptized and became one of the Witnesses. My mom and my brother soon followed.

My dad, who had stayed in Poland, was sending us books written by former Witnesses in an attempt to save us from joining what he felt was a cult. We threw away the books and dismissed his warnings as we were told by our Witness community that his words came from Satan. But did they?

We were one happy God-serving family, with the full god protection, like the best insurance you could buy; blessings falling on us just like manna on hungry Israelites. After all, we were followers of the one true religion, and we were surrounded with the only truly spiritual—the best— the crème de la crème of all the people on this earth. But were we? Was this really the spiritual paradise we had read so much about in *The Watchtower*? And were the books my dad sent us really meant to steal our faith?

How Life Verifies Beliefs

> *"I talk to God, but the sky is empty"*
> ~Sylvia Plath

I was busy, giving every moment of my life to *The Watchtower* and working part-time in some job I hated, so I could be working as a pioneer (In the Jehovah's Witness organization, pioneers are volunteer workers who spend unpaid hours -used to be 90 hrs. a month, then it got changed to 70 hrs. a month-promoting Jehovah's Witness literature, among other tasks.). For many ears I also volunteered one day a week at the Canadian Bethel (the country's branch office), working in a construction crew, or in orchards during harvest season. Most of my summer vacations I spent working in the Polish Bethel. For many years I was serving the Polish-language congregation in Toronto, and in Russian-language as well as in English congregations. I had 'privileges' of interpreting at talks and assemblies for Polish group. I took part in meetings, interviews and magazine presentations, and I loved taking last-minute theocratic ministry school dialogues. Maybe it was partially because I had always loved the stage, since I was a child. I should have been an actress!

I knew from the explanation of the scriptures why women don't give talks, but deep inside I did not agree with that. Why can't a woman speak up? Why not in this organization? There are women working as prime ministers and judges. Oprah is a woman and even the Witnesses watch her show and respect her views. Surely my God, whom I loved, wouldn't mind if a woman had a talk about him, or would he?

My mom was trying to do her best in what the organization was demanding, but somehow, she never felt accepted. And I saw it but would dismiss it into a deep corner of forbidden thoughts. After all, these were God's people, the most loving humans on earth! My mom was very hospitable and almost every Sunday we had members of the congregation over for dinner, even though she was a single mom with two teenagers, trying to make ends meet. She was trying to follow what the organization was teaching but she was also speaking her mind. If she did not agree with or like something, she would speak up, and that was something you don't do in this organization. But why? Where is the love and acceptance? Where is the help for the single mother? Where is the support of which Jesus taught when he talked about widows and fatherless children?

My brother was a wonderful, kind and loving person. He could have been an inventor of many things. Since he was a child, he was a genius. At a few years of age, he made his own radio, from scratch. He could remember a text after just reading it once, where I, had to repeat it ten times to memorize it. Surely a loving God would want the talents He gave him to be furthered and used for the good of mankind? Why would this organization then discourage him from going to university and using those God-given talents to the full?

Unfortunately, his life was cut short. God's protection of his people did not reach Dominik, his faithful 23-year-old servant, my brother. Somehow God's angel did not spread his wings over the highway and did not stop the truck from killing him. Where was the promise of those blessings we were supposed to have under the condition of enrolling in full-time service? We were told our families would benefit from our faithful wholehearted service. Where was the blessing? Why did my happy God let him die? Why didn't he keep his promise? I did my part; I gave him all I had. Where was his side of the deal? Or was there a deal? Or was there even a God ...?

And here all along I had thought that by putting aside all the desires of my age, and doing ninety hours a month of door-to-door, by putting a roof on a new Kingdom Hall, by vacuuming assembly hall, by washing fruits in Bethel, by making coffee for morning service group in my apartment every Wednesday ... The list is endless. By doing all this and by studying all possible old and new articles of *The Watchtower* and *Awake!* I thought I was spreading a sort of umbrella over all my loved ones. We were told God promises his protection to those who serve him! And where was that umbrella? Where was that God? What was I doing? Was it all just a man-made lie?

This tragedy shattered our lives. This felt like a carpet pulled from under my feet and I was falling into the abyss. Maybe it had always been there, underneath?

How would I keep on going? How would I regain that trust in the happy all-caring God I loved so much?

Would I?

My Personal Armageddon

"Shards of broken glass don't hurt as
bad as shattered dreams."
~ Naazneen Samad

If you ask me, "How was it? What was it like to be in this organization?" I will tell you with an honest heart that I was happy. I did not experience any abuse, not the most horrific kind which I learned later, through accounts of my friends, exists in this religion also. I genuinely liked preaching, especially in those days where we still had debates with people at the door, when they would invite us in for tea and we would talk about the trinity, and cross and all other interesting topics using scriptures. (But I enjoy people in general, so the preaching was just something that gave me that opportunity to just be me).

I had tons of friends, I really enjoyed making new acquaintances and was good at keeping in touch. I remember saying and I hoped it would be possible, in the future—in that godforsaken promised paradise—to know and be friends with every living person on the planet. For the longest time, I thought, or I was fooling myself into thinking, that all Witnesses are as genuine and honest, although many times I saw otherwise. But it was another one of those forbidden thoughts I would be putting into the dark corner of my mind.

When I served in Bethel, especially in the Polish one in Nadarzyn, I had such a wonderful time with people my age. I was in my 20s and I should have been in university pursuing law or an acting career, but I was busy with "more important things": ironing shirts for the brothers, cleaning showers in the rooms, peeling potatoes for supper. But it was all for the greater purpose, for the Highest Power! At least I was part of a higher plan: a collective waste of life!

I saw so many depressed souls. They were trying to console themselves with the vision of this godforsaken promised paradise. They must had been also pushing forbidden thoughts into the corners of their minds. Does it ever get too full in those corners?

I heard of some committing suicide, of some leaving and becoming apostates. Turning against the organization, it was said. But were they? Or maybe their corner of forbidden thoughts got filled to the point where the door to it wouldn't shut and they had to be acknowledged.

Would my dark corner of forbidden thoughts fill up one day?

After my brother's tragic death, I tried to get back to that state of high faith and devotion to the God and the greater-than-life mission once again, but it was hard. I started going to my father in Poland more often. Spending time in the familiar surroundings of my happy childhood, each visit brought a sense of much-needed soothing comfort and freedom to dream, to be me. Not being judged, unmonitored. For that brief time, during each visit to my old home, I was again that carefree girl, the one left behind when I left home. She was still there chasing butterflies in those fragrant fields, while the other me was on a busy set schedule made up by some giant multimillion-dollar publishing corporation. Promising that I would see my brother again if I did what they tell me to do.

And maybe this vision of perfect paradise and the return of the dead would have been enough to keep me in the rat wheel, still running in circles, chasing my tail in the la-la land of my mind. But one event shook me and left me open to allowing my forbidden thoughts to slowly come out of the hiding places. What was it?

When metro-witnessing started (a pilot project only in big cities, for pioneers who positioned themselves by magazine stands on the street corners) myself and a number of single pioneers, we wanted to try this new kind of preaching. We applied. (To get this 'privilege' to stand on a street corner, you must be reviewed and approved by the service committee ... Yes, unbelievable! But true.)

Surely, I thought, my application was just a matter of formality. But was it?

When one elder called to let me know they wanted to visit me, I thought they would commend me for applying and let me know when I could start. I had just taken a cake from the oven and was eagerly awaiting their arrival. The most encouraging visit ever, right?

Far from it! It wasn't a happy visit. I couldn't contain my tears once they left. I wished the cake had been a flop and the tea so hot that it would have burned their tongues before they spoke. These were their words: "Didn't you read on the metro-witnessing application? It says it is only for exemplary pioneers!" These words were all I could hear that evening, the next day, and the day after. And still now when I write this, I can hear this harsh, demeaning, dismissive tone of voice from that day, which shattered my heart into a multimillion pieces. What else could I do? What else could a woman in this sect do?

At that time I was doing all that a woman in this religion could do: pioneering, being involved in building a Kingdom Hall with regional committee, commuting to Bethel, having service groups at my apartment every Wednesday, and working part-time at a job I hated, to pay for all my expenses. At meetings I had last-minute parts, always commenting, visiting the elderly and when I had a free evening a glass of wine to relax.

And I was not qualified to stand on a corner?! It turned out that I wasn't the only one received this loving, lifesaving (as it turned out for me in the end!) visit. All the single pioneers, girls only, got this disqualification visit. Turned out our God prefers married women, because he can't trust the single, sex-crazed ones. After all, we might start promoting the magazines naked, or get the donations doing something other than standing. Right?

This event made me consider this forbidden thought: maybe it is humans, not some higher being, making decisions and managing this organization? Slowly, I started revisiting more of the forbidden thoughts I had been putting away into the dark corners of my mind and I allowed myself to express my doubts to some close friends.

I was introduced to Ray Franz' book *Crisis of Conscience*. I read it in one sitting. I had flu that week, so it was a blessing: being home I read all day and night. While I was reading, I wasn't sure if it was the flu intensifying or it is the reaction to the information. Up till then, I had been having some doubts, of course. I was wronged and felt hurt sometimes, for sure. And I was allowing the possibility that this religion was not what for so long I had thought it was, that is one thing, but having it black on white now, pure facts showing that it actually wasn't, that gave me high fever and a strange sensation. I felt like I was losing my mind. I felt numb. I felt disgusted. I felt confused. While reading, I remember checking with myself, asking myself, "Do you want to continue reading? You know there is no going back." And it was that much more exciting and terrifying, the fact that I was crossing the point of no return, the edge of the abyss, drinking the poison of Satan with unknown effect, but known punishment for such action. What would happen to me now? I had crossed over to the dark side!

To my surprise, nothing happened. Demons did not start attacking me. Somehow God did not strike me with lightning. In fact, He did not react at all. Nothing changed around me. I was still given parts at meetings; I even accepted the role of permanent Bethel commuter. I could attend morning worship and lectures just like all live-in Bethelites. But here I had dipped into Satan's book. I had sinned. Surely God knew! Why wasn't He reacting, why was He giving me all the privileges NOW?

The hard realization was that God has nothing to do with this organization to which I had given my youth. I had wasted my time, sacrificed love, worn out many pairs of shoes. It put me right back to the time when I was seven years old girl, who felt betrayed and cheated by the man of God, the religion she knew. But this time, I felt also betrayed by the God I thought I was serving.

For my last convention, all three days I dressed in black. And even now I don't know whether I was mourning or I just felt that I didn't want to waste colorful dresses on this dark, godforsaken organization. All I knew was that it felt right to do so. Maybe it was in a way a funeral of my former life. A three-day long funeral full of holy nonsense spoken and sang. Pure mental torture.

My mom, who was sitting beside me, looked surprised that I was not taking notes and not singing songs. I couldn't hide how I felt. I couldn't repeat the programmed lyrics with the collective. I would rather strip and run naked in front of the whole audience than utter one more of those cultic hymns.

How would she react? I was afraid to tell her that I was done with this paradisiacal cult, but I didn't know that at the same time she was feeling the same. As a result, we both were going to the meetings and went to the convention, dreading it, doing it not to lose the other, not to be rejected by our blood. But after the painful convention I didn't care anymore. Imagine my surprise when I told her that I was done with this, she told me that she was done with it too, but she had just been afraid to tell me. Such a relief!

I decided to exit slowly. At that time, I was in a Polish group. I was well known and liked and doing a lot as one of the youngest in the group. I was interpreting English talks at meetings, a task I really enjoyed. As I did it, I realized that I could do this as a career.

Why hadn't I thought of it twenty years before?

Obedience, is the answer. "All of us must be ready to obey any instructions we may receive, whether these appear sound from a strategic or human standpoint or not." Watchtower 2013 Nov 15 p.20

We were told during pioneer meetings that we should choose jobs we didn't like, because it is dangerous to like what you are doing for work. What a bunch of utter nonsense!

And what did I choose? Being a dental assistant, because there was a part-time job possibility and I could spend more time volunteering for The Watchtower.

I wasted time on medical college and spent money on this darn diploma. I was the worst assistant you could imagine. I hated that work. Besides being spit on and having fingers bitten by patients, I faint when I see blood. Great spiritual choice I made! And I made my God happy by making myself unhappy! Yay!

I left that profession for another, an office job. Payroll. I worked there seventeen years with the same people that preached with and roomed with at some point. I was suffocating in never changing demographics and slowly awaiting my death in the gray cubicle. It was a live version of a coffin.

My department was made up mostly of Witnesses, but fortunately at the time of my awakening from the paradise dream, I wasn't in the same congregation with any of them. But still, how could I now function among them? Could they see that I had dipped into forbidden material? I was listening on my earphones to John Cedars videos while a Witness beside me was also working on payroll. I felt like a naughty school-kid again. But this time it seemed as if I was surrounded by teachers, ready to discover my dark secret. No one to share it with. No one to collaborate with. I started to look for other jobs, other options. I needed to leave this place. Here I was trying to leave one Kingdom Hall ... But at work I was entering a place that felt like a second Kingdom Hall. Was there a way out of this lion's den?

If there was a God, who was watching my sinful act of discovering facts and digging for more information about his multimillion-dollar publishing corporation and pedophilia heaven, then he used His mighty hand towards me in a surprising way at the right time. Suddenly, a situation with management arose that added to my already weakened health, and my doctor gave me a note for three months' leave from work. Was this the doing of that Mighty Being? One might wonder which Being? But I didn't care. I needed a break from those paradise devotees, no matter if it was God, Satan or just my doctor helping me in this crisis, this most confusing time of my life. Now I had time to digest what I had discovered. Now I could be safe from the surveillance at work, and slowly exit the religion.

Becoming an interpreter meant going to college. That meant missing midweek meetings. The excuse was well taken, since I would be an even better interpreter for the brainwashing sessions after graduating. So, it was for the greater good! For a couple of months, I still attended meetings on Sundays, but after one Sunday talk at which I was interpreting, and a brief meeting with the elders regarding moving from Polish group to English meetings, came the moment when I knew I was closing the door behind me for the last time. It was that moment I mentioned in the beginning. What happened at that meeting?

The talk was about 1914 ... I had such a hard time interpreting it, not because of my lack of vocabulary. I myself could give that talk, I knew all the information by heart. I had a hard time, because now, consciously, I was delivering lies! I felt like a traitor, like I was passing a spoon filled with poison to a friend looking at me with hope and love in his eyes, trusting me to be giving him life-saving medicine. I still remember that horrible, uncomfortable feeling. This moment I knew it was my last day, that my feet would never again walk through that door. Still, I was unsure what would await me on the other side. How would I live? What would happen now? I had no clue, but one thing I knew was that my life as I knew it was over, and there was no going back, there was not even looking back. It was over. Just like when I was seven years old and found out that I had been believing in a lie.

Kintsugi – Golden Seams in My Shattered Life.

*"A bridge of silver wings stretches from the
dead ashes of an unforgiving nightmare to the
jeweled vision of a life started anew"*
~ Aberjhani

"*Kintsugi* or *kintsukuroi* ('golden mend') is the Japanese art of mending broken pottery using lacquer resin laced with gold or silver. As well as a nifty form of repair, *kintsukuroi* has a deeper philosophical significance. The mended flaws become part of the object's design, and some people believe the pottery to be even more beautiful having gone through the process of being broken and repaired." – (*What Japanese Pottery Can Teach Us about Feeling Flawed* from BecomingWhoYouAre.net)

Once shiny and beautiful, here I was, shattered into a thousand pieces. Once happy and full of life, now a depressed and lonely soul. I had lost my hope, my paradise, my friends. I had lost my God, or had He lost me? That I wouldn't know, but He didn't seem to be looking for me or missing me.

Due to the combination of stress at work, and stress of losing my life as I knew it, I ended up in the emergency room with symptoms of a heart attack. It felt that the doctor who prescribed me three months off work, cared more than that God whom I had served for the past thirty years.

I stayed in bed for many days, leaving only to buy some milk and bread. I was listening to all I could get on YouTube, from all different sources about *The Watchtower*. I needed to do that, and my exhausted body needed to rest. My parents were great, calling me every day. Checking up on me and trying to help me somehow, the best way they could. At some point I realized that maybe I needed to see some professional, because I couldn't keep on going like this. I wanted to be happy again, I wanted to keep living, I wanted to laugh again.

The psychiatrist I got referred to suggested group therapy in Mount Sinai Hospital, and I happily agreed to that. I needed to reenter society, get acquainted with the outside world, make new friends. This group was a safe place, and slow introduction to this unknown which I was facing ... the big, vast, wicked world of Satan. (One of Witness teaching is, that everyone and everything outside of The Watchtower organization, belongs to Satan and will be destroyed) I went to a few of those meetings. In one of them we had to draw with crayons. I don't remember now exactly what, but this made me think of what I always wanted to do: paint.

Now I had time, all day, every day to do whatever I wanted. It was one of those days, a sunny spring day, when I decided to buy those brushes, paints and canvas. I came home with all of it, and I set it up on a table in front of my huge window. As those warm and happy sun-rays were entering my room and shining on me, I started putting colors on the canvas. No rules, no plans, no thinking ... just letting my heart express itself, allowing it to show me its colors ... if they were still there. And as I was painting, or putting colors on the canvas, it felt as if each new color was a feeling my heart was letting out and into my soul. It felt like a rebirth had started, that golden mending of that shattered bowl had begun. My personal *kintsugi* of my life.

I will always cherish one memory during my now regular time with the canvases. I broke more rules! I decided that day I needed a cigarette! I had my wine in a glass, but all famous artists didn't only drink, they also smoked. I needed to go and buy cigarettes before I started painting! My walk to the corner store, in that spring sunshine, was so swift and happy, I was almost skipping. I felt like a child going to get her favorite candy.

My heart was beating with excitement. And as I asked for a pack of Camels, I felt like I was committing a criminal offense, but I was happy to do it. A crime with a smile. I put the pack in my pocket and quickly left the store, looking around to see whether anyone had seen this transaction. I lived in an area highly populated with Witnesses, the same ones I used to work with.

You couldn't see a happier person walking on that sidewalk that day. I felt that I had joined the worldwide society of humans; I was finally an adult, now, at 40! This realization was sad, but so profound. My choices, my decisions till not long before, had not been mine. I was kept a child, programmed to just obey. I was deprived of normal aspects of life, of lessons and experiences in which I could have made up my own mind. My life hadn't been mine. But that had changed now.

Going for the first time to the ex-JW meet-up was exciting but also scary. Exciting to meet other rebels, "mentally diseased" like me, but scary in case someone still active might be there and could tell on me to the elders. I didn't want to be bothered by them, just wanted to be considered ... missing. My fears were quickly allayed, and I met wonderful people, and so started my new collection of friends. It was so comforting to know and see for myself now that there are others who understood what I was going through.

Freedom is Mine to Keep

"Liberty, when it begins to take root,
is a plant of rapid growth."
~ George Washington

Not all birds end up flying. Some are afraid to leave the cage, not even realizing that they can fly. Kept in an artificial, controlled environment, they think that is all there is. This is how they were meant to live. Until one day, the owner leaves the cage open, and the nearby window as well. We all know the outcome of this story ... The canary is never to be seen again.

This is how my story ends. This one

But that's only the story with me and *The Watchtower*, because there are many more chapters of my life that await to be written. There are still blank pages to be filled, and that's why I would never go back.

There is so much more to experience, to discover, to learn. That chapter is done and closed, and there is nothing more I could add to it. I love my weekends now, I love Sundays. I can just do nothing and not feel that I am disappointing some invisible being, and that I will have to answer questions at the next meeting. Leaving wasn't easy; it was very hard. The process of discovering what this was that I was in, realizing that all I was looking forward to and waiting for was not going to happen. That all my best years had been given away to nonsensical activities, instead of using them to pursue my passions, a career. That I could have had different choices in men, chances of love and a family of my own. All that and much more, it hit like a ton of bricks. For a little while I thought I would lose my mind. I lost purpose in life and any motivation to go on. Fortunately for me it was just for a brief while.

My heart goes out to those who did not survive this hard awakening.

It takes time and support from others to get through the harsh reality, that we were in a cult. Some of us had no choice, being born into it. Others, like myself, were an easy target while of tender age and in a vulnerable state. But despite how we ended up in it, once we realized what it was, we needed to move forward, we needed to fight to not fall into bitterness and regrets.

Do you remember *kintsugi*?

I want to be the bowl which, after being broken, gets to be repaired with golden resin, to be even more beautiful, more valuable. I don't want to stay broken and chipped. Find what makes you happy, find your passions, explore your interests. Focus on that. It will add value to your life and in turn it will heal your wounds.

I found the answers to my questions I had at the time when I was closing the Kingdom Hall's door for the last time. What's better out there? Freedom. Freedom to make my own decisions, to make my own mistakes, to do nothing, to be who I am, who I can and want to be.

Where am I going to go? Wherever I want to. It is my life and mine alone.

The feeling of freedom and joy was stronger than any doubt and fear, as I closed that door to my former life.

One thing we might be forgetting, because we want to make up for the years that have passed us by, is patience. It's really important to remember to be patient with oneself and allow oneself the time to heal.

Sometimes I still must remind myself of that. You too: be patient with yourself. You can still achieve all you want. There are 90-year-old university graduates out there!

It is never too late to start living the way you want to!

My Adventure Continues

"… so that I can start a new path, my own path,
the one that will make me whole again."
— Jack Canfield

My journey of life continues.

Since I was a child, I looked at life as a one big adventure. And I still view it this way. Being in a cult was one of the episodes in it. I lost my whole social network, but I am slowly building a new one.

To help myself slowly disappear from the meetings, as I mentioned, I started college courses to get a diploma and become a certified language interpreter. I have obtained that diploma and currently I am a freelance interpreter working for agencies such as University Health Network in Toronto, United Health and others. For once I enjoy what I am doing. You can do what you like for work and it feels awesome!

My passion for painting continues. I have made many wonderful creations. I discovered and am pursuing energy healing, which I am also combining with my artwork. Recently I started the process of putting up a website with my artwork and different spiritual portals on it.

Traveling is second nature to me, and therefore I am exploring more possibilities of earning money remotely and visiting more of the places on my list.

And my heartfelt wish to all who read my story is: live without regrets, follow your dreams and each day try to make someone smile!

Love to all and may all of us at the end of our life's journey be able to sing along this song: —

> "And now, the end is near
> And so, I face the final curtain.
> My friends, I'll say it clear,
> And I'll state my case, of which I'm certain.
> I've lived a life that's full,
> I traveled each and every highway.
> And more, much more than this,
> **I did it my, my way**..." -Paul Anka

Chapter 8

On the Upward Spiral

"Blindness does not cause the sun to cease from shining."

by Gary Alt

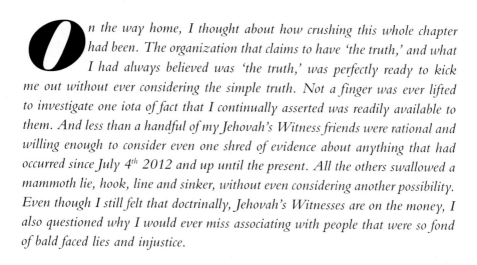

*O*n the way home, I thought about how crushing this whole chapter had been. The organization that claims to have 'the truth,' and what I had always believed was 'the truth,' was perfectly ready to kick me out without ever considering the simple truth. Not a finger was ever lifted to investigate one iota of fact that I continually asserted was readily available to them. And less than a handful of my Jehovah's Witness friends were rational and willing enough to consider even one shred of evidence about anything that had occurred since July 4ᵗʰ 2012 and up until the present. All the others swallowed a mammoth lie, hook, line and sinker, without even considering another possibility. Even though I still felt that doctrinally, Jehovah's Witnesses are on the money, I also questioned why I would ever miss associating with people that were so fond of bald faced lies and injustice.

The remainder of the two-hour trip home, I was overcome with an unusual, almost surreal sense of peace, relief, and happiness. But having time to think meant that my mind would periodically turn to the great hypocrisy of what had just happened, and what it means for my relationship with my kids. When I got *home to Judy, I was feeling all at once serene and washed out. I made a beeline for Judy, who was in our bedroom, and before she could ask, "How did it go?" I hugged her tightly, rubbed my right hand across her back, and said, "Honey, can you sing to me?"*

After holding each other for just a few seconds short of eternity, Judy said, "I'm sorry. It didn't go well, did it?"

"It depends upon your point of view. In one sense, no it didn't go well... it couldn't have gone worse. But on the other hand, I'm free. That decision they made tonight, that is the last decision they will ever be able to make about me. They have absolutely no authority over me anymore."

Those excerpts are from one of the final chapters of the book *Force of Will*[1]. I have always experienced life through music and sounds, so my first thoughts upon returning home at once exhausted and exhilarated were for my wife of three months to sing me our wedding song[2].

The appeal committee, made up of three elders with whom I had varying degrees of familiarity, decided to uphold the decision of the original committee, which in turn was made up of two elders I had served with in the past and one elder I had never met before.

It didn't surprise me that all six of those men felt I needed to be disfellowshipped. In fact, I expected it. My only reason for attending the hearings was that I knew that I would never be able to live with myself if I didn't do everything in my power to preserve my ability to associate freely with my three grown children.

That's not to say that I agreed with their decision. I knew that I had attempted to provide one of the members of the original committee with all the contact information and documentation necessary to prove that I was free to remarry. Their outright refusal to even look at the documents in order to have a glimpse at so much as their basic nature, if not their substance, had convinced me several years prior that their minds had already been made up. Truth had been rendered unnecessary by them.

How did some forty years of loyal service to my God and his earthly organization come to this? More importantly, how would I navigate the uncertain waters of my new life?

Shock of a Lifetime

In hindsight, I had unwittingly started preparing for this moment years ago. Or perhaps the universe was preparing me. I still believe that it was Jehovah who was providing the guidance, he being the God I still believe in and love, despite the religious organization that has slanderously co-opted his name. You may prefer to call it the universe, karma, or even something less specific. That is fine with me. I am no longer a JW[3], and have learned to fully respect all belief systems and not criticize or judge.

The preparations began in earnest on the night of Independence Day, the holiday that is celebrated each July 4th in my country, the United States of America. And that is the date when the story of *Force of Will* started[4].

That night, events would begin to unfold that very quickly led to my ostracism from the "brotherhood." That abashed condition normally would have been, I thought, reserved for someone in a state of disfellowshipment or disassociation. Yet I would not officially experience that circumstance for another three and a half years, in February, 2016. Therefore, while it was a huge shock to my system when my network of associates collapsed all around me, it nevertheless allowed me to consider the realities of the so-called brotherhood, and make adjustments in my life to cope with the present as well as the future.

On the night of July 4th, 2012, I picked myself up from the dinner table, said goodbye to my wife Marta[5], and began the 45 minute journey to Centenary College in Hackettstown, New Jersey, from which the FM radio station I had a weekly musical show called *The Cavern* was broadcast.

My hour-long, mostly-Beatles show went without a hitch, ending on time at 9:00 PM. However, after my broadcast I had to remain at the studio to help with a technical problem that was preventing the show after mine from being broadcast.

Around 11:00 PM, with the broadcast issue under control, I decided to take a break. I turned my phone on and noticed that I had gotten a call from my son, Derek. When I called him back, he asked me an exceedingly odd question.

"Dad, why did you hit Mom?"

A very bizarre conversation ensued, almost completely devoid of facts. All that was clear was that Derek was very upset, and he wasn't about to tell me anything about Marta's welfare or whereabouts.

I recommended we get a decent night's sleep and think about things in the morning.

When I got home well after midnight the house was empty. Within minutes I received a call from the State Police requesting that I come down to the station, which I did, thinking that Marta was there for some reason connected with her frequent jags.

Call me naïve, but the fact is that I was quite surprised to find myself under arrest for domestic abuse.

"Brothers" vs True Friends

The fact that the alleged crime was ostensibly committed at my house at the same time I was doing all the aforementioned activities at the radio station never seemed to matter to anyone. I suppose that if a fact is going to interfere with a cherished preconceived notion, that fact must of necessity be ignored. I further suppose that if a fact is ignored by enough people, especially respected authority figures, that fact automatically morphs into a lie in their minds.

That Friday, just two nights after July 4th, I began to learn how complex a web my wife had been spinning for a long time. A quick perusal of emails and social media, along with a complete absence of text messages and phone calls from erstwhile friends I had tried to reach out to, revealed that I had already lost scores of friends. Those estrangements would become more and more entrenched until finally achieving permanence when I was disfellowshipped in February, 2016. During the intervening years, I could count on one hand the number of meaningful contacts I had with any JW. Only a finger or two less would be required to count the number of true friends with whom those contacts occurred.

There were a number of people associated with the radio station that I considered friends, albeit not yet with the depth of my erstwhile JW associates. Those were the people I reached out to.

CC was already a dear, trusted friend. But her friendship would soon blossom into something quite extraordinary and wonderful. CC is an atheist who happens to have more moral sense than anyone I know who has based their moral values on a draconian set of rules supposedly culled from the Bible. She is quintessentially kind, non-judgmental, and open-hearted.

CC and I have an uncommon ability to make each other laugh. But there have been times when I could not summon any laughter. At those times, when things were the hardest, and I had no idea what to do next, I would call on CC. Typically, it would be in the form of a text message.

One day, while driving home from work, I started to feel overwhelmed with problems that came from different areas of life, hitting me all at once like a ton of bricks. Four separate things happened in quick succession. I learned that my temporary derailment from my chosen line of work had become permanent due to the legal difficulties forced upon me. Then I had a very negative experience visiting an insurance office while making my rounds in my new low-paying, menial job. On top of that, problems with my phone, laptop and car were letting me know that some big repair or equipment replacement bills were in the offing.

The final blow was getting some very bad news from a woman I had recently met whose attraction to me became mutual, and with whom a very nice relationship had subsequently been developing.

On occasions such as these I would just text two words to CC:

"Say something."

CC always knew what that meant. Her responses typically had absolutely nothing to do with discovering what difficulties I was currently navigating, or offering a solution to those difficulties. They would be related to whatever she was experiencing at the moment, from the mundane to the hysterically funny – but her choice of words always highlighted the humor. Sometimes I would have to pull over lest I prang into the car in front of me during a fit of hysterical laughter. In no time at all, my mind was off my myriad troubles, once again able to perceive the joy of life. Once I returned to the realities of the day, I was able to focus on one thing at a time and put everything else where it belonged, on the back-burner.

On the occasion of the quartet of problems that rained down on me all at once, for some providential reason, CC decided to change course and write something different.

"The world is okay, because Gary Alt is still in it."

At least that's the way it was reported in *Force of Will*. I actually don't remember the exact words. But the way they entered my brain and settled in my heart touched me so deeply, and made my spirit soar so high, that my problems all melted into nothingness in that moment.

That's what I needed more often than not in those days, because my problems were too thorny and too multitudinous to really grapple with effectively. My life spiraled downward so quickly from that July 4th night on, and I was now attempting to remain on the upward spiral. Yet for every small step upward I made, it seemed like three huge ones downward were eager to greet me. I don't know how I would have made it through that dark period without friends like CC. I just know that whether it was the medicine that is laughter, or the more sober emotional jolt she delivered at the end of that dark day, I accepted it all as the blessing that it was.

Trevor is another friend from the radio station. I had only known him for a few months by the time July 4th had rolled around.

Occasionally, on an otherwise lonely Friday night, I would stop by the station to hang out with Trevor during his show. Frequently he would invite me back to his house to hang out, play guitars, sing, and talk... and talk... and talk. Those activities would typically carry on until 2:00 AM or so, once in a while resulting in me staying the night.

I don't recall talking at length with Trevor about what I was going through, but it didn't matter. Being able to pass the time with my new good friend, doing something I loved most, that is playing music, was all I needed to ameliorate the acute loneliness felt due to the collapse of my "brotherhood." And that, just like my interactions with CC, helped me to focus on my game plan, whether he knew it or not.

I became a regular at his relatively frequent parties, meeting scores of new people and adding some of them to my growing circle of friends. I brought my guitar to one of those parties. Few people knew that I played. New acquaintances at my table, mostly women, started asking Trevor to, "let Gary play" with his band that didn't need any help. So, I played.

That's when this new coterie of friends discovered my musical abilities. If they knew anything about me before that day, it was probably just that I was the Wednesday night host of *The Cavern* on 91.9 WNTI-FM. Things really started to change from that moment on.

Life Under a Microscope

With notoriety comes scrutiny. The visibility of being a DJ with a regular show at a popular station with a wide radius, augmented by my frequent substitutions for other DJs at various times during the week, and now further augmented by a growing reputation as a musician, meant that more and more people were finding out about the JW who had been arrested on false charges (they all knew where I was on July 4th 2012), who was homeless, jobless and penniless for a period of time, and who received absolutely no help from his supercilious religious community.

Exactly how the word spread as far and as fast as it did, I may never know. What I do know is that because of me and my situation, Jehovah's name was being reproached among many people over a significant geographical radius. *Because of me.* That absolutely broke whatever was left of my heart. I could not live with it.

That situation dovetailed with another problematic circumstance. Since I could no longer legally attend meetings in Sussex, New Jersey, where I had worshiped for nearly thirty years, I had begun visiting other Kingdom Halls randomly. Very early on I perceived some extremely negative treatment both from people I knew and those I did not. The shunning that had started in Sussex, and was beamed to pockets of friends in various parts of the US and Central America, had started radiating into congregations closer to home. People I had known for years ignored me. People I had never met before automatically acted strangely around me.

The following is an edited excerpt from *Force of Will:*

> *"One day after a meeting at the Kingdom Hall in Byram[6], I went to a convenience store to get a drink. I saw a family from the congregation. I instinctively smiled at the Mom and her little girl, who looked to be about five years old or so. Neither of them smiled back, but the little girl hid herself in the folds of her mother's skirt, and said, 'Mommy, it's him!' I was stunned, and didn't know how to react. The mother, like a typical mother trying to do a little shopping with a demanding kid wrapped around her, was, I guess startled at first, and said*

something like, 'honey, let go of me,' and then, 'it's him?
Him who?' The little girl started saying, 'it's him, Mommy,
the brother that killed his girls. It's him, Mommy, it's him!'"

Thus, began some three years of attending meetings outside of the
broadcast range of WNTI, where no one would know me. Congregations
within a 250-mile radius from Sussex NJ became my itinerary.

In hindsight, attending meetings under any circumstances did nothing
to help me cope with the estrangement from the organization. Rather,
it was like a recovering addict using his drug of choice just enough to
prolong the withdrawal process and increase the pain. But since I still
firmly believed that JWs had the truth, I continued my strident efforts
to remain connected. Somehow.

The Greatest Loss of All

Contact with my three kids became increasingly icy and awkward on
and after July 4th.

Marta had used my son Derek as a liaison and unwitting rabble-rouser
during the whole process, certainly because she knew how easy it would
be to seal him into her corner, and probably because she recognized his
temperate personality as the perfect foil for her nefarious plan. What she
failed to appreciate is how much internal anxiety he suffered by being
placed squarely in the middle of the raging conflict she had created.
Before my being disfellowshipped I could talk to him relatively freely,
even though it was clearly painful for him.

My eldest child, Lindsay, had become prone to anger in her mid-
teens. Something deep inside her, something that she refused to ever
discuss with anyone, was eating at her more and more as time went
by. I now believe it had to do with something of a nature that puts the
person she is inside at odds with the strict and inescapable moral code
of the Watchtower. Be that as it may, her deep-seated anger became
measurably more palpable from the first time that I saw her after July

4th. She had clearly decided that it was necessary to take one parent's side in the matter, and that parent was not me.

Nikki, my youngest, has always presented a cheerful demeanor. She also is the Person-Most-Likely-To-Speak-First-Think-Second. Those diametric tendencies played havoc on our new relationship.

Damage control became a slippery slope. For my kids to understand that their father is not the monster they were told about, I would have to, at the very least, prove where I was the night of July 4th. But every bit of the abundant proof I could offer to them would, by definition, contradict their mother's story. Hence, I would indirectly be either calling her a liar, crazy or both. Therefore, any discussion about recent events would only make the situation worse, while silence would only allow it to fester.

Several times I either met them at a diner for a meal and a chat, or had them over to the house where I was living. The results of those times together were at best inconclusive, at worst... well, something worse than inconclusive.

I began sending brief notes to them, especially to Lindsay. Just little messages that said, "I love you," or, "Thinking about you." At times I would send them gifts. At one point I had transferred all of our home videos from VHS to DVD at considerable expense, since the tapes had become all but destroyed by mold. I sent copies of them all to each of my three kids.

It would seem that these efforts made during the three years that I was estranged but not disfellowshipped amounted to nothing. But something was accomplished. At least for me. I was able to realize that I was doing all that I could possibly do. Whether or not those efforts achieved the desired effect, doing them gave me at least a modicum of peace of mind, so that I could live another day and think about the next problem I had to deal with.

Coping, Setting Priorities, and Progressing

One day at a time.

I wish there were another, less cliché way of expressing it. But it may be the only way. It certainly was the only way for me to *do* it. One day at a time.

One day at a time *and* one thing at a time.

The morning after my arrest and interrogation, then a psychiatric evaluation at nearby Newton Memorial hospital, I came face-to-face with a plethora of losses. I had lost my home, my car, my cell phone, all of my financial accounts, my job, my ability to get a new job, my wife, my kids, all but a handful of my friends, and my reputation. In addition, I had only the clothes I was wearing and no access to the house where the rest of my clothes were, as well as no way to even pick up my mail. Under those circumstances one would expect one's mind to be rather clouded and compromised in the area of problem solving.

It's humanly impossible to tackle all of those tasks at once. In fact, it's human impossible to really attack even two tasks at once. We may imagine we multi-thread, but in actuality none of us ever do. I'm not talking about walking and chewing gum at the same time. I'm talking about, for example, preparing this year's tax return and having a heart-to-heart talk with your kids at the same time. No human can do it.

So why can't we just stop being overwhelmed by a multitude of necessary tasks and realize that we can only work on one at the moment? Perhaps it's because, as humans, we have the ability to imagine that we can, and that we have to.

When a bird is looking for food, it is not also thinking about building or repairing its nest. Nor is it thinking about where the food is going to come from tomorrow. Nor moving up to a bigger nest within five years. Nor providing for its nestlings' future nestlings. Nor anything else. It is just looking for food.

Of course, we have bigger problems than the scavenging bird. As humans, it's a requirement that we plan for the future. But that still doesn't mean that thinking we can and have to multi-task is going to help matters.

When I was finally released from the hospital around 6:00 AM, July 5th, after having passed the psychiatric evaluation with flying colors[7], I had to think about what I was going to do next. All the things already mentioned were on the table – my home, car, phone, finances, job, etc.

So, here's my secret.

Since I can only worry about and tackle one thing at a time, I have to pick one. How? It boils down to just two factors. The most obvious factor is actually my second factor: What is the most important problem I'm facing?

The slightly less obvious factor is my first: What are the problems that I can change, that I can actually *do something about?*

So *first* I pick all the *things I can do something about, then* pick the *most important one* from that list.

Not the hardest, or the most fun, or any other quality. Just the most important one of all the things I can do something about.

My first task in order to leave the hospital was to call a taxi, since I had been chauffeured there by the NJ State Police, and I didn't even know what happened to my car. Presumably it was at the police station. (As it turns out, it wasn't.) Since my cell phone was still at the police station, along with my wallet, keys and probably the lint that had been in my pockets, I had to borrow a remote phone from the nursing station, and have them help me find the number to a taxi service. And I called that taxi service.

Task number one complete.

The next two tasks, once I arrived at the police station, were to get my cell phone and other accouterments back, then my car. One task at a time, of course. But first I was reminded of the damage my interrogators at the police station had done to my rectum[8]. Lowering my 6'2" frame into that taxi was not a pleasant experience.

The police handed me my cell phone with a depleted battery. They not only had left it on all night, but played with it, removing the record of several phone calls that proved my innocence[9]. The trooper at the window kindly allowed me to use the barracks phone to call Derek, whom they said was to deliver my car to me. Then they gave me back my wallet and the key to the older car that was to be mine from now on, by order of the NJ State Police.

Tasks numbers two and three complete. One at a time.

Ancillary to task number two became charging my phone. So, task number four was now buying a charger, since the car that Derek had brought did not have one in it. There was a car parts store not far from the police station. For that day, at least, my debit card still worked – it would be a little later that I would learn that my wife had drained all of our financial accounts and closed them. I bought a charger that plugged into the car's cigarette lighter socket, since the car was a pre-USB model. Then I charged the cell phone battery.

Task number four complete. On to task five.

Task number five was something I had started thinking about before all the others. But logically, I couldn't complete it until I got through the first four tasks. I had to find a place to sleep for that night. And hopefully the weeks ahead. But I could only worry about that night for now.

I spent quite a bit of time calling people in the congregation to see if I could just sleep on their couch or anywhere. No one answered my calls or returned my voicemails.

I finally tumbled to the fact that I hadn't communicated with my parents, brother or sisters yet, none of whom have ever been JWs. A conversation with my older brother led to having an early dinner with him at a local restaurant, his treat. Since, at the time, Ed was commuting every week from New Jersey to Rochester, New York, he had lots of hotel perks built up. He put me up in a Hampton Inn in Newton, NJ.

Task number five complete. And with a full stomach!

When I talked to my parents, we made arrangements for me to visit them in Delaware for the weekend. I realized my next tasks were to be more complex, including beginning the gathering of evidence for my criminal trial, as well as retaining an attorney, but would have to wait until Monday. For now, my only plan was to get a good night's sleep after about 40 hours with very little of that precious commodity.

During that weekend at my parents' house, among other things, we discussed legal representation. By the time I left for home, I had a check in my hand that would cover my soon-to-be-attorney's retainer. They also provided some cash for daily expenses.

The tasks that followed, too numerous to delineate, occurred over many months. They all have one thing in common: they were accomplished one at a time. Just a few will be mentioned.

The following Monday afternoon I arrived at the radio station and began collecting evidence of my innocence. Then I met with the attorney that would represent me in both family and municipal court.

With those tasks done, it served no further purpose to think about them. So, I began to think about other things.

Provisions From... Whom?

Over the next three years and change, I continued attending meetings where I could. I continued trying to establish and maintain contact with old friends who were JWs. Neither of those two activities turned out to be healthy, but I tried.

I also continued making new friends. On occasion I received unsolicited help from some of them.

Force of Will compresses the many experiences with my new friends into just a couple. I will relate one, not mentioned in the book, that appeared anonymously as part of a consolidation with other people and events.

One day, for reasons I do not recall, I agreed to meet CC and her eventual-soulmate Brad at a favorite restaurant of ours. As the waiter took our orders, I simply asked for water, indicating nothing else was needed, rather than revealing my impecuniousness and significant hunger.

When their food arrived, Brad offered me some of his bread, ostensibly because he wasn't going to eat it all. I accepted graciously and ate just one slice.

My honest recollection of the conversation is that we did not discuss my situation. Unbeknownst to me, something touched Brad's heart. Perhaps it was my lack of a poker face combined with an unconsciously and unintended voracious attack at the bread and water.

Brad reached into his pocket and pulled out a wad of ten $20 bills and gave them to me.

I awkwardly yet quickly acquiesced, deciding to not look this gift-horse in the mouth. And I promised to pay him back when possible, even though he did not intend his gift to be a temporary loan. By the following week I had received my meager paycheck which afforded me the ability to pay Brad back in full and have a little left over for the next tank of gas and perhaps another meal.

Whether or not the reader believes that there is a spirit person who makes such events happen, I believe that is often the case, and probably was in this instance. As a JW I always believed that Jehovah influenced people who were willing to be moved by his holy spirit to perform acts of kindness toward their fellow believers. A shift in my thinking had now occurred. If Jehovah was responsible for coming to my aid at the restaurant, and not one of my former brothers and sisters cared enough to even ask about my welfare, let alone assist, then Jehovah was no longer using that ersatz "brotherhood" in my case. Rather, he was using people like Brad, CC, Trevor, and many, many others.

I prefer to be grateful for positive deeds. I prefer to not dwell on omissions of such, nor on inconsiderate, even wicked deeds. My gratitude starts with thanking Jehovah. Next come the humans that acted. Not everyone believes in the same god, or even any higher being, as I do. That's OK with me. But regardless of beliefs, it is possible, indeed advisable, for all of us to be grateful to the humans that help us in even small ways.

The Greatest Secret Weapon

Gratitude makes not only its recipient feel good, but also the person who is extending the gratitude. Among other things, it helps the grateful person forget the negativity caused by their problems, and clears their head in order to make room for solutions. Gratitude, just by accident, happens to be a great coping mechanism.

I even learned to remain grateful to the very ones who got me into the mess I was in. Admittedly, it is extraordinarily difficult to feel gratitude toward the woman who had me arrested and turned my own kids against me. I have certainly tried. No technique comes to mind, and the process tires me, so it remains on a distant back-burner. Similarly, I can summon no positive thoughts about those elders who railroaded me out of what was once my religion of choice. But they did unwittingly do me a favor, so at least I don't hold on to resentment.

I concentrate on things I was taught throughout my life. Granted, some were wrong, even egregiously so. But some were good. Very good.

Naturally, I learned many things in my forty-year association with the JWs. A number of positive things stand out. The sterling example they set of treating people of different ethnic backgrounds equally is one life lesson I will always be grateful for. Even though there are myriad problems associated with the JWs' ancient attitudes toward women, I did learn to respect all women and treat them accordingly from the JWs. It has been just a matter of recognizing where the JW view of women becomes mired in Puritanical extremism, and avoiding that thinking. I overcame a terror of speaking in front of a group thanks to the Theocratic Ministry School. And although making new friends and conversing with people one-on-one was always relatively easy for me, my increased degree of comfort in new situations with new people must go back to the dreaded, mandatory door-to-door ministry.

Did I really need the JWs to learn all of those things? Maybe not. But I will never know, because the incontrovertible fact is, that is where I learned them. I prefer to be grateful for things I have received, regardless of from whom I received them. Gratitude frees me from the prison created by bitterness.

I remain grateful for the fact that I was still breathing on July 4th, 2012 and am now doing more than just breathing. I am grateful for the scores of new friends who helped me in ways that they are not even aware of. I am even somewhat grateful for my forty-some-years as a JW because it is part of who I am today, and I like who I am. But I am most grateful that today I am not Gary Alt the JW, or Gary Alt the ex-JW, but just Gary Alt.

The Truth About the Truth

Judy and I separated in February, 2018, and I moved to a town about fifteen miles closer to my job as a Financial Advisor for Bank of America in Allentown, PA. Our divorce was finalized three months later in May.

Even during this time, two years after I attended my last Kingdom Hall meeting, I still thought that JWs had "the truth." The condition that causes this curious thinking, "malignant optimism," is discussed in *Song of Gil*[10], the sequel to *Force of Will*. In my defense, I maintain that since I was too jaded from the experience of the previous nearly six years, and still tasked with putting my life back together, it was best to not have 'researching the Watchtower' as an item on my agenda.

I still believed that we were living in the last days, and that the earth will soon be a paradise. However, as a result of the spiritual, emotional, and mental torture my elders had subjected me to during the final years of my marriage to Marta, I decided that it didn't matter whether I was going to be there to enjoy that paradise – the fact that it was going to happen is what really gave me joy. Whether or not the end would come in my lifetime never mattered to me either; I always thought that living as a JW was the best way of life anyway.

Being a creative person who may at any moment experience a spark to write a new song or some prose, I sometimes am inspired to do other things at odd times also.

One day, about a year after settling into my new apartment, for some inexplicable reason the idea of researching the Watchtower anew entered my mind. It was finally time.

I used many publications in my research, including the Watchtower Library, going back as far as that resource would take me. I also researched out-of-print Watchtower publications wherever they were available, going back to the first edition of *Zion's Watch Tower and Herald of Christ's Presence,* as well as other earlier writings of Charles Taze Russell and his associates.

I tried to maintain an open mind, but I confess that I was really trying to prove that JWs *do* have the truth.

I do not come to major conclusions lightly. I do not believe things just because someone tells me to, no matter who they are.

As I came to understand some of the problems with the methods the Governing Body has used in determining doctrine after that organ began operations in 1971, I also started to see problems with the doctrines themselves.

But being accustomed to accepting the concept that "...the path of the righteous is like the bright morning light that grows brighter and brighter until full daylight[11]," I continued to defend Watchtower's position in the universe as being God's earthly organization. My thinking went like this:

> *Suppose that they are wrong about 10% of their teachings. That means they are right about 90%. Since they are the only religious organization on earth that can be said about, they are still the only organization with the truth.*

As time went by and I discovered more and more problems with Watchtower teachings, I changed those statistics to perhaps 40% wrong, 60% right. That is a disturbing statistic, but still an acceptable ratio to declare that they have "the truth."

The final epiphany that made me realize that they do *not* have "the truth" was when I realized that the authority that the Governing Body claims to have been granted as the faithful and discreet slave by Jesus himself depends on grossly inaccurate chronology and interpretation of it.

As was previously stated, I do not come to major conclusions lightly. Later I did some studying on the subject of cults[12]. Comparing that information with my experience and what I already knew, I decided that the term "cult" cannot apply to the JWs.

The reason for that was not that my research was incorrect. It was my limited view of my experience that was incorrect. I once again adjusted my thinking.

One of the most gloriously freeing things I have learned since leaving the JWs is that it's not important to always be right, to always have an answer to everything. In fact, it's not even possible. For that and other reasons, it doesn't matter whether or not my personal answer to the "cult" question is 100% correct. What does matter is that I now have a better personal understanding of the Complex Post Traumatic Stress Disorder caused by my stint as a JW from 1974 to 2016.

Again, I do not come to major conclusions lightly.

Like most or all people, I have experienced physical injuries at various times in my life. A few times those injuries and the events that caused them have been traumatic. At those times the body has a way of spreading the pain of those injuries over time, so that trauma is more readily dealt with, especially at the beginning.

If there can be a reason why it took me so darn long to appreciate the reality of the organization I had been a part of for all those years, perhaps that reason is that the trauma was reduced by being spread out over time. Maybe I did that favor to myself subconsciously. Or maybe it was my malignant optimism that only let "The Truth About The Truth" seep into my mind gradually.

I honestly don't know. Some people leave the JWs because they realize it is not the truth. I realized it is not the truth because I left the JWs.

I thereby unwittingly prolonged the trauma, but perhaps that is what I personally needed to do. I don't know, because I don't have all the answers. For that I am gloriously grateful.

What Next?

The most exciting thing about this brief story is that it's not over yet.

References:

1 Written pseudonymously by Tan Swiftwater, available at store.bookbaby.com/book/force-of-will. The only changes to these excerpts are the switch from the book's point of view to first person and the use of my then-wife's real first name.

2 "Never Ending Always," written by me and performed by Lori Klein with the Gary Alt Jazz Trio. Available at store.cdbaby.com/cd/lorikleinthegaryaltjazztrio.

3 From hereon, rather than the name "Jehovah's Witnesses," the acronyms "JW," "JWs" and "JWs'" will be used.

4 Any facts related are an extremely condensed summary of just parts of the story presented in *Force of Will*.

5 Not her real name, but the name that is used in *Force of Will*. The name "Marta" will be used throughout this story.

6 There was no Kingdom Hall in Byram NJ. Because *Force of Will* is a novel based a true story, most proper nouns had been changed. However, the story that is told is true in every key way.

7 *Force of Will*, Chapter 7

8 *Force of Will*, Chapter 5, which also explains why this wasn't taken care of at the hospital.

9 *Force of Will*, Chapter 10

10 *Song of Gil* picks up where *Force of Will* left off and fills in some of the gaps in the story. It is available as a free PDF by writing to goodleafpublishing@gmail.com – however it is highly recommended that the reader first read *Force of Will*.

11 Proverbs 4:18, *New World Translation of the Holy Scriptures*, 2013 edition

12 All research referred to and subsequent conclusions are discussed in detail in *Song of Gil*.

Chapter 9

Kicking Against the Goads

by Eric Wilson

Freed from Indoctrination

ommy, am I going to die at Armageddon?"

I was only five years old when I asked my parents that question.

Why would a five-year-old child worry about such things? In a word: "Indoctrination". From infancy, my parents took me to all five weekly meetings of Jehovah's Witnesses. From the platform and through the publications, the idea that the world would shortly end was hammered into my child brain. My parents told me I'd never even finish school.

That was 65 years ago, and Witness leadership is still saying that Armageddon is "imminent".

I learned of Jehovah God and Jesus Christ from the Witnesses, but my faith does not depend on that religion. In fact, since I left in 2015, it is stronger than it has ever been. That isn't to say that leaving Jehovah's Witnesses has been easy. An outsider may have trouble understanding the emotional trauma a member of the Organization faces upon leaving. In my case, I had served as an elder for over 40 years. All my friends were Jehovah's Witnesses. I had a good reputation, and I think I can say with modesty that many looked up to me as a good example of what an elder should be. As the coordinator of the body of elders, I had a position of authority. Why would anyone give all that up?

Most Witnesses are conditioned to believe that people only leave their ranks out of pride. What a joke that is. Pride would have kept me in the Organization. Pride would have caused me to hold onto my hard-won reputation, position and authority; just as pride and fear of losing their authority drove the Jewish leaders to murder God's Son? (John 11:48)

My experience is hardly unique. Others have given up much more than I have. My parents are both dead and my sister left the Organization along with me; but I know of many with large families—parents, grandparents, children, et cetera—who have been totally ostracized. To be completely cut off by family members has been so traumatic for some that they have actually taken their own lives. How very, very sad. (May the leaders of the organization take note. Jesus said it would be better for those who stumble the little ones to have a millstone tied round the neck and to be pitched into the sea—Mark 9:42.)

Given the cost, why would anyone choose to leave? Why put oneself through such pain?

There are a number of reasons, but for me there is only one that really matters; and if I can help you find it, then I will have accomplished something good.

Consider this parable of Jesus: "Again the kingdom of the heavens is like a traveling merchant seeking fine pearls. Upon finding one pearl of high value, away he went and promptly sold all the things he had and bought it." (Matthew 13:45, 46)[1]

What is the pearl of great value that would cause someone like me to give up everything of value to acquire it?

Jesus says: "Truly I say to you, no one has left house or brothers or sisters or mother or father or children or fields for my sake and for the sake of the good news who will not get 100 times more now in this period of time—houses, brothers, sisters, mothers, children, and fields, with persecutions—and in the coming system of things, everlasting life." (Mark 10:29, 30)

So, on the one side of the balance we have position, financial security, family, and friends. On the other side, we have Jesus Christ and everlasting life. Which weighs more in your eyes?

Are you traumatized by the idea you may have wasted a large portion of your life inside the Organization? Truly, that will only be a waste if you do not use this opportunity to grab hold of the everlasting life Jesus is offering to you. (1 Timothy 6:12, 19)

The Leaven of the Pharisees

"Watch out for the leaven of the Pharisees, which is hypocrisy." (Luke 12:1)

Leaven is bacteria that causes the fermentation that makes dough rise. If you take a tiny morsel of leaven, and put it into a mass of flour dough, it will slowly multiply until the entire mass has been infected. Likewise, it only takes a small amount of hypocrisy to slowly permeate every part of the Christian congregation. Real leaven is good for bread, but the leaven of the Pharisees is very bad within any body of Christians. Nevertheless, the process is slow and often difficult to perceive until the full mass is corrupted.

I have suggested on my YouTube channel (Beroean Pickets) that the current state of the congregation of Jehovah's Witnesses is much worse now that it was in my youth—a statement sometimes contested by some channel viewers. However, I stand by it. It is one of the reasons I didn't start to wake up to the reality of the Organization until 2011.

For example, I can't imagine the Organization of the 1960s or 1970s ever engaging in an NGO affiliation with the United Nations as they came to do for ten years starting 1992 and ending only when exposed publicly for hypocrisy.[2]

Further, if, in those days, you got old in the fulltime service, either as a lifelong missionary or Bethelite, they would care for you until you died. Now they are putting old full-timers on the curb with barely a slap on the back and a hearty, "Fare well."[3]

Then there is the growing child abuse scandal. Granted, the seeds for it were planted many decades ago, but it wasn't until 2015 that the ARC[4] brought it into the light of day.[5] So the metaphorical termites have been multiplying and eating away at the wooden framework of the JW.org house for some time, but for me the structure seemed solid until just a few years ago.

This process can be understood through a parable Jesus used to explain the state of the nation of Israel in his day.

"When an unclean spirit comes out of a man, it passes through parched places in search of a resting-place, and finds none. Then it says, 'I will go back to my house out of which I moved'; and on arriving it finds it unoccupied but swept clean and adorned. Then it goes its way and takes along with it seven different spirits more wicked than itself, and, after getting inside, they dwell there; and the final circumstances of that man become worse than the first. **That is how it will be also with this wicked generation.**" (Matthew 12:43-45 NWT)

Jesus was not referring to a literal man, but to an entire generation. God's spirit resides within individuals. It doesn't take many spiritual persons to exert a powerful influence on a group. Remember, Jehovah was willing to spare the wicked cities of Sodom and Gomorrah for the sake of *only ten righteous men* (Genesis 18:32). However, there is a crossover point. While I have known many good Christians in my lifetime—righteous men and women—little by little, I have seen their numbers dwindle. Speaking metaphorically, are there even ten righteous men in JW.org?

The Organization of today, with its shrinking numbers and Kingdom hall sales, is a shadow of the one I once knew and supported. It seems the "seven spirits more wicked than itself" are hard at work.

My Story

I was a pretty typical Jehovah's Witness in my teens, meaning that I went to meetings and participated in the door-to-door preaching because my parents made me. It was only when I went to Colombia, South America, in 1968 at the age of 19 that I began to take my spirituality seriously. I graduated high school in 1967 and was working at the local steel company, living away from home. I had wanted to attend university, but with the Organization's promotion of 1975 as the probable end, attaining a degree seemed like a waste of time.[6]

When I learned my parents were taking my 17-year-old sister out of school and moving to Colombia to serve where the need was great, I decided to quit my job and go along because it sounded like a great adventure. I actually thought of buying a motorcycle and travelling through South America. (It's probably just as well that never happened.)

When I got to Colombia and began to associate with other "need greaters", as they were called, my spiritual perspective changed. (There were over 500 in the country at that time from the US, Canada, and a few from Europe. Oddly enough, the number of Canadians matched the number of Americans, even though the Witness population in Canada is only a tenth of that in the States. I found the same ratio persisted when serving in Ecuador in the early 1990s.)

While my outlook became more spirit oriented, hobnobbing with missionaries killed any desire to become one or to serve at Bethel. There was just too much pettiness and infighting among the missionary couples as well as at the branch. However, such conduct didn't kill my faith. I just reasoned it was the result of human imperfection, because, after all, didn't we have "the truth"?

I began to take personal bible study seriously in those days and made a point of reading all the publications. I started with the belief that our publications were thoroughly researched and the writing staff was comprised of intelligent, well-studied Bible scholars.

It didn't take long before that illusion was dispelled.

For instance, the magazines often delved into extensive and often ridiculous antitypical applications such as the lion that Samson killed representing Protestantism (w67 2/15 p. 107 par. 11) or the ten camels that Rebecca received from Isaac representing the Bible (w89 7/1 p. 27 par. 17). (I used to joke that the camel dung represented the Apocrypha.) Even when delving into science, they came up with some very silly statements—for instance, claiming that lead is "one of the best electrical insulators", when anyone who has ever used battery cables to boost a dead car knows you connect them to battery terminals made of lead. (*Aid to Bible Understanding*, p. 1164)

My forty years as an elder means I endured approximately 80 circuit overseer visits. The elders generally dreaded such visits. We were happy when left alone to practice our Christianity, but when we were brought into contact with central control, the joy went out of our service. Invariably, the C.O. would leave us feeling we just weren't doing enough. Guilt, not love, was their motivating force used and still used by the Organization.

To paraphrase the words of our Lord: "By this all will know that you are not my disciples—if you have guilt among yourselves." (John 13:35)

I remember one particularly self-important C.O. who wanted to improve the meeting attendance at the congregation book study, which was always the most poorly attended of all meetings. His idea was to have the Book Study Conductor call up any individual who didn't attend right after the study was over to tell them how much they were missed. I told him—quoting Hebrews 10:24 mockingly—that we'd only be "inciting the brothers to guilt and fine works". He smirked and chose to ignore the jibe. The elders all chose to ignore his "loving direction"—all but one gung-ho young elder who soon gained a reputation for waking people up who missed the study to go to bed early because they were overtired, overworked, or just plain sick.

To be fair, there were some good circuit overseers in the early years, men who were really trying to be good Christians. (I can count them on the fingers of one hand.) However, they often didn't last. Bethel needed company men who would blindly do their bidding. That is a perfect breeding ground for pharisaical thinking.

The leaven of the Pharisees was becoming increasingly evident. I know of an elder found guilty of fraud by a federal court, who was allowed to continue to manage the Regional Building Committee funds. I've seen a body of elders repeatedly attempt to remove an elder for sending his children to university, while turning a blind eye to gross sexual misconduct in their midst. What is important to them is obedience and submission to their lead. I've seen elders removed simply for asking too many questions of the branch office and not being willing to accept their whitewashed answers.

One occasion that stands out was when we tried to remove an elder who had libeled another in a letter of recommendation. Slander is a disfellowshipping offence, but we were only interested in removing the brother from his office of oversight. However, he had a former Bethel roommate who was now on the branch committee. A special committee appointed by the branch was sent to "review" the case. They refused to look at the evidence, even though the slander was clearly laid out in writing. The victim of the slander was told by his circuit overseer that he couldn't testify if he wanted to remain an elder. He gave way to fear and refused to come to the hearing. The brothers assigned to the Special Committee made it clear to us that the Service Desk wanted us to reverse our decision, because it always looks better when all the elders are in agreement with the direction from Bethel. (This is an example of the "unity over justice" principle.) There were only three of us, but we didn't give in, so they had to overrule our decision.

I wrote the Service Desk in protest for their intimidation of a witness and for directing the special committee to deliver a verdict to their liking. Not long after, they tried to remove me for what was essentially non-compliance. It took them two tries, but they did accomplish it.

Just as leaven continues to permeate the mass, such hypocrisy infects all levels of the organization. For instance, there is a common tactic elder bodies use to vilify anyone who stands up to them. Often, such a person cannot advance in the congregation so they feel motivated to move to another congregation, one with—they hope—more reasonable elders. When that happens, a letter of introduction follows them often filled with positive comments, and one small telltale statement about some "matter of concern." It will be vague, but enough to raise a flag and prompt a phone call for clarification. That way the original elder body can "dish the dirt" without fear of reprisals because nothing is in writing.

I detested this tactic and when I became the coordinator, I refused to play along. Of course, the C.O. reviews all such letters and will inevitably ask for clarification, so I would have to get it. However, I wouldn't accept anything that wasn't put in writing. They were always miffed by this, and would never respond in writing unless forced to by circumstances.

Of course, all of this is not part of the written policies of the Organization, but like the Pharisees and religious leaders of Jesus' day, the oral law supersedes the written one within the JW community—further proof that the spirit of God is missing.

Looking back, something that should have woken me up was the cancellation of the Book Study arrangement in 2008.[7] We were always told that when persecution came, the one meeting that would survive was the Congregation Book Study because it was held in private homes. The reasons for doing this, they explained, was because of rising gas prices, and to spare families the time spent in travelling to and from meetings. They also claimed this was to free up a night for a home family study.

That reasoning didn't make sense. The Book Study was arranged to cut down on travel time, since they were spread around the territory at convenient locations rather than forcing all to come to a central Kingdom hall. And since when does the Christian Congregation cancel a night of worship to save us a few bucks on gas?! As for the family study night, they were treating this as a new arrangement, but it had been in place for decades. I realized they were lying to us, and not doing a very good job of it either, but I couldn't see the reason why and frankly, I welcomed the free night. Elders are overworked, so none of us complained about having some free time at last.

I now believe the main reason was so that they could tighten up control. If you allow small groups of Christians managed by a single elder, you are sometimes going to get a free interchange of ideas. Critical thinking could blossom. But if you keep all the elders together, then the Pharisees can police the rest. Independent thought gets squashed.

As the years rolled by, the subconscious part of my brain took note of these things even while the conscious part fought to preserve the status quo. I found a growing disquiet within myself; what I now understand to have been the beginnings of cognitive dissonance. It is a state of mind where two contrary ideas exist and are both treated as true, but one of them is unacceptable to the host and must be suppressed. Like the computer HAL from *2001 A Space Odyssey*, such a state cannot continue without doing serious harm to the organism.

If you have been beating yourself up because you were like me in taking a long time to recognize what now seems to be as plain as the nose on your face—Don't! Consider Saul of Tarsus. He was there in Jerusalem while Jesus was curing the sick, restoring sight to the blind, and raising the dead, yet he ignored the evidence and persecuted Jesus' disciples. Why? The Bible says he studied at the feet of Gamaliel, a prominent

Jewish teacher and leader (Acts 22:3). (He had a "governing body" telling him how to think).

He was surrounded by people speaking with one voice, so his flow of information was narrowed to a single source; like Witnesses who get all their instruction from Watchtower publications. Saul was praised and loved by the Pharisees for his zeal and active support of them, just as the Governing Body claims to love those with special privileges in the Organization like pioneers and elders.

Saul was further screened from thinking outside of his environment by training that made him feel special and that caused him to look down on others as beneath contempt (John 7:47-49). In the same way, Witnesses are trained to view everything and everyone outside the congregation as worldly and to be avoided.

Finally, for Saul, there was the ever-present fear of being cut off from everything he valued were he to confess the Christ (John 9:22). Likewise, Witnesses live under the threat of shunning should they openly question the teachings of the Governing Body, even when such teachings are contrary to the commands of Christ.

Even if Saul had doubts, to whom could he turn for counsel? Any of his colleagues would have turned him in at the first hint of disloyalty. Again, a situation all too familiar to any Jehovah's Witness who has ever had doubts.

Nevertheless, Saul of Tarsus was someone Jesus' knew would be ideal for the work of expanding the gospel to the gentiles. He just needed a push—in his case, a particularly big push. Here are Saul's own words describing the event:

"Amid these efforts as I was journeying to Damascus with authority and a commission from the chief priests, I saw at midday on the road, O king, a light beyond the brilliance of the sun flash from heaven about me and about those journeying with me. And when we had all fallen to the ground I heard a voice say to me in the Hebrew language, 'Saul,

Saul, why are you persecuting me? To keep kicking against the goads makes it hard for you.'" (Acts 26:12-14)

Jesus saw something good in Saul. He saw a zeal for truth. True, a misdirected zeal, but if turned to the light, he was to be a powerful tool for the Lord's work of gathering the Body of Christ. Yet, Saul was resisting. He was kicking against the goads.

What did Jesus mean by "kicking against the goads"?

A goad is what we call a cattle prod. In those days, they used pointed sticks or goads to get cattle to move. Saul was at a tipping point. On the one hand, all the things he knew about Jesus and his followers were like cattle prods that should have been moving him toward the Christ, but he was subconsciously ignoring the evidence, kicking against the spirit's goading. As a Pharisee, he believed he was in the one true religion. His position was privileged and he didn't want to lose it. He was among men who respected him and praised him. A change would mean being shunned by his former friends and leaving to associate with those he was taught to view as "accursed people".

Does that situation not resonate with you?

Jesus pushed Saul of Tarsus over the tipping point, and he became the Apostle Paul. But this was only possible because Saul, unlike the majority of his fellow Pharisees, loved truth. He loved it so much that he was willing to give up everything for it. It was the pearl of high value. He thought he had had the truth, but when he came to see it as false, it turned to garbage in his eyes. It's easy to give up garbage. We do it every week. It is really just a matter of perception. (Philippians 3:8).

Have you been kicking against the goads? I was. I didn't wake up due to a miraculous vision of Jesus. However, there was one particular goad that pushed me over the edge. It came in 2010 with the release of the revised generation teaching that expected us to believe in an overlapping generation that could span well over a century of time.

This wasn't just a silly teaching. It was blatantly unscriptural, and downright insulting to one's intelligence. It was the JW version of "The Emperor's New Clothes"[8]. For the first time, I came to realize that these men were capable of just making stuff up—stupid stuff at that. Yet, heaven help you if you objected to it.

In a backhanded way, I have to thank them for it, because they got me wondering if this was just the tip of the iceberg. What about all the teachings I thought were part of "the truth" that I had come to accept as scriptural bedrock all my life?

I realized I wasn't going to get my answers from the publications. I needed to expand my sources. So, I set up a web site (now, beroeans.net) under an alias—Meleti Vivlon; Greek for "bible study"—to protect my identity. The idea was to find other likeminded Witnesses to engage in deep Bible research. At that point, I still believed I was in "The Truth", but I thought that we might have just a few things wrong.

How wrong I was.

As a result of several years of investigation, I learned that every doctrine— every doctrine—unique to Jehovah's Witnesses was unscriptural. They didn't get even one right. I'm not talking about their rejection of the Trinity and of Hellfire, because such conclusions are not unique to Jehovah's Witnesses. Instead, I'm referring to teachings like the invisible presence of Christ in 1914, the 1919 appointment of the Governing Body as the faithful and discreet slave, their judicial system, their prohibition of blood transfusions, the other sheep as God's friends with no mediator, the baptismal vow of dedication. All these doctrines and many more are false.

My awakening didn't happen all at once, but there was a eureka moment. I was struggling with a growing cognitive dissonance—juggling two contrary ideas. On the one hand, I knew that all the doctrines were false; but on the other hand, I still believed we were the true religion. Back and forth, these two thoughts went ricocheting around my brain like a ping pong ball until finally I was able to admit to myself that I wasn't in the truth at all, and never had been. Jehovah's Witnesses were not the true religion. I can still remember the overwhelming sense of relief that realization brought to me. I felt my whole body relax and a wave of calm settled upon me. I was free! Free in a real sense and for the first time in my life.

This wasn't the false freedom of licentiousness. I didn't feel free to do whatever I wanted. I still believed in God, but now I saw him truly as my Father. I was no longer an orphan. I had been adopted. I had found my family.

Jesus said that the truth would set us free, but only if we remained in his teachings (John 8:31, 32). For the first time, I was truly starting to understand how his teachings applied to me as a child of God. Witnesses had me believing that I could only aspire to friendship with God, but now I came to see that the path to adoption was not cut off in the mid-1930s, but is open to all who put faith in Jesus Christ (John 1:12). I was taught to refuse the bread and wine; that I was not worthy. Now I saw that if one puts faith in Christ and accepts the life-saving value of his flesh and blood, one must partake. To do otherwise is to reject the Christ himself.

Learning to Think

What is the freedom of the Christ?

This is the crux of everything. Only by understanding and applying this can your awakening truly benefit you.

Let's start with what Jesus actually said:

"And so, Jesus went on to say to the Jews that had believed him: "If YOU remain in my word, YOU are really my disciples, and YOU will know the truth, and the truth will set YOU free." They replied to him: "We are Abraham's offspring and never have we been slaves to anybody. How is it you say, 'YOU will become free'?" (John 8:31-33)

In those days, you were either Jew or Gentile; either someone who worshipped Jehovah God, or someone who served pagan gods. If the Jews who worshiped the true God were not free, how much more so would that have applied to the Romans, Corinthians, and the other pagan nations? In the entire world of that time, the only way to be truly free was to accept the truth from Jesus and live that truth. Only then would a person be free of the influence of men, because only then would he or she be under the influence of God. You cannot serve two masters. Either you obey men or you obey God (Luke 16:13).

Did you notice that the Jews were unaware of their enslavement? They thought they were free. There is no one more enslaved than the slave who thinks he is free. The Jews of that time thought they were free, and so became even more susceptible to the influence of their religious leaders. It is as Jesus told us: "If the light that is in you is really darkness, how great that darkness is!" (Matthew 6:23)

On my YouTube channels[9], I have had a number of comments ridiculing me because I took 40 years to wake up. The irony is that the people making these claims are just as enslaved as I was. When I was growing up, Catholics didn't eat meat on Fridays and didn't practice birth control. To this day, hundreds of thousands of priests cannot take a wife. Catholics follow many rites and rituals, not because God commands them, but because they have submitted themselves to the will of a man in Rome.

As I write this, many fundamentalist Christians avidly support a man who is a known shyster, womanizer, adulterer, and liar because they have been told by other men that he has been chosen by God as the modern-day Cyrus. They are submitting to men and so are not free, because the Lord tells his disciples not to mix in company with sinners like that (1 Corinthians 5:9-11).

This form of enslavement is not restricted to religious people. Paul was blinded to the truth because he limited his source of information to his immediate associates. Jehovah's Witnesses likewise limit their source of information to the publications and videos put out by JW.org. Often people who belong to one political party will limit their information intake to a single news source. Then there are the people who no longer believe in God but hold science to be the source of all truth. However, true science deals with what we know, not what we think we know. Treating theory as fact because learned men say it is so is just another form of man-made religion.

If you want to be truly free, you must remain in the Christ. This is not easy. It is easy to listen to men and do what you're told. You don't really have to think. True freedom is hard. It takes effort.

Remember that Jesus said that first you must "remain in his word" and then "you will know the truth, and the truth will set you free." (John 8:31, 32)

You don't need to be a genius to accomplish this. But you must be diligent. Keep an open mind and listen, but always verify. Never take anything anyone says, no matter how convincing and logical they may sound, at face value. Always double and triple check. We live at a time like no other in history in which knowledge is literally at our fingertips. Do not fall into the trap of Jehovah's Witnesses by restricting the flow of information to a single source. If someone tells you the earth is flat, go on the Internet and look for a contrary view. If someone says there was no flood, go on the Internet and look for a contrary view. No matter what anyone tells you, do not surrender your ability to think critically to anyone.

The Bible tells us "to make sure of all things" and to "hold fast to what is fine" (1 Thessalonians 5:21). The truth is out there, and once we find that we have to hold onto it. We must be wise and learn to think critically. What will protect us as the Bible says:

"My son, may they not get away from your eyes. Safeguard practical wisdom and thinking ability, and they will prove to be life to your soul and charm to your throat. In that case you will walk in security on your way, and even your foot will not strike against anything. Whenever you lie down you will feel no dread; and you will certainly lie down, and your sleep must be pleasurable. You will not need to be afraid of any sudden dreadful thing, nor of the storm upon the wicked ones, because it is coming. For Jehovah himself will prove to be, in effect, your confidence, and he will certainly keep your foot against capture." (Proverbs 3:21-26)

Those words, though written thousands of years ago, are as true today as they were then. The true disciple of Christ who safeguards his thinking ability will not be trapped by men nor will he suffer the storm that is coming upon the wicked.

You have before you the opportunity to become a child of God. A spiritual man or woman in the world populated by physical men and women. The Bible says that the spiritual man examines all things but he is not examined by anyone. He has been given the ability to see deep into things and understand the true nature of all things, but the physical man will look at the spiritual man and misjudge him because he does not reason spiritually and cannot see the truth.

If we extend the meaning of Jesus' words to their logical conclusion, we will see that if anyone rejects Jesus, they cannot be free. Thus, there are only two kinds of people in the world: those who are free and spiritual, and those who are enslaved and physical. However, the latter think they are free because, being physical, they are incapable of examining all things as the spiritual man does. This makes the physical man easy to manipulate, because he obeys men rather than God. On the other hand, the spiritual man is free because he slaves only for the Lord and slavery for God is, ironically, the only way to true freedom. This is because our Lord and Master wants nothing from us but our love and returns that love superabundantly. He wants only what is best for us.

For decades I thought I was a spiritual man, because men told me I was. Now I realize I was not. I am thankful that the Lord saw fit to wake me up and draw me to him, and now he is doing the same for you. Behold, he is knocking on your door, and he wants to come in as sit at the table with you and eat the evening meal with you—the Lord's supper (Revelation 3:20).

We have an invitation but it is up to each of us to accept it. The reward for doing so is surpassingly great. We may think we have been fools to allow ourselves to have been deceived by men for so long, but how much greater the fool we would be were we to turn down such an invitation? Will you open the door?

References:

[1] Unless otherwise stipulated, all the Bible quotes are from the *New World Translation of the Holy Scripture, Reference Bible*.

[2] See https://www.jwfacts.com/watchtower/united-nations-association.php for full details.

[3] All district overseers were sent packing in 2014, and in 2016, 25% of worldwide staff was cut, with a disproportionate number being among the most senior. Circuit Overseers are not dismissed upon reaching 70 years of age. The majority of Special Pioneers were also dropped in 2016. Due to the requirement for all to take a vow of poverty upon entering "fulltime service" so as to allow the Organization to avoid paying into Government pension plans, many of these sent packing have no safety net.

[4] Australia Royal Commission into Institutional Responses to Child Sexual Abuse.

[5] See https://www.jwfacts.com/watchtower/paedophilia.php

[6] See "The Euphoria of 1975" at
https://beroeans.net/2012/11/03/the-euphoria-of-1975/

[7] See "End of the Home Book Study Arrangement"
(https://jwfacts.com/watchtower/blog/book-study-arrangement.php)

[8] See https://en.wikipedia.org/wiki/The_Emperor%27s_New_Clothes

[9] English "Beroean Pickets"; Spanish "Los Bereanos".

Chapter 10

Finding Freedom

by Sarah Elizabeth Lund

I dedicate this to the people who have given my life so much meaning and joy. To my kids, you are my everything. To my brother in law Joe, you are the reason I woke up when I did, which began my road to mental freedom. To my ex-husband Darcy, although our marriage didn't work out, we continue to raise our kids with love and friendship. To Bryden, you have been there from the beginning of my journey, and have always been quick to help and support me when I needed a shoulder and advice. To Kyle, you have been my constant rock. You have taught me not to give up on love, and not to give up on myself. I love you with all my heart, and I feel so blessed to call you family.

> *"Expose yourself to your deepest fear; after that, fear has no power, and the fear of freedom shrinks and vanishes. You are free."*
> *-Jim Morrison*

Many people see Jehovah's Witnesses as just another religion, a bit odd, but ultimately, harmless. While there are kind, empathetic

Jehovah's Witnesses, those qualities of human goodness are restricted and suppressed by their peculiar doctrines and policies in ways not found throughout the rest of Christianity. The inhumane experiences I endured within this religion, brought me to the brink of insanity and almost made me end my life. It took me years to recover from the psychological damage.

Yet here I am, alive and strong, telling my story. I hope that anyone who reads this will know that they are not alone. No matter how difficult life may seem, no matter how many challenges are thrown at you, you can keep going and find a place of strength, peace, acceptance, and love. You can look to the future with positivity, hope, and love in your heart, celebrating the life that you have in front of you. Today, I share my story in the sincere hope that it will help others find the peace of mind that I was finally able to find.

Where It All Began

I grew up in a home where the "rod" was not spared. My parents became Jehovah's Witnesses before they married and had us kids. Before that, they were just a couple of happy hippies. My sister Aimee was the eldest, and my brother Daniel was the youngest. I was the middle child. We were good kids, yet somehow, we were always getting yelled at. Aimee was the quiet one, and I was the louder energetic child that was mostly always in trouble. Daniel was diagnosed as having special needs and needed full-time care. This additional burden on my parents only made matters worse, and caused them to cling more tightly to the hope found in the doctrines of the Jehovah's Witnesses.

When I came to learn in my adult years of the tumultuous life my dad had growing up, I understood why he would be drawn to religion. It explained why he was always so angry and frustrated. Looking back, I believe he had mental health issues that were left unidentified and untreated. He suffered alone and in silence, possibly not even understanding it himself. Before becoming indoctrinated with the Witnesses, my dad was on a quest to find meaning and life's answers.

I remember him telling me he was looking into Buddhism when his coworker approached him and told him about "the truth". He was drawn to the promises held out by the Witnesses, and when he converted, he finally found a purpose. But little did he know this purpose came with many conditions attached. This put a lot of pressure on him to behave a certain way, live up to the Witnesses' absurdly high standards, and forcefully make his family live up to them, too. We were under so much pressure to conform under the threat of losing God's favor and everlasting life in Paradise. This made life at home quite tumultuous, to say the least.

Us kids were always in trouble for not dedicating enough time to Jehovah and the organization. I remember some softness from my mother, but my dad was always so stressed. My mom played the part of a good, submissive housewife, doing everything she could to not provoke my dad's frustrations. There was little love between them, and it was heartbreaking to see. My dad worked hard to provide for the family, and I do believe he loved us very much. But because of the demands of the religion, he was under a lot of pressure to do everything he was taught at the Kingdom Hall. After experiencing so much tension and turmoil at home, I'd go to school and live out a second nightmare. Because I was so different and wasn't allowed to make non-JW friends, I was bullied all through school and treated like a worthless outcast. The stress of everything made me fail a lot of my school work, so I fell behind. I felt like a failure, both at home and at school. I didn't receive any encouragement to do better in school, because Armageddon was around the corner. Back then it was taught at the Kingdom Hall and conventions that education was a waste of time because paradise was around the corner. I didn't think I would see adulthood in "this system of things".

I got baptized into the religion at the age of 14, with absolutely no idea what I was signing up for. At the time, I truly believed everything I'd been taught, and I wanted to give my life to being a servant of God. I hoped that this would finally make my parents proud of me. For a brief moment, I felt happy, like I had found my purpose in life. But that dissolved quickly. I continued to be a disappointment to my parents, and I never understood why. I tried so hard to be a good Jehovah's Witness girl. Maybe I could have read more Watchtower publications instead of novels and poetry. Maybe I could have spent more time preaching and less time hanging out with friends or listening to music. Who knows. It sure seems silly to think about now. I just remember that, through all of it, I stayed close to Jehovah. He was all I had. I would talk to Him every day, several times a day. But still, nothing I did was ever good enough for my parents.

At the age of 19, my older sister Aimee was disfellowshipped (excommunicated) for smoking cannabis. I was 17 at the time. She tried to get reinstated (the process of undoing ex-communication) which involves sitting at the back of the Kingdom Hall and being shunned (ignored) by everyone. No one was allowed to make eye contact with her. She wasn't even allowed to eat at the family dinner table. She had to eat alone in her room. This was all done as a show of repentance. Her life was micromanaged by my dad, and if she did anything outside of the JW world, she wouldn't hear the end of it. When her attempt to become reinstated became too much for her, Dad told her to move out of the family home.

Aimee moved in with her high school boyfriend that she had been seeing secretly, and his family helped her get on her feet. After she left home, she and I had no contact, except for a few brief phone calls. She tried to warn me that we were raised in a cult and that I should do some research for myself, but I was too scared to listen to her. I could hear my mom's words: "Apostate lies will bring Satan into the house." The fear of Satan and his demons were instilled in me from a very young age, so I ignored my sister's warnings. I quit high school a few credits short of my diploma, to preach full time in hopes that I would get closer to Jehovah, finally gain my parents' approval, and keep Satan out of my life. I did everything I could to remain loyal to Jehovah. But the heartbreak of losing my sister became too much, so I stopped preaching full time and found a job working in an office. Along with my parents, I had fallen into a deep depression over the loss of my sister, and my parents felt the need to be even more strict. Life at home became unbearable, so I moved out and found a place of my own.

About two years later, something happened that would spark deep fear. I was out with some friends at a public arena for a wrestling event. I was followed into the women's washroom by a man twice my size. He dragged me into a stall with his hand over my mouth. I managed to get his hand off my mouth to scream, and that scared him off. I was in shock as I watched him walk away. I couldn't believe that a moment ago, his hands were up my shirt. Luckily, I snapped out of it, chased after him, and a security guard caught him at the door. I later found out that he was a convicted rapist out on parole. Because he assaulted me, his sentence was prolonged. This incident shocked me so much that I asked my parents if I could move back home. I was now 21 years old, so I thought that the dynamic between my parents and I would be different since I was no longer a child. Though things were better at first, they were still judgmental of me. They showed their disappointment if I did anything other than study and prepare for JW meetings and the door to door preaching work.

Getting Disfellowshipped

I had been dating my boyfriend for about three years when I "slipped up" and made one of the worst mistakes you could make as a Jehovah's Witness. I had sex. Rather than it being the beautiful, magical experience that I imagined it would be, I was consumed with guilt and shame for what I had done, and we eventually broke up. I was so distraught about this horrible sin I had committed that I knew I had to confess it to the elders. I was terrified of getting disfellowshipped like Aimee, but it was the only way to clear my conscience and gain back God's favor. I had been taught that, as long as you were truly repentant, the elders would sense your remorse and support you instead of disfellowshipping you. I was taught only unrepentant people were disfellowshipped. Feeling hopeful, I met with trusted elders for the loving guidance I'd been promised. But instead, I got the boot. I was disfellowshipped on the spot, and my world crumbled.

At age 22, it was now my turn to find out about the horrors of being shunned. Unlike my sister, I was determined to get reinstated as soon as possible. I was not going to turn my back on Jehovah. Trying to get reinstated was a grueling process, but I was determined. I was so ashamed of myself and felt like the worst human on Earth. I was forbidden to attend my best friend's wedding, as well as other important events. I came to learn just how heartbreaking, humiliating, and dehumanizing shunning truly is. Though I did everything to prove to the elders that I was worthy of reinstatement, my request was denied. I felt hopeless. The stress and pressure I felt at home once again caused me to move out.

Alone and Desperate

Two years after being disfellowshipped, I had long given up the process of trying to get reinstated. Because of this, I lived in agonizing guilt and shame. But I didn't feel strong enough to go through the process of getting reinstated. I'd convinced myself that I wasn't worthy of God's love. Then life took another turn. I had been having sex with a friend of mine and became pregnant. I didn't consider how this was about to change my life and the life of the baby's father. I was just so happy about this little being growing inside me. When I realized that I would have to raise this child alone, I didn't care. I was used to being alone. I was desperate for love, and in my eyes, having a baby would fill that void. My parents were deeply saddened by the news of my pregnancy and continued to shun me. My mom wouldn't even let me in to use the washroom the one time I went to visit her. I was so excited to show her my growing belly, but she closed the door in my face. At that moment, it dawned on me that if I ever wanted my family back, my only choice was to get myself reinstated. I was 25 years old, nine months pregnant, and ready to try again. I was too deeply brainwashed to realize the depth of this emotional manipulation. At least now, I was living in a new town and found it was easier to be shunned by strangers than by friends and family. I had moved to Woodstock Ontario to live with the baby's father and his mother. Being in a new congregation far away from home helped me cope with being shunned.

My son was born amid the SARS outbreak of 2003. I was terrified and alone. Not even my mom would come and be with me while I gave birth. With the help of the nursing staff, I delivered my beautiful little prince whom I named Sebastian. When he first came out, the doctors rushed him over to the table to pump his chest and give him oxygen. He wasn't breathing. I was terrified. Was he dead? "This is what I get for leaving Jehovah," I told myself. I couldn't breathe at that moment, but then he finally cried! They wrapped him and put him in my arms. I never thought I could love someone so much. My little boy was finally here, and I vowed to be the best mom he could have. At this moment, I couldn't understand how a mother could shun her child. I pushed those thoughts out of my head and focused my attention on getting reinstated and get my family back. One positive thing I will always remember is a forbidden phone conversation I had with my mom while I was still in the hospital. I was having a hard time with breastfeeding, and she encouraged me not to give up. She was kind and loving, and she gave me the courage I needed to continue breastfeeding. It was the nurses that taught me the proper technique, but it was my mom that gave me the will to continue.

The Road to Reinstatement

The congregation in Woodstock was kind to me. As soon as Sebastian was born, I had JW sisters helping me with him during the meetings, and sometimes, I'd even feel a squeeze on my shoulder, as if to say, "Hang in there." The elders helped me get to all the meetings, and they eventually were able to convince my parents to let me move back home while I looked for an apartment close to them, despite still being disfellowshipped. I was reinstated soon after to the congregation in Richmond Hill. I felt so happy, and it was such a huge relief to be back in the good graces of family and friends. There were a few people in the congregation that continued to avoid me and look at me in disgust, but I just ignored them. I told myself nothing could hurt me now. I settled into my new apartment and enjoyed every second of my role as a mother. My parents were so in love with Sebastian that I felt like

I had finally done something they were proud of. Even though they disapproved of how I went about it, they loved Sebastian very much. Now, all I had to do was be a good Jehovah's Witness and wait for Armageddon to come.

The Marriage from Hell

Not long after being reinstated, Derek, a brother in my congregation, started paying attention to me. He was also raised as a Jehovah's Witness but hadn't been baptized yet. Shortly after we started dating, he was baptized and immediately started putting on the pressure to get married. He threatened to break up with me if we didn't get married because it was getting "too hard to be around me without having sex". That was his grand marriage proposal, and I blindly went along with it. I believed that we loved each other. Now, looking back, I had no idea what love actually was. We had a lot of fun times together, and he seemed good with Sebastian, so when he promised he'd take care of us, I fell for it. He would say things like, "No one else would want you now that you have a baby", putting himself on a pedestal and making it seem like he was such a big person because he was willing to take us on. I was too naive to see through the manipulation. It all happened so fast, and we were married just a few months later. I was about to find out that I had just married a sociopath. All the signs were there, but I was too blind to see them.

January 2005

Soon after the wedding, Derek wanted me to get pregnant. I thought we should wait a bit because we were fighting all the time, and I was concerned about his drinking and spending. But he insisted, and I didn't dare argue with him. Life with Derek may have been difficult, but I loved being a mother. I was finally good at something, and if that was all I could get out of this life until Armageddon came, I'd take it. I had accepted that this was my life now, and because "God hates a divorce", I felt stuck. So, I tried to make the best of it. Three months after the wedding, I became pregnant. My due date was the following winter. I was finally feeling hopeful again, but the day the doctor called me to confirm my pregnancy at nine weeks along, I had already begun to miscarry. The grief was too much to bear. It took me a long time to get over this loss. Even worse, I had to hide my grief from Derek because whenever he saw me crying, he'd tell me to "get over it, already". I secretly named the baby Winter and continued to grieve alone and in silence. He wanted to try to get me pregnant again right away, but I told him that my body needed to heal. He didn't care about any of that, so I was only able to keep him away from me for so long before having to fulfill my "wifely duty", as the Bible advises.

I got pregnant again a few months later. When my sweet little girl, Sekora, was born, I had hoped that Derek would be nicer now that he had a child of his own. But the abuse only got worse. He continued drinking every day and had us in so much debt that we could no longer afford to pay our rent, and were forced to move into his parent's basement. To make our financial matters worse, he wouldn't let me go back to my office job after maternity leave. He said my job was to be at home looking after him and the kids. I was submissive and gave up a very well-paying job to be a stay-at-home mom. Derek later quit his job, forcing us to go on welfare. His spending habits and excessive drinking continued to the point that we could no longer pay our bills. I had to go to the food bank every month, and my parents were buying diapers and other necessities for us. When he found out that I had an education savings plan for Sebastian, he made me cash it in so that he could pay off some of his unpaid bills.

Over the years, I left him twice. Once, I took the kids to my parents' house, and another time, to a woman's shelter. I kept going back to him because I didn't want to displease Jehovah, and I was fooled every time that things would be different this time. I had hoped that by leaving, he'd smarten up and realize how badly his actions were affecting the family. This was not the case. The Jehovah's Witnesses' control over me as a woman had only enabled Derek's control over me. I tried to get help from the congregation elders, but they always managed to turn it around like Derek's problems were somehow my fault. The elders would also remind me that if I ever did leave him for good, I would not scripturally be able to remarry. It was constantly drilled into my head that if I left my husband, I would be alone and a disgrace to God, possibly losing my chance to be in paradise. I pleaded with them for help and told them that I was scared for my life and my kids. I told them that he beat Sebastian and even beat my cat. He'd broken all my treasured possessions, and I was truly terrified of him. But in the end, the elders just kept reading me scriptures on why I should be a submissive wife and stick it out. They'd give examples of other women who were submissive and eventually "won their husbands over without a word", as the Bible advises. I was expected to do the same, to put up and shut up. They suggested that maybe if I gave him more sex, lost some weight, and put on a little makeup that things would get better. I couldn't believe what I was hearing and thought I was losing my mind. All I wanted to do was make Jehovah happy so that I could get into Paradise with my kids. I was stuck and never felt more helpless. I was so deeply indoctrinated that I just couldn't see how deeply I was being controlled.

Hopelessness Sets In

In our almost four years of marriage, Derek had become abusive on all levels: physically, verbally, mentally, emotionally, sexually, financially, and even spiritually. No, he never hit me, something he was quite careful about. He did everything but. He'd go to punch me, but I'd move just in time for him to leave holes in the drywall where my head was. When he realized that my friends and family were finally seeing what he was doing to me and the kids, he informed me of his plan to move us to a town eight hours away. I said I didn't want to move, but he said that that was too bad and that I had to obey him. I was numb. He was going to take me far away from what little support I had. One evening, when he was out and the kids were at my parents', I drank a bottle of wine as I filled the bathtub. I was feeling defeated, and my will to live was slipping away. With a sharp razor blade in my hand and with thoughts racing, I laid down and put my head under the warm water, thinking that I just wanted this to end. Derek's voice was loud in my head. I was useless, good for nothing, ugly, stupid, fat... No one would ever love me. I'd never be good enough for Jehovah... NO!

I quickly sat up and gasped for air. I put the razor down. Derek was wrong; I was not any of those things! And my kids! I was clearly out of my mind for even thinking about leaving them to be raised by that psycho! If nothing else, I had my kids to live for, and they saved my life that day. I quickly got out of the water, dried myself off, and started to plan. I was done with this life of fear and terror. I was done with all things Derek. I left him for the third and final time. I got a therapist and was diagnosed with battered woman syndrome and Stockholm Syndrome. I was able to get on my feet fairly quickly, thanks to all the help from community services. Being a victim of spousal abuse, I got into government housing very fast. The kids and I got settled into a nice three-bedroom townhouse in Markham, and we were ready for a fresh start. Derek wouldn't let me pack up my things, so he put them all out on the lawn. A lot was missing but I didn't care, I was just so happy to be free of him. Some members of the congregation avoided me because I had left my husband without "scriptural grounds", but for the most part, the congregation in Markham was very kind to me, and I'll never forget it. One sister even gave me a car! Derek went quiet for a long time, refusing to see His daughter. He thought he was punishing me, but the only person affected by his neglect was her.

A year after I left, I managed to get scriptural grounds for divorce. I had intimate relations with someone other than Derek, and this loophole gave me my freedom to remarry within the congregation. The Markham elders didn't disfellowship me. Rather, they showed mercy because of my abusive situation and privately reproved me. Derek still refused to take Sekora regularly. He saw her just enough to keep her from forgetting him. He knew that I would have to deal with her questions and her sadness. Thankfully, she took his absence better than could have been expected. I eventually took him to Court to get an official separation agreement, which laid out a visitation schedule for him. He was self-employed by now, and he lied about his income so the child support amount would be lowered. I was not at all surprised by this, but I didn't care. I was just happy to be away from him. Sebastian was especially relieved that he didn't have to see him anymore. When the separation agreement was finalized, Derek could have Sekora every other weekend from Friday to Sunday. I was hoping to give her more stability with the regular visits, but his words to me were, "They can't make me take her." He was right; they couldn't make him love his child and want to spend as much time as possible with her. They couldn't make him be a decent human being or a responsible parent. So, he continued to see her only occasionally, whenever it was convenient for him. We were fine without him, and at least now he couldn't say that I tried to keep her from him. It was only when I began a serious relationship that Derek suddenly showed an interest in his daughter.

A Safer Environment

In 2010, shortly before my divorce was final, I reconnected through Facebook with an old friend, Darcy. Since I was about 14 years old, my family had vacationed often at the resort owned by Darcy's parents. He was also raised as a Jehovah's Witness, so we had that in common. We fell in love and began dating. As soon as Derek found out, he could not hide or contain his rage. One time, he even attacked my mom because I wasn't home when he brought back Sekora at the end of the weekend. He strangled her with his forearm and only stopped when the neighbor came over to help. He didn't care that five-year-old Sekora was standing there, watching him hurt Grandma. Later, he tried to tell Sekora that he was protecting her from Grandma, but Sekora quickly saw through his lies. Through the years, he continued to try very hard to make life difficult for me, but in the end, he only made a fool of himself. By this point, everyone knew what he was all about, and they saw through his lies. I even had his friends contact me to tell me that they were glad I got away. "We hoped that by marrying a nice girl and having a family would be good for him, but we are sad to see that he is never going to change..." Despite all that Derek put me through, he was never held accountable for his actions, and to this day is considered to be a "good Christian."

In 2011, Darcy and I got engaged and married. Sekora was 5 years old, and Sebastian was 8. In 2013 our son, Maxwell was born. Darcy was and is such a good dad. He loved Sebastian and Sekora as if they were his own and was such a huge help when Max was born. It seemed I'd finally found happiness, but it was short-lived. Something felt off. My faith was constantly brought into question when I heard something at the Kingdom Hall that didn't make sense or was a contradiction of other teachings. Instead of thinking about it, as always, I did as I was told and repressed these doubts. The words "trust in Jehovah" were drilled into my head since birth. Over the years, Darcy and I couldn't help but drift apart. The stress of trying to live up to the requirements of a highly controlling religion made it impossible for us to thrive as a couple. We were viewed as a spiritually-weak family, and therefore, we were not included in most of the congregation's social life. I had a strong feeling that the congregants were being hypocritical and two-faced. They were kind in my presence, but they planned gatherings without inviting me or my family, and they talked about us behind our backs. There were several kids in our congregation that were the same age as my kids, but they rarely were included in events. I tried to preach more to prove myself worthy, but nothing changed. Gossip about my family always came back around to me, and I realized just how fake these people really were.

Waking Up

It was rumored that my brother-in-law Joe whom I worked with was an apostate. I decided to ask him about it because I felt close to him, and I wanted to see if there was any hope of him returning to Jehovah. "Is it true that you're an apostate? Do you really not believe anymore?", I asked. And that's when he told me everything, all his reasons for why he didn't believe and that yes, that makes him an "apostate". All of a sudden, every doubt I ever had about the religion surfaced. Everything that didn't make sense before, all the doubts I'd ignored and stuffed down so deep, suddenly made sense. It was as if my eyes were open for the first time. It all clicked into place for me in that small moment. I drove home in tears saying out loud, "It's not real. It's all lies. It's not real! I can't believe this. Jehovah is not real!" For the months that followed that conversation, Joe and I would go into work early and watch John Cedars (Lloyd Evans) videos. The more information I took in, the more awake and aware I felt. It was bitter-sweet. I was finally gaining control of my thoughts, but it came at a great cost.

I knew that the life I'd known for 37 years was about to change dramatically, more than I could even know at that moment. Not only was I about to lose all my friends and family, but I had lost my conception of God. I loved Him with all my heart, and I had lived my life entirely for Him, but he died that day. For a year, I tried to make sense of everything and even attempted to cling to my faith, but it all felt so wrong. I was still fearful of Satan, but I continued to do the forbidden research. The more I read, the more it became clear to me that my entire life was based on lies. One year after my official wake up, I stopped calling myself a Jehovah's Witness. By that time, I had met a few other ex-Jehovah's Witnesses and found out that there is a large online community and many support groups to help those who "wake up". Darcy tried to be supportive about my leaving the faith, but we just couldn't make it work. We were arguing all the time. I know what it's like to grow up with parents who were always fighting, and this was not the example of love and marriage I wanted to set for my kids. It felt like an impossible situation. How could I stay married to a man that believed I was going to die at Armageddon? How could I stay married to someone that I can't talk about my deepest thoughts and feelings with? I was learning so much, but I couldn't share it with him because although he was inactive, he still strongly believed. His mind was closed. It just didn't work, and we became unbearably disconnected. He became more of a roommate than a marriage partner. I believe that if circumstances had been different, maybe we would have had a chance, but I knew I was now faced with another big decision.

More Challenges

Before I knew it, Witnesses started unfriending me on Facebook and avoided eye contact when they saw me. It was a small town, so this was frequent and painful. The feeling was reminiscent of being disfellowshipped, but I wasn't disfellowshipped, and I hadn't formally disassociated myself either. Simply because I no longer believed that Jehovah's Witnesses had the one and only "Truth", I was labeled an apostate and therefore shunned. I eventually lost my parents all over again. They made several attempts to keep the kids indoctrinated, but gave up as soon as they realized they were not getting anywhere. It was heartless treatment.

When the shunning and arguing became too much, Darcy and I officially separated. I moved back to the city where I grew up and found work and housing with ex-Jehovah's Witnesses I met through the local support group. I was now ready to start a new chapter. Darcy and I agreed to share equal custody of Maxwell, and we now have a more agreeable relationship than when we were married. To this day, Darcy is one of my best friends, and I love him dearly. He has remained an important part of Sebastian and Seroka's life. To them, he will always be Dad. I cannot say enough good things about him and I will always hope that maybe one day, he will wake up and have freedom from the mental slavery I believe is causing him much inner conflict. Derek had made several attempts at turning Sekora against me, but things did get peaceful for a time. Then he ramped up his efforts again after I left Darcy. Every visit she had with him, he'd try to fill her head with negative ideas about me. He would tell her that I don't love her, that I'm going to die at Armageddon, and that she would die along with me if she didn't live with him. My poor girl was tormented for years. He had her convinced that she should go live with him. Her misery and confusion got so bad that I told her she could go live with him and see what the grass was like on the other side. I know what it's like growing up in a Jehovah's Witness house, and I know my daughter is a free spirit like her mother. You can't control a free spirit, so I just had to let it play out. Not two weeks went by and she asked to come home. That wasn't enough time though. I wanted her to get a good feel for what life with Derek would be like. Less than two months went by, and she was now begging me to come home. I knew she'd seen enough and told her I would be more than happy if she came home. Soon after moving back home with me, she told Derek that she no longer wanted to be a Jehovah's Witness. Not surprisingly, he didn't respect her choice and still forced her to preach and go to the Kingdom Hall with him. One day, she confessed to me that she had been cutting herself after each visit. When she showed me the scars, that was the last straw.

Enough is Enough

Finally, I'd had enough of Derek's antics. We all had. I called the Children's Aid Society and told them how he was acting and asked if this is something they can help me with. They said that it was, and they arrived soon after to get Sekora's testimony. After, they went to talk to Derek. Instead of changing his behavior, he texted Sekora and told her that she no longer had to see him. Sekora was hurt for a moment when she first got the text because she felt rejected, but then, she was overcome with relief. She immediately became a different child. She became more open, more willing to share in family activities, and most importantly, she stopped cutting herself and having suicidal thoughts. She felt free to speak her mind and be herself. She started going to school every day voluntarily, and has even been improving her grades. She has blossomed into a beautiful young lady, and I couldn't be prouder. It's been almost a year, and we haven't heard from Derek. All we know is that he is still a member of the congregation of Jehovah's Witnesses, and to this day, the elders have done nothing about his years of tormenting my family. After all that he did to me, the kids and even to my parents, my parents have forgiven him because he is still a "worshiper of Jehovah."

The healing process

Over time, the depression lifted, and I was able to feel hopeful again. My best friend, roommate, and fellow JW survivor, Kyle, introduced me to the Unitarian Universalists. I'll never forget the first time I attended their service. It was the most empowering, heartwarming, genuinely beautiful thing I had experienced to date. The choir sang beautiful harmonic hymns. Soulful, inspiring poems were read, and the sermon reached deep into my soul. The minister, Reverend Shawn Newton, was a gay man. This was so refreshing because the Jehovah's Witnesses are mercilessly against homosexuality, which was one of the many things that never sat right with me. The other minister was a woman! Growing up as a Jehovah's Witness, women were treated as lesser beings, a "weaker vessel". So, there I was listening to sermons by a woman and a gay man, and it was wonderful! After each service, I walked away feeling uplifted, inspired, and full of hope. I started attending regularly and even joined the choir. It was a busy time for me, so I was only in the choir for a few months, but I loved every second. Reverend Lynn Harrison and Reverend Shawn Newton, were both there for me when I was feeling at my lowest. Their kind words of encouragement were just what I needed to keep moving forward. During a phone conversation with Rev. Lynn, I had opened up about my sadness regarding losing everyone I ever loved, including God. I wanted to hang on to Him, but I couldn't find any proof that He existed, so I became agnostic. I missed praying and felt lost because I no longer knew what or whom to pray to, so I'd stopped completely. Lynn gave me a new perspective that helped me immensely. She told me that God is different for all of us and that there is no right or wrong way to pray or to worship. We have to find what feels right for us and follow that path. This was so different and refreshing from what I'd previously been taught, and was just the thing I needed to hear to find peace and healing amongst my tormented thoughts. How do you thank someone for giving you that kind of peace of mind? I will be forever grateful.

Kyle and I went to check out several different churches besides the Unitarians to see what they were all about. It was so fascinating, and I was full of wonder as I entered the "churches of Satan", as the Witnesses would call them. The Quakers, Catholics, Buddhists, and Baptists were among some of the ones we visited. I was in search of answers, but mostly, I was filled with curiosity and awe about religion in general. The answer I found is that I am not interested in religion, or whether or not God exists. I have discovered that I do not need all the answers. I now believe that all of the answers I've been searching for are right in front of me, inside myself. There is a certain beauty in the fact that the fundamental nature of reality is mysterious. Maybe I don't have all the answers to life's questions, but at least I'm no longer feeling so desperately lost, empty, alone, and loveless. I am no longer controlled by a panel of men claiming to be inspired by God.

I took Rev. Lynn's advice and began Praying and meditating in forests or anywhere in nature, saying out loud what I am thankful for, and what I am most concerned with. This filled the "God" void I'd been feeling. When I am near a body of water, especially while the sun is rising or setting, I feel the most at peace. I have traveled to the most beautiful parts of Canada and have been humbled by what I saw and experienced along the way. The mountains in British Columbia and Alberta were a site of beauty I never could have imagined. I climbed one of those mountains with Kyle, and as I stood at the top and looked down at the view, I was forever changed. It became clear to me that I don't need to belong to an organization in order to be a good person. I have chosen to set religion aside and just focus on how wonderful it is to be alive. I continue to sometimes attend the Unitarian Congregation in Toronto because it is non-denominational and gives me the most peace. I am moved to tears at each service, not because I am sad, but because I am just so touched with gratitude and inspiration to do more with my life. I do not feel judged, and rather than being told what to believe, I feel free to figure out what feels right for me. And I did. I will never forget that my healing began with the Unitarian Congregation in Toronto.

Letting Go of the Past

The definition of freedom is the power to act, speak, or think as one wants without hindrance or restraint. It is the state of not being imprisoned or enslaved. For 37 years, I was living my life under the mind control of the governing body of Jehovah's Witnesses. When I finally woke up, it took a lot of time to adjust to this kind of freedom. I was completely lost with no idea what to do with myself. I felt I had such little knowledge about the outside world, and because I was so deeply saddened by all I had lost, the Watchtower corporation still had some control over me. It has been five years since that first day I woke up, but it hs been in this last year that i've seen the most progress in myself. I haven't felt truly free until recently. I realized that I'd wasted a lot of time feeling sorry for myself, beating myself up for not waking up sooner, and feeling such deep sadness over everything. I knew that I could never go back to that life now that I knew the truth about "the Truth".

I was diagnosed with PTSD and was left with some pretty strong triggers, but I have finally come to a place of peacefulness. I have so many good things in my life that it just seems pointless to focus on anything else. To truly be free from my past, I had to stop dwelling on it, and focus on the fact that I had gained more than I'd lost. With the continued help of therapy, the love and support from the Unitarian congregation, and so many incredible friends, I was finally able to let the past go.

To this day, my parents still shun me and the kids, but we are not concerned with that anymore. We now have a "chosen" family and friendships that are deeper than those that are possible within the conditional relationships Jehovah's Witnesses tend to have. I am now surrounded by people who value growth, open-mindedness, and kindness. Every day, I feel blessed to wake up, excited to see what adventures the day will bring. I am so happy that my kids and I have stood strong through this, only making us that much more connected. We no longer live in fear of what others might think. I am blessed with so many incredible humans who love me and support me on this crazy, incredible journey. For the ones who don't like me -- oh, well. They no longer have power over me because I no longer need their approval. I live for myself and for the people who have proven worthy of my heart.

Positive Thoughts

As I sit here and reflect on this story, it feels like I've lived so many lives, and I wouldn't change a thing! I am the person I am today because of every single challenge I faced and conquered. I feel like a fierce warrior who can survive anything. When you leave a high-control group, there are several stages of healing, and these may vary for everyone. It is important to seek help, and not give up.

It has been a very long road, but now when I look back at my life, I try to think about the happy times, like when my dad picked up his guitar and taught me "Mr. Bojangles" when I was about 6 years old. My love for music and guitar is definitely thanks to him. I'll always remember how comforting his voice was as he sang Eric Clapton, sounding almost exactly like him. I also remember that time he worked extra hours so I could buy myself a new dress for a wedding. We were very poor, so this had meant so much to me. I remember my mother always working so hard around the house, and no matter what, she'd always stop and listen when I needed to talk to her. I used to love sitting in the kitchen helping her make supper while my dad sang and played guitar in the other room. She was also a very good listener and would sit and knit while I'd tell her about my day and my latest crush. It still makes me smile as I remember her saying, "Don't tell dad." I always wondered if she ever did, but didn't dare ask him. I also have many good memories of my brother and sister on family vacations. Those and other happy memories are the ones I will carry with me. Nothing good can come from dwelling on the pain.

Other Inspirations

A few books I have enjoyed are, The Power of Now and A New Earth, by Eckhart Tolle, Man's Search for Meaning by Viktor Frankl, Conversations with God, by Neale Donald Walsch, The four agreements by Don Miguel Ruiz, Change your Thoughts, Change your life by Wayne Dyer, Supernatural by Graham Hancock, and A Return to Love, by Marianne Williamson. These are just to name a few of the many books that inspired me and helped to open my mind and heart. This may seem silly, but my absolute favorite book is called The Little Prince by Antoine de Saint-Exupery. I got a tattoo of the little prince flying away with a flock of birds leaving his planet b612. I have been deeply inspired by so many cool things on my travels in this second and most incredible half of my journey.

Though I continue to struggle with occasional sadness, I am finding it much easier to focus on what is important, and move past it. I have learned the true meaning of love, and that no matter how many people come in and out of my life, the most important love I can have is for myself. I am finally free to have an open mind and heart with the ability to see beauty in everything. And most importantly, I no longer ignore that little voice inside me that says something isn't right.

Final Thoughts

My favorite time of day is the quiet early hours of the morning when my family is still deep in slumber. I sit in my backyard, coffee in hand, feeling the warm breeze on my face. I listen to the birds cheerfully waking up and the water rushing down the stream through the trees behind my house. I feel so peaceful as I watch the sun come up, and it is in these quiet moments that I reflect on all that I am grateful for. I am no longer plagued with constant guilt, or fear of never being good enough for "God". I choose how I spend my time, what clothes I wear and what I do with my partner in the bedroom. When I think about all the silly made up rules, all I can do is laugh, and be grateful that I am no longer controlled by the governing body. I am especially grateful for having my sister back in my life after 20 long years of absence. Our bond could not be broken after all this time, and I hope she knows that she is my hero. I am so thankful for learning the real and true meaning of spirituality, friendship, and love. To those who talked me down from the proverbial ledge and those who helped me see my value in this life, thank you. Thank you for not giving up on me, for loving me, and helping me learn to love myself. For you amazing people who are within my circle of friends, know that you've been carefully selected, and I am truly honored and humbled to have you in my life.

When I look up at the sky, I take a deep breath in and smile. I am finally and truly free, and I look forward to all of the adventures that the Universe has in store for me.

"If you realize all things change, there is nothing you will try to hold on to......... Life is a series of natural and spontaneous changes. Don't resist them, that only creates sorrow. Let reality be reality. Let things flow naturally forward in whatever way they like."
-Lao Tzu

Chapter 11

Re-own Your Power

by Kimberly Sherry

*"The secret in handling fear is to move yourself
from a position of pain to a position of power."*
Susan Jeffers ~ <u>*Feel the Fear and Do It Anyway*</u>

It's a warm summer afternoon, and both of my children, ages five and seven are in school. Feeling numb, hopeless, and as though all the blood had drained from my face, I stand in front of the gun case in Big Five Sporting Goods wondering which one would do the job. *Would it leave me drooling for the rest of my life, or would death be immediate,* I wondered.

I'm shocked to my senses when the salesman asks if he can help me. Suddenly, I know I can not end my life and do this to my two children. *What am I doing here? How could I have gone this far?*

How I Lost My Power

Born and raised as a Jehovah's Witness (JW), I was a baby when they knocked on our door one day in the mid-fifties and love bombed us with their acts of kindness. Going to the Kingdom Hall, their place of worship, several times a week became my mother's refuge from her alcoholic husband, my father. While my mother had the best of intentions for her five children, she had no idea we are being deeply programmed and controlled with fear, guilt, and shame — the traits of a cult that contribute to feeling powerless.

Every year I was not allowed to celebrate my birthday. As a child, this annual insult became a reminder I was not worth remembering, or worth-less. We're not allowed to celebrate any holidays for that matter. Their justification was that these had pagan origins, and they would always find some bible text to support their views. My most dreaded question every year from outsiders was, *"And what did you get for Christmas?"* I watched the puzzled look on their face when I'd say in hushed tones, *"The same as last year... nothing."*

As a child, I always felt left out. While the entire school enjoyed dressing up on Halloween, I contemptibly waited for my mom to pick me up at lunch before the parade. I longed to be like everyone else, but every morning not being allowed to say the flat salute was just one more reminder I was different, in a shameful sort of way.

My non-believing, alcoholic father was thankful not to celebrate holidays since we were on welfare and food stamps most of the time. Supporting five children in the 50's was not an easy task. I eagerly looked forward to the one new dress my mother sewed each year since my two sisters' hand-me-downs were usually all I had.

We got a respite from my dad's drinking binges when my mom called the police and had him hauled away in handcuffs. Other times, she would wake me in the middle of the night to accompany her on the hour drive to either Napa or Mendocino State Hospital where he would spend a week or more drying out. I'm not sure why she always chose me. Maybe even back then I was an unrecognized grounding force for her.

We weren't allowed to have friends outside of the religion. I'm lucky to have two JW friends my age — twins — from the fourth grade on. In high school, we got baptized together at sixteen, graduated six months before the rest of our class of 1973, and had our diplomas mailed to us — we never went to a school dance and certainly no prom. Instead we pioneered, spending thirty to sixty hours a month knocking on doors, hoping to save the world from Armageddon, expected in October 1975.

The Witnesses will tell you today they never said Armageddon would come then. This is not true. I got married in September, 1975, a week before I was twenty and with high hopes of slipping under the Armageddon wire as a married couple. We had no idea how devastating this destruction would be and we wanted to make sure we faced it together. We also wanted to have sex, and pre-marital sex was not allowed.

Beyond my knowledge or comprehension at the time, I brought all my childhood distortions into my marriage. I'd been sexually abused by my father from two-and-a-half until I went to kindergarten and was forbidden to masturbate — the JWs call this self-abuse. I did my best to be perfect, a submissive, obedient Stepford wife. I performed my sexual dues whether I wanted to or not. I was revered as a pillar in the congregation.

My JW husband has his share of distortions as well. He'd been raised in a more entitled family than mine. His father was married to actress Bette Davis before marrying his mother, the nanny they had employed.

Because of his own sexual repressions being raised as a JW, he became a sex addict. According to the JWs, he was considered "weak" and barely attended meetings. In the twenty-five years we were married, he joined me in service knocking on doors, only once or twice. He admits later to leaving during congregation bible meetings to get blowjobs from prostitutes and coming back like nothing happened.

He became controlling, wanting me to account for my whereabouts, what I was doing, and who I was with. He kept insinuating I was guilty of what he later admitted he'd been doing. My witness friends became uncomfortable coming to visit since they never felt welcomed by him, and over time, I began to feel very isolated, alone, and powerless.

The only way out of a JW marriage is a partner committing adultery, however, between the "two Witness" rule and his lying, I could never prove it to the elders.

From this hopelessly depressed state, I ended up in front of the gun counter. As I drove home that day, instead of feeling the deep depression I had sunk into, I energetically stepped up a notch and started to feel a burning rage. I felt the resentment, the wasted time, and that I deserved better than this. Anger became the fuel to start moving me up and out of this toxic relationship.

This process of trying to leave the relationship and him wanting to work things out went back and forth over many years. He eventually got disfellowshipped for admitting his adultery, meaning he needed to attend all meetings without anyone speaking to him for a year before he could return in good standing and have privileges returned, like answering at meetings, going out in service (knocking on doors preaching), and talking with those in the congregation. After about six months I convinced the elders to allow him to return, which they did. However, he was never welcomed back by anyone in the congregation and instead treated like a leper.

My Breaking Point

It became very apparent my spiritual family was as toxic as my biological family. The biggest wake-up call for me was realizing I could be fine all week and then, when I would attend our meeting and sing a song, tears would well up for no apparent reason. By that time, I had spent many years working on myself and healing childhood stuff. I watched Oprah, read and listened to Leo Buscalia and the inspirational Les Brown. I stopped stuffing my emotions and the floodgates were releasing. My body was screaming, "this is not a healthy place to be!" The book that pushed me over the edge of leaving this cult was, *Feel The Fear And Do It Anyway*, by Susan Jeffers.

I knew I needed to get out, but fear kept me paralyzed. Susan's book helped me realize that pushing through fear would be less frightening than living with the underlying fear that comes from feeling powerless. If I pushed through the fear and took some inspired action, I would feel tremendous relief. When the pain of staying surpassed the fear of leaving, I took some bold actions.

I finally listened and sent in a letter of dissociation denouncing my affiliation with Jehovah's Witnesses. It felt important and empowering to be the one deciding my fate instead of allowing them to hang me in the gallows. Writing this letter was for me, not for them. I needed to take a stand for my life and what I was choosing to do. Even so, this was one of the hardest decisions of my life.

When I left, everyone I had ever known and loved was required to shun me and never speak to me again, including my mother, unless it was for important family business. I felt alone in the desert and only had my jealous adulterous husband and children, nine and eleven, for support.

Although I was the last of five kids to leave the cult, I'd estranged my siblings because they were already on the outside. Even though I was now out, the huge chasm became apparent when I tried to celebrate my first birthday at the age of fifty. I invited all my family (except my mom) and distant relatives thinking I am now *"free."* But *no one* came. Devastated, I vowed to never celebrate my birthday again.

Creating a Support System

Even though I felt a newfound sense of freedom, I also felt more alone than ever. I was soon contacted by an ex-JW therapist, Kaynor Weishaupt, who had seen an article I had submitted to the FreeMinds Journal by Randall Watters, a monthly newsletter that advocated for former JWs. Kaynor and I decided to start a support group for ex-JWs.

Initially, we had small meetings in the back of a metaphysical bookstore in Larkspur, California. As I told bits of my story every month, I kept healing and taking the energetic charge off of all the ways I had felt powerless — from the little girl who never got to experience the joy and wonder of holidays, birthdays, and team sports, to my young adult who was trained into submission under the Governing Body and my husband as the head of our household.

After about four years, Kaynor left to start her own family. I continued running the group like a lone soldier to the cause of helping cult survivors and drew from the valuable traits ingrained in me from being a JW, namely dedication, commitment, persistence, reliability, and perseverance. I told my story month after month for a total of nine years. This helped me to discharge boatloads of anger and resentment. It felt equally rewarding to see week after week others healing, feeling heard and understood, and no longer alone. No one understands what it is like to be born and raised into a religious cult like others who have been there. Some said I had saved their life, as they too had contemplated suicide. Knowing that most JWs are on antidepressants and how common suicide is for those who leave and are shunned by their families gave me purpose in my life again and great inner fulfillment. Others had been out for 20 years, and for the first time, were able to finally talk about what had unknowingly been bottled up for years, unaware how it was still the overriding cloud in their life.

It was this group that provided support for myself as well when I finally divorced my husband. I didn't know how I would support myself and my two children since we lost our family janitorial business during the breakdown of the marriage, but I kept moving forward in the ways I felt directed. Even though I stopped believing in the JW version of Jehovah, I continued to feel guided by a benevolent power that felt true and had my best interests at heart, and I kept listening.

I recall one evening before I was divorced and still a JW, reading Susan Jeffers' book and being visited by a very powerful guide. As I was reading, I got a whiff of some perfume that reminded me of an elderly woman, like Chanel 5. I smelled my hair and shirt to see if this is where it had come from, but it was not. I continued reading and smelled it again, only this time it was accompanied by two other senses. I felt the sensation of someone petting my hand and simultaneously heard the words in my head, *"You're doing a good job, you're doing a good job."* I began to cry because I no longer felt alone. I knew I was being guided by something higher than, or other than, the JW version of Jehovah. I later came to understand that this guidance was Mary, Jesus' mother. She is just one of the many guides with whom I continue to work to this day.

This continued guidance led me to become certified as a massage therapist. Three months after I was certified, it was time to pull the plug on the marriage and file a restraining order. I also started working for a financial planner, and my father died, leaving me enough money to buy out my husband and keep the house.

I Discovered My Life Purpose

Another contributing factor to my recovery from Jehovah's Witnesses was attending a previously forbidden psychic school every week for twelve years. This helped reverse decades of cult programming.

I always had an attraction to the healing arts, but these were considered demonic. I decided to test if this was true. I went to a psychic fair a couple hours away, hoping no one would recognize me, and got a psychic reading.

I was fascinated by a man who, though I had never met him before, told me things about my father that made me cry. *"How can he know these things?"* I wondered. When I returned home, I looked up the psychic school with which he was affiliated in my city. I wanted to see for myself if this was actually where the demons lived or not.

I walked into this psychic school and noticed a man sitting in a chair and a woman waving her hands around him as though she was smoothing something out. The director asked, *"would you like to feel an aura?"* I had no idea what this meant, but it sounded intriguing so I say, *"sure."* What I found is not scary at all. Instead, I discovered an exciting world of energy and wonder.

As I do what the previous woman did, I am amazed to feel sadness in my hand in only a couple places around his body, but nowhere else. The man confirms his sadness. No one could have convinced me I did not feel what I felt. I was fascinated, instantly hooked, and wanted to know more.

I began attending Aesclepion Intuitive Training Center in San Rafael, California. Attending this psychic kindergarten became a playground. It also became my cult in reverse. Every person that came into the clinic and sat in front of me for a reading or healing became a mirror for all the places in me that longed to be seen, healed, and loved. This helped to deprogram a lifetime of cult programming. After attending this school every week for twelve years, I went through a massive shift and my life imploded.

The director sent me away with a healing package so I could take care of myself for a change. This meant that I would receive a healing for myself and then would go and process this healing over the next month. I came back only once a month for six months. During this time, I cleared so much of the clinic from my energy field, that I never went back. While I was forever grateful for the foundation of energy healing I learned there, I knew it was time to expand and grow beyond this school.

A Change in Direction

By then I had finalized my divorce and the children were grown and out of the house. I sold the house and bought a motorhome so I would never have to worry about having a place to live.

Since I was wearing my body out doing massage, I opened a retail eco-flooring store with my new partner who I met at my support group for former JWs. He was a flooring contractor who wanted to get off his knees. We combined forces, I ran the office and he ran the crews. In any another economy, this would have been a home run. In fact, we made three quarters of a million dollars in our third year. But it was not meant to be. We filed for bankruptcy after five years in 2009 during the great economic downturn. Everyone was using the store to touch and feel what they would then go buy online.

While my partner and I continue as best friends today, he had more family drama than I wanted to cope with, including a tragic event that left his teenage son paralyzed from a bullet lodged in his neck.

A New Angle to My Life Purpose

Having lost everything, I spent the next few years struggling to get back on my feet while I lived in my motorhome — sometimes parked on the side of the road — and going back to doing massage at a private gym. I got tired of the police banging on my door at three in the morning telling me I could not park where I was. I knew I was meant for more than this.

My tearful prayers were answered with a voice that said, *"Check out ayahausca."* I didn't see how this would help my urgent situation of more money now. I heard the voice again, *"Kimberly, check out ayahausca."* I went online and didn't find what I was looking for. However, a week later I received an email from the Children of the Sun Foundation[1]. I had been following them for about a year.

They were looking for twelve participants as ambassadors of light for a humanitarian mission, but all I hear is *ayahausca*. I sent in my application, and out of more than one hundred and fifty applicants from around the world, I am one of twelve chosen, and one of seven from the U.S. It felt like such an honor — and I had no money. So, I decided to do an Indie-Gogo campaign and raised enough funds for me to attend.

After this journey - fifteen days deep in the Amazon jungle with no running water, electricity, a very simple diet and five ayahuasca (shamanic plant medicine) journeys – spirit directed me to lead my own mission and bring a group back after three years of integrating this first journey. This was a big step. I'd never done or organized anything like this.

I received a skeleton of an outline of what I would need to do and pack from the director of the Children of the Sun. I started telling people about it and, before I knew it, someone had purchased their airline ticket. *"Oh shit, it's happening!"* Now it felt like there was no turning back. People were relying on me to be their fearless leader. A knot in my stomach reminded me I was scared, worried, and excited all at the same time.

Since I only speak a little Spanish, I brought an interpreter. He was so transformed by his experience that he decided to bring back his own group six months later. I joined him again. When we emerged from the jungle for *my* third time, it just so happened to be my birthday, where I had one of the most magical experiences of my life.

My First Birthday

It's September 2015. We emerge from the jungle, extremely elevated after detoxing with daily herbal tonics, a simple clean diet, no electronics, and doing shamanic journeying with Ayahuasca every three days for fifteen days. We arrive to the airport and discover our flight is delayed due to fog. All eight of us will now miss our connecting flights home. Avianca Airlines sticks to their policy which states, *"if a flight is missed due to weather"* they are not responsible.

At first, we think we are out of luck and will have to figure where all eight of us will spend the night since the next flight is the following day. My interpreter gently persists for other possibilities while the rest of the group holds space for a better outcome. After about 40 minutes, the best news ever!

They upgrade all of us to first-class on the next flight out to Lima where our connecting flight will be the following morning. We're ushered to the front of the line ahead of a packed airport of disappointed travelers who have also been delayed.

Upon our arrival, we're transported from the airport in a luxury van to a Five Star Hotel an hour away just outside of Mira Flores and given food vouchers for breakfast, lunch, and dinner. Greeted like kings and queens with fruit smoothies served in tall champagne flutes, we are blown away, knowing twenty-four hours before we were deep in the sweaty Amazon jungle without electricity or running water sleeping on crappy air mattresses. Now we each had an air-conditioned private room with a king size bed and a bidet.

To add to our excitement, the shamana accompanying our trip contacts her mentor and fellow shamana who lives in Lima. She joins us for lunch and dinner. I'm pleasantly surprised by the group with a dessert that has a trick birthday candle that keeps re-lighting every time I blow it out. Like a giddy little girl, I keep making wish after wish. *"How does it get any better than this?"* I laugh.

After dinner, the shamana surprises us with a powerful sound healing ceremony using the sacred plant medicine, *San Pedro*. She wants to help ground our Amazonian experience for a smoother integration when we returned home. We all spread out on the floor and bed in my room. This turns out to be such a profound experience with even stronger, more colorful visions in this twenty minute ceremony than all the previous journeys on Ayahuasca. She uses eagle feathers, rattles, chimes and whistles carved from eagle bones as she channels a male and female voice singing indigenous songs. I don't want it to end. When I think about how far I've come from vowing to never celebrate another birthday, this somehow makes five decades of uncelebrated birthdays feel irrelevant. Happy birthday to me!

My Keys to Empowerment

In summary, the main things I did that helped me overcome my loss of an entire belief system, hope for the future, and the only friends I was allowed to have and find my life purpose were:

I started a support group to create a new community where I felt loved and accepted. This empowered me to find my life purpose helping others. Today, I am a member of the largest and most successful former Jehovah's Witness group on FaceBook, called Empowered Minds, started by Rodney Allgood[2], where I offer support and mentorship to exJWs.

I read non-JW books that were self-help in nature. Besides those previously mentioned, I also read *Crisis of Conscience*, by Raymond Franz and cult expert, Steven Hassan's, *Combating Cult Mind Control*. These empowered my mind to challenge what I had been told and helped me to start questioning. When I finally left, I needed to challenge everything I had been taught. I needed to figure out what ideas, programs, and beliefs I wanted to keep that were helpful, and what didn't work that I needed to throw out.

I applied the new things I was learning to start doing some self-healing, like feeling the fear and doing it anyway... doing things that scared me. I purposely challenged myself to skydive when I was fifty so I could release fears of dying. Beginning to release my fears empowered me to continue doing more things I was previously afraid of, like speaking up for myself. I no longer tolerated what was not in my best interests.

I joined a psychic school to become an expert at something I had a keen interest in. This empowered me to find my life purpose and innate gifts I had been given. I discovered my super powers. I used these gifts on myself first as I became my own guinea pig to experience success within.

I was inspired to work with plant medicine and shamans to reach additional layers of healing and higher dimensions of knowledge and information. Stepping outside of my comfort zone helped me expand beyond my tiny box of limited, oppressed, and fearful thinking. This empowered me to step more fully into my gifts with confidence.

I started working with Dr. David R. Hawkins' scale of human consciousness as outlined in his book, *Power vs Force*. This empowered me to tap into a newfound gift of being able to measure vibrational frequencies. After twenty-five *ayahuasca* journeys, I was able to break through his scale to reach new heights and create a new scale of human consciousness to access higher levels of infinite possibilities.

This is outlined in my book, *Access YOUR Ultimate Power: The Blueprint To Infinite Intelligence*. In this book, I demonstrate the Infinity System I created with the help of my spirit guides. This is a method of accessing your inner healer to empower yourself to speak up for your wants and needs, stop settling for less, and to end the JW programs of unnecessary guilt, fear of everything, and the hard working martyr that keeps you struggling to prove your worth, as well as overcoming the lack mindsets that contribute to financial struggles. You can learn how to make the Law of Attraction work in your favor. Suffering is now optional.

I keep asking the question: *How does it get any better than this?* Then I stay in that blissful question of... *I wonder?* It's a question that allows the universal Law of Attraction to show you how things get better. It could show you a little better or a lot better, but things can ALWAYS get better. This allows me to stay in a positive outlook of focusing on what is better. This is similar to staying in a state of gratitude. What you focus on expands.

180 Degree Turn Around

In February 2018, I sold everything. I keep a small storage in Sonoma, California, and today I am a digital nomad, international inspirational speaker, and number one best selling author, traveling the world, exploring the reality of our planet rather than what's on the news, seeing the endless wonder of lush nature and world heritage sites, and meeting amazing people.

I've visited the jungles in Peru, the Great Wall of China, the ancient temples and healing centers in Greece, Istanbul, ridden a camel at the pyramids and hot air ballooned over the Valley of the Kings in Egypt, snorkeled in the Great Barrier Reef, lived in a castle in Scotland, to name a few of the more than dozen countries I've visited.

While traveling, I work with clients from all over the world thanks to advanced technology, helping them access new levels of their ultimate power and infinite intelligence. In addition to connecting with clients via Wifi, I also visit clients in person, allowing me to explore even more places on this amazing planet. In between all of this, I write.

If you'd like to explore more of what I do, you can visit these sites:

Website: https://www.kimberlysherry.com

Intellectual Property: https://kimberly-sherry.mykajabi.com

YouTube Channel: https://www.youtube.com/user/ShamakimProductions

Instagram: https://www.instagram.com/KimberlySherryOfficial/

FaceBook: https://www.facebook.com/KimberlySherryOfficial/

If you'd like to break through your limiting beliefs to access a much more fulfilling and rewarding life, the best place to start is with a Vibrational Altitude Report. I use my highly intuitive gifts to scan and read your energy field no matter where you are in the world, without ever speaking to you or knowing anything about you. This report will give you the calibrations of about forty energies that could be adversely affecting your life, such as how much hard working martyr energy you have, how much anger you have pushed down in the background affecting your relationships, how high your money vibration and deep the container that holds it, how open your heart center that allows you to self-generate love, to name a few. You can find more information about the report and how to obtain one here: https://kimberly-sherry.mykajabi.com/store/7o69EXk7

If you are just leaving a high control religion, or contemplating doing so, I hope my story has provided some hope that healing is not only possible, but necessary to live a rewarding life. The only way out is through.

If it's been decades since leaving, but you still feel the effects of this dark cloud, get some expert help. Suffering is now optional. I have turned a lifetime of misery into my passion for helping others transform their life. It's what I've done for more than two decades helping thousands and I know I can help you as well. Check out the links above and I look forward to helping you lift the dark clouds to a much more rewarding life.

References:

[1]   Children of the Sun Foundation – founder, Tiara Kumara https://iamavatar.org/tiara-kumara/

[2]   Empowered Minds (Empowered ex-Jehovah's Witnesses) – founder Rodney Allgood. https://www.facebook.com/groups/1412960118760984/

Chapter 12

Tell Me Why the Caged Bird Sings

by Bess Kristie

"The cage bird sings with a fearful trill of things unknown but longed for still"
~ Maya Angelo

Captured by the bird catcher, an easy target. I willingly walked into my cage, unbeknownst to me the door would be randomly slammed shut. The bird catcher's control. I was let out but not to venture far, I would be quickly returned to my cage. My bars made of guilt and shame enforced by the same repetitive Bible verses. The Bible verses of being submissive. The Bible verse of God hates a divorcing. When my voice belted out my sorrows, a dark blanket was thrown over the cage to silence me. A sleepwalk state is where the bird catcher liked me. Teaching me the words I was to say. Trying to teach me the thoughts that should occupy my mind. It worked for a while on the surface. A look deeper within, the struggle was ever present. My thoughts recorded in the annals of my own journals. A sense of enslavement glorified by my religion's words 'Slave for Jehovah', inside a yearning to feel free. Journals no one heard but my eyes could see. Blank pages filled with the writings from my own hand. My voice silenced. Even censoring my own pen, afraid someone would find it and read what was inside. I adjusted my vision, my mom's words also echoing in my ears to make the best of a situation. One day, I slowly lifted the blanket. I saw light. Light at first blinding me. I had to squint and take it in slowly. It started piercing the dark. I looked up. I saw the sky. It seemed so out of reach. I saw the blues and the ever changing colors of the sunset. I started carrying those colors within, my inner palate awakening. During the night while everyone slept, I saw the stars, what a vast universe I longed to be a part of. I dreamed of freedom. I wanted more than the perch that became my home. I wanted more than the dreams I was to put off until some new system, that so called paradise that became more and more elusive. I was lost in a hope that kept me in an endurance race of apathy. The paradise that I looked forward to now relegated to a fairytale.

Do you know why the cage bird sings? It's all she can do. She listens to the solace her own voice brings. She knows the longing of her heart. How will she break free, her wings clipped. Her voice stifled to a decibel those around her are comfortable with, stifling the scream within. One day she realizes the cage no longer serves her. She has to break free, broken wings and all. Terror hits but her soul wants to grow. She feels the fear. To preserve the little life that is left within, escape is her only option. Her path unknown. She calculates the losses not realizing the full spectrum of emotions she will go through. She took flight not with wings that were strong but on wobbly legs. She kept walking. Fearful but she did it anyway.

Judge and Jury

I heard a knock on my apartment door. I didn't look out the peephole, my dog led the way down the long stairway. I opened my door. There was an Elder from the Kingdom Hall I didn't recognize. He was accompanied by a Ministerial Servant I did recognize. It was November of 2018. A soft mist outside. If I had looked out the peephole, I pro... ...bly wouldn't have answered. I felt safe and at peace in my new haven. ... was surprised they were even there.

The Elder said "Sister, we haven't seen you at the Kingdom Hall ... a while, is there anything we can do to get you back?"

It had been over a year since I had walked into a Kingdom Hall. The last meeting, I attended was in May of 2017. It had also been over a year since I walked out on my thirty-three year marriage. I was now legally divorced. I was already shunned. It wasn't the first time I was cast aside. I was disowned for a short time by my father for becoming one of Jehovah's Witnesses. My dad was a staunch Greek Orthodox. He was the first generation from his family to come to the United States. He carried his Greek heritage with him. My dad expected me to carry on the traditions of the Orthodox Church and that Heritage. Being born and raised in the United States, those expectations felt like my first prison. My first cage. Growing up, I wasn't allowed to spend the night with my neighborhood friends. I wasn't allowed to go to movies and birthday parties of my schoolmates. Becoming a teenager, I surely wasn't allowed to date. I was to grow up and marry a Greek and stay in the Church. From young, all I wanted to do was to be with my friends. I wanted to fit in. Inside I yearned for a sense of belonging. I yearned to be loved for me. My dad's love expected perfection from me. Perfection is not something I was capable of attaining. Criticism is what that kind of love breeds. I was criticized for the way I dressed. I was criticized if I didn't look like I was paying attention in church. I was even criticized for not studying enough when I brought home straight A's. As I got older, I also wondered what was the meaning of life. I wondered if there was a spiritual truth. I thought I had found it when I started dating my high school boyfriend who would become my husband. I had to sneak every time we met for a date. He had to do the same. He was born and raised as one of Jehovah's Witnesses. Dating me was wrong. I was not a Witness.

I was 19, I thought I was in love. I started studying with the Witnesses and going to their meetings. I thought I had found truth. I was always greeted with warmth when I attended meetings at the Kingdom Hall. But the more I studied and defended the beliefs I was adopting by the Witnesses, the more the arguments at home escalated. I decided I would move out. I was making a hundred dollars a week. I moved in with another Witness, I remember my first night in my new apartment crying on the curb in the rain. I left with my dad yelling at me. Nothing had prepared me for the total rejection from my father for wanting a different belief. Nothing had prepared me for being hung up on when I called home. Now I was going through it again from a religion that demanded their members shun me if I disagreed, if I walked away, if I broke my marriage vows. It also brought back memories from the Baptist School I had been expelled from in the eleventh grade. My parents sent me to that school in the seventh grade. A rebellious child was to be controlled. If at home didn't work a Baptist School surely would help. It had the opposite effect. I just learned how to sneak. I found comfort in smoking, mostly alone in the woods. My quiet spot. I was also learning something else. If my words and thoughts and beliefs didn't match the adults and institutions that surrounded me, I would be rejected from those places, even if those places were supposed to be safe havens. The havens that taught love, but for those asking questions and not fully conforming, it was a place where I learned I was expendable. My Orthodox beliefs were so different from the Baptist beliefs. I did start to do more research into Bible teachings. There were too many teachings that didn't make sense to me. Inside I wanted to know if there was a truth and if not, I was ready to be an atheist. The thought of a God burning me in hell for a different belief didn't resonate with my idea of a loving God. With my new studies I was learning there wasn't a burning hell. There was going to be a paradise on earth. Even though my dads rejection hurt, he did return to my life. He was also dying from a brain tumor. I looked forward to the hope of the resurrection where he could live with me in paradise, both of us perfect. My new teachings bringing me comfort.

Now these teachings I had learned were showing me a different side. The ugly side. I knew that the close friendships I had developed among the Witness friends were unlikely to continue. We were taught that shunning is love, designed to make you miss your friends and family so they'll return. It is not love. It didn't feel like love when I saw others who were disfellowshipped sitting among me at the Kingdom Hall treated like they didn't exist. It breeds feelings of isolation and rejection. The feelings I had experienced.

The shunning that hurt the most was from my own daughter. I had sent her a present soon after I separated from her dad. She had moved overseas. I saw a bracelet made of rose gold, it had a dainty quality that reminded me of her. I knew it would be something she would like. I packaged it and took it to the post office. It took a month for it to make its way back to me, 'Return to Sender' written on the outside of the package. In that month I wondered if she got it, I wondered if she liked it. I wondered if she knew how much I loved her. I sent her a message, asking if I had her right address. I received no response. My answer. I was shunned. This is the ugly face of shunning. The other ugly face is that I had a part in calling this religion the truth. I had a part in taking her to meetings and reinforcing Watchtower's doctrines. I wanted to apologize but I knew the label that awaited me if I did. The worst sin was to speak out against their teachings. I don't know how many tears I cried, too many to number.

Now here is an elder before me. I had already experienced my greatest loss. I had already experienced shunning. What did he hope to accomplish? What was the real reason they were at my door?

My dog Riley either felt my discomfort or their intention. I had to put a choke collar on her to keep her from lunging. This is a dog who loves almost everyone.

I told the elder "I will not be returning to the Kingdom Hall".

It didn't take long for the reason they were there to become apparent.

"We have accusations of adultery against you and we need to set up a judicial hearing".

I took a deep breath to calm the nerves that were already rising up within. I calmly replied "I will not be there".

He looked at me and said "We will have the hearing without you".

As these words came out of his mouth, I sensed the discomfort of the ministerial servant that was with him. He looked down at his feet. I knew anything I said would be disregarded. To argue doctrine would be pointless. Hadn't I learned to do the same when my beliefs were being questioned and disagreed with.

I looked at him and said "You have over 1000 cases of child sexual abuse being investigated by the Australian Royal Commission, you have million dollar lawsuits against you in the US because of your organization's coverups of child sexual abuse. I think you have more important things to discuss at your judicial hearing". My voice was shaking. I wanted to tell that brother accompanying the elder to do his research, but no other words came out. I was too shaken inside. I closed my door.

Anger welled up inside. Who did they think they were showing up at my door? To me they were like puppets on a string doing the bidding of the Watch Tower Bible and Tract Society. They were cut off from the emotions someone who left feels. But to even share those feelings, the blame would have been placed on me for leaving. They didn't see the blanket they were under. The blanket that prevents research outside of their own literature. Their information controlled. Any contrary information would be ascribed to Satan, "the ruler of this world". Information from those who left and did research would be called lies, "food from the table of demons". A blind man can't see through a looking glass neither can a bird see outside his blanketed cage. I knew the fear their leaders instilled. I experienced it myself. It is what kept me in my cage for so long. But now, was I the example for other wives who wanted to leave? Was my 'hearing for adultery' absolution for my ex-husband?

It wasn't until I walked away that my research started. It wasn't until I walked away that I understood the full manipulation of the leaders of

Watchtower Bible and Tract. I had also seen how others who had walked away or were disfellowshipped were talked about. I saw how they were used as examples for the congregation. Now I would be the example. Would it be blamed on worldly association, not studying enough, not going out in service enough, not being submissive enough, not being obedient enough. Even as a Witness I use to say if everyone felt loved and supported and refreshed, I doubt anyone would leave. I doubt anyone leaves a happy marriage. I knew now, the blame, the example, the judgement would be directed toward me. I would be the example. I had been around enough whispers and car groups to know what would be said. I had heard enough local needs talks. It didn't matter how many decades of faithfulness I had. It didn't matter to them why I left. It would be information they would have been unwilling to hear.

A week later, obviously the coverup of the child sexual abuse in the organization was not as important as the accusation against me. A knock upon my same door, the same elder, the same brother. No longer would I be considered a sister.

"We are here to inform you that you will be disfellowshipped and you have seven days to appeal"

I was rather dumfounded they were even there much less the words that came out of the elder's mouth. My unexpected response? I wished them a good day and closed my door. I suddenly felt such a sense of freedom. I danced with abandon around my apartment. George Michaels blasting "Freedom" through my bluetooth speaker. The blanket not only lifted from my cage but the door wide open, I had walked out physically, now I felt mentally almost out too. I had to learn a few things to be mentally free.

> *"You want to fly, you got to give up the*
> *shit that weighs you down".*
> ~ *Toni Morrison*

I felt stifled by my marriage and by my religion. I felt like life was constantly being choked out of me. I would journal for my sanity's sake. I found this journal entry made 10 years ago. It was 4 months after my mother's death. She had spent the previous 4 years in the hospital and in an assisted living facility. I also had a mentally challenged brother I was responsible for. He was in a group home but I was his only living immediate family. The years of caretaking had taken its toll, yet I was grateful my moms last years were happy ones despite her health challenges. This was my journal entry. This was a reflection of my life.

January 24, 2010

"Inside I feel so empty. Even at the Kingdom Hall, I'm tired of the judgements. I'm tired of not being me. I'm suppose to feel love, I don't feel it. Maybe I never felt it. Is that what life is, is that what love is Conditional? Criticism? I'm enjoying being in my studio, even with minimal heat it is warmer than my house. My husband says I give him dirty looks. He and my daughter whisper behind my back. What do they want from me? I have been there for everyone else. Maybe I don't want to be there for anyone anymore. Maybe they can find their own socks.Maybe they can cook their own dinner. Maybe they can do their own laundry. Maybe they can solve their own problems. I need time for me. I'm tired of hearing complaining. Maybe I'm in the middle of something that is important to me. Life feels empty".

This was the cage. This was the pain that was ever present from the time I said I do. I was baptized the year before I married, I was twenty. Both became my cages, both intertwined. Now I was to have the self sacrificing spirit of a wife. I was to have the self sacrificing spirit as a Witness. It meant just that, I was to sacrifice my 'self'. It would be 7 years after this was written before I walked out.

How did I get to that day.

From the day I left, I knew I had to start building my life. Fear had kept me in the confines of my marriage, fear had kept me in the confines of a religion. That cage provided protection too. I didn't have to worry about bills. I had a home, half of it gifted by my mother. I was mostly a stay at home mom and wife. Staying at home though and doing those 'wifely' duties and just going to meetings always brought me into a depressive state. I also hated knocking on doors. I never found it joyful, I never found it refreshing. I loved being with some of the others in the car group but it was the social aspect. Knocking on doors, I felt like I was bothering people, counting time so I wouldn't be considered inactive. To cope with the depression, I started taking art classes at a local technical school. It became my therapy. My love of photography reignited from high school. I had to still squeeze it into my schedule because everything else was suppose to come first. Putting me first was not a concept I was familiar with. I was good at sacrificing my 'self' and the things I loved.

Walking out meant shunning but there is another aloneness. Becoming a Witness meant pulling away from friends and family who were not Witnesses. They are the worldly association I was suppose to just witness to, not become close to. Being a Witness separated me from celebrating holidays with my friends and relatives. Birthdays, Christmas, Easter and Thanksgiving rarely ever saw me at the table with my relatives. If I did go, it came with a lecture from my husband about not looking like I was participating and definitely not letting anyone in the Kingdom Hall know. I just wanted to be with my Greek family. So, leaving meant even a hesitancy on my part in confiding with my relatives when I first left.

I was fortunate in that I continued taking classes. This time at a college campus that had a program geared toward senior citizens. They weren't college credit classes so there were no demands as far as studying, taking test and writing papers. I was in my early 50's. One class entitled Dynamic Aging taught at Furman University through the Olli program became a strong support. Every Wednesday, I saw the faces that had been with me the year before I left. The year I was still a Witness and a wife. Every week, I learned about aging dynamically. I saw in my class retired men and women, kindness in their eyes, a warmth and acceptance not because I was the same religion. It was here I saw we could have a discussion on death where the the Buddhist tradition was discussed, the Christian tradition was discussed, the Energetic theory discussed and we all participated and listened, each taking what was useful. No one arguing about who was right and who was wrong. A mutual respect for all beliefs. Week after week we had different topics. It was here I started to learn what love is suppose to be like. It was here I heard about self love. It was here I heard the phrase Unconditional Positive Regard for others, and also for yourself. It was here I saw gratitude and growth. The Witnesses talk of love but I soon saw how conditional that love was. When I was studying and had to move out of my house, a Witness couple offered me a room in their upstairs. Yes, it was loving. They actually became like family. Would they offer me a room now? Now that I wasn't studying. Now that I no longer wanted to be a Jehovah's Witness. When my class heard I was leaving my marriage and religion, I had 3 offers of rooms from my fellow classmates. This is what love is supposed to look like. I saw dynamic living. I saw dynamic loving. I saw learning that inspired positive change. I heard the term personal development over and over. The blanket on my cage now lifting like a curtain on a stage. Me, the marionette, was learning I had strings, I no longer had to let anything or anyone else control them. My tune, my song, is the only song I need to dance to. It was the song I needed to sing. The key was now in my hands.

There Is Power in Observation

This contrasted so dramatically with the Kingdom Hall. The spirituality I sought had been missing from the seat I sat in at the Kingdom Hall. How we dressed seemed more important. It was a constant topic to look "modest and well arranged". How much time we spent knocking on doors was also a constant topic. The shaming tools were used well. It sounded like the Pharisees in the Bible, putting heavy loads on the people. The message, we were never doing enough.

One day I was sitting in the back of the Kingdom Hall just observing. It was a Sunday. We always did the Watchtower Study, an elder and a reader up on stage. A question would be asked, taken directly from the Watchtower after the reader read the paragraph. Generally there were about twenty paragraphs to a Watchtower study. When the question was asked it was the audiences turn to answer. Hands would go up and the elder would call on someone. The answer would be a repeat of what was just read in the Watchtower article. Sometimes there would be some elaboration from another publication by Watchtower. It reminded me of a parrot repeating what was read. Repeating what was in the literature. My mind did a flashback to Elementary School and how we would raise our hands hoping it would be seen and we could espouse what we just learned. Maybe we would get a pat on the back. There were pats on the back in the Kingdom Hall, for following, for remaining within the confines of their dogma and beliefs. For repeating. Pats on the back for placing magazine or a book at a door. This was suppose to be happiness? All of a sudden it felt like I was back in Elementary School. Where were the pats on the back for personal development and developing your gifts and talents. If it wasn't something to be used by the religion, it wasn't a pat on the back but a consternation

I had my Dynamic Aging Group but nothing prepared me when the shunning hit. I had spent so much time in tears because of it. I did miss my friends who were closest to me. But I knew If I told them I was never returning they would shun me. I just started fading away from their life after I moved out of my home. I stopped answering the phone calls because the question always became when are you coming back. They were shunning their own children. I knew I would eventually be dating someone, no matter if I was separated or divorced, it would be adultery. Until death do you part is the marriage's life time sentence. What about when something inside you dies during the marriage? That death is not talked about. What about when love feels dead because of the words and criticisms that were directed to me. What if the love is killed by putting me last in the relationship, work coming first, not only work but everything else. What if your love is killed because of the things said behind your back. How would you like to hear what your husband thought of you through your daughter's words?

When she was a teenager, she looked at me and said, "Wow mom, you really are smart, dad had me convinced you were dumb." These words stayed with me. These words cut me like a knife. This is death. My marriage felt dead to me long before I left. It was an endurance race. At one time I thought to myself, can life be brought back when the death is inside. My mantra was love hurts. I had wounds and scars. It was now time to heal. The hurt from a marriage and the hurt from a religion. Even the hurt that went farther back, to a dad's rejection.

My Own Resurrection

Now it was time I looked for support in dealing specifically with leaving a high control group. I found a group of Ex Jehovah's Witnesses that focused on empowerment and moving forward. It's easy to just feel the loss and the anger of the injustice. Moving forward for me was my only option. I didn't leave to stay in grief and bitterness. I left for betterment.

One of the Life Coaches had put a program together for Ex Jehovah's Witnesses called "The Twenty-one Day Deprogramming Bootcamp". It almost sounded like something out of science fiction when I first started the journey, mind control? But as I learned and read, it is real. By the time the elder came to my door. I had lost my fear of their judgements. I had lost my fear of their labels. My coach likened it to playing sports. If I walked away and was not on the ball-field does the referee's whistle apply to me? No, I am no longer in the game. Their rules do not apply to me, their labels do not apply to me. Learning that what others think of me is none of my business started releasing me from the mental constraints I had learned not only as a Witness but from growing up. My legs no longer wobbly, my wings no longer clipped.

To expand our capacity to learn from all disciplines is to start the path for our personal freedom.

I searched for teachings that would move me forward. I took a class entitled Wisdom of the Mystics from the same Olli program. I learned about different religious traditions, different beliefs, different so called spiritual growth practices. I read poetry and novels. I looked at art work and found music that spoke to me. I started spending more time in nature. I started to incorporate what resonated. The question, what nurtured me today? How can I grow from this? What are my appreciations today? These were my new journal entries. These questions shifted my focus. My past losing the hold it had on me. My direction was today and what it takes to go forward. One of my most important lessons I had to learn was to love myself.

To learn to love myself sounded like it should be easy. I sat one day in my new home crying. It was after my divorce. My boyfriend's arms around me asking me what was wrong. I was clueless about so many things. I didn't even know how to write a resume. My work experience was just various part time jobs. I was attaching lack of skills to a lack in me. He looked at me with a perplexed and sincere look. What? You are so talented, you are so kind, you are an amazing human being. Those were not words I had been use to hearing. I had to first learn to see myself through others eyes. I had to learn a skill is just that, a skill, something to be learned and with work is mastered. I had to learn to not look through the eyes of those who had tried to control me, who tried to keep me down. Those were eyes distorted by their own fears and insecurities. I didn't want those eyes in my life anymore. Neither did I want my own eyes looking at me in that way. They say we should love ourselves first and while I do believe that, I was glad I now had those in my life who believed in me. One day I just looked in the mirror and saw who I really was. What was my inner being. Who am I? I starting loving and appreciating the being that I am. Perfectly imperfect. I got in touch with my authentic self. My loves, my likes, what brought me joy and even what makes me cry. I looked at my past wins. Awards I had won for art and photography. Poetry I wrote that I loved. I looked at pictures I have taken where I captured emotion, the pictures I loved, my wins. I clung to words that honored my gifts and talents. I doubt the teachers that had the biggest influence even knew what their words meant. To be acknowledge for something I loved and worked hard at meant the world to me inside. My previous world, would relegate it to something that took me away from preaching, discounting what gave me joy.

I learned the masks I was suppose to wear did not belong to me. They were mask that were suppose to make me fit in someone else's narrative.

Those narratives are not the stories I want to be in. I know now I get to write my own story. I get to be me. I remember the day a teacher took my hand as I thanked him for his class. He said I see great things for you one day. These are words I clung too. Inside I knew there was more to me than the cages those who said they loved me tried to keep me in. My huge win, claiming me. Walking away. Feeling the fear and doing it anyway, I see the warrior spirit that resides within me. The spirit that didn't give up, the spirit that kept going and still keeps going.

Through another life coach I learned to set targets. To me it sounded less daunting than goal setting. What did I want to feel with this target. What was the emotion. Happy and accomplished is what jumped out at me. Those feelings had remained illusive throughout my life. I remember turning 30 and sitting in a therapist office wanting to feel happy. Now happy is my reality. It is not that everyday I'm giddy but everyday I can ask myself what will make me happy today. I can also ask that for feeling accomplished. What can I do today to feel accomplished. What inspired action can I take. These are doable targets that add up to some great results.

When I look at my past, I realized I looked outward to feel a sense of belonging. I looked outward to find love. I looked outward to find meaning. I looked outward to find spirituality. I looked outward to find this elusive thing called enlightenment. The search that came from my own darkness. The darkness of grief, of loneliness, of feeling lost, of not feeling good enough. Out of that darkness came the unexpected light. The light that is within. The light that illuminated the key in my own hand. The light that tells me I was never meant to be a parrot just to repeat the words of another. The light that tells me I am the creator of my own life. I am the the spiritual thing I sought. My job is to always tap into that uniqueness that makes me who I am. It's not the life I was born into. It's not the constraints society tried to keep me in. It's not the buildings I sought for enlightenment. They turned out to be my dark places. The answers were in the questions that come out of those dark places. The darkness where I searched for answers to my own life, my own narrative. The answers that got me in touch with my 'self'.

The best life coaches helped me find that. They didn't tell me how to live, they helped me look within. They helped me find my light. My light that is to be illuminated from within. Pouring out who I am. Pouring out my dreams. Pouring out my words, my song, maybe it touches another. I embrace the freedom to be me. That is my definition of living an enlightened life. That is the life I want to live every day. Now I find when tears mist my eyes, it is tears of gratitude, tears of joy, tears of feeling connection. Tears that I found me. Tears knowing how wonderful love is supposed to feel. Tears that there are so many beautiful people in my life. People who build up. People who showed me what unconditional love means. Now I don't search for truth, I ask what is useful to me and the life I want to live. Nature still my quiet place.

Being the keeper of my journals, when I find an entry like this, I know dreams do come true.

From 1995: My number one dream: to live on a mountain and be self sufficient. That is where I find me writing this. It takes work, it takes struggle, it takes tears and grit, but what a breathtaking view.

Chapter 13

How Fearlessly the Mouse Roars

A story of losing and then restoring my voice and my power

by Libby Pease

"Remember to breathe"
— Mom

I was told in a meeting with the elders that my husband's affairs with other women were my fault. I was not submissive enough. I spoke up too often and therefore he is justified in his actions. I could not believe what I was hearing. Not only had my husband left the country, but I was underemployed with a toddler, a mortgage and now I was to bear the sins of another person. This was when I knew that I could not be one of Jehovah's Witnesses any longer.

How could I build a life when my world was crumbling all around me?

Marrying In – How I Became a Witness

In 1989 I was an active 17-year-old thinking about my final years of high school and what I could do next with my life. I had just broken up with my high school sweetheart who I had dated for 3 years. He had been my first lover and the first person to truly break my heart.

In that year of high school, I had accomplished an Award of Merit, given to those who earned 75% or higher in all classes. This was quite an accomplishment for me. While I always loved learning, I had struggled with reading for my entire academic career. At the award ceremony, my mother said, "You can accomplish a lot when you are not distracted by men". That little comment has stayed with me for 30 years.

It seemed like I was getting a footing on life. I was working for a local summer day camp and started also working for a therapist and partner on their 150-acre property as their groundskeeper.

I was a typical teen. My mom and I were always at odds with each other. Sometimes I wonder how dad managed us during that time. I spent time with my geeky friends. I was "that girl" who played Dungeons and Dragons (D&D) with a group of boys; mostly my brother's friends. There were 4 consistent players and Richard was a younger brother of one of the consistent players. He was my age and we had known each other in grade school. I had not seen him for a long time because his family had moved a lot, but his grandparents still lived in our small town. Richard's family were Jehovah's Witnesses and his grandfather was an elder in the local congregation.

One thing that is glaringly apparent now, but was not obvious to me at the time was my low self-esteem. I exuded confidence, but I needed others to feed my self-worth. I had internalized a poster I had received as a child to post on the door of my rabbit room in the barn that said, "you are no bunny until some bunny loves you". It was a cute innocent poster with a lop-eared rabbit on it and I took it as gospel. I was always in the market for the next person to date, so I could be "somebody" again and Richard fit the bill.

We had not seen each other since grade 5. He had grown from a gawky boy who was shorter than me, to a man just over 6 feet tall. He had played Rugby for a while, so had filled out considerably. I had been a swimmer at camp and also doing a lot of physical work with property maintenance. We were two teens in the prime of their lives who instantly clicked.

That summer we hung out a lot, played D&D, went for walks and to the movies and talked for hours.

For those familiar with Jehovah's Witnesses, you have probably noticed a couple of things right out of the gate. He played sports, played D&D and hung out unsupervised with a woman, and a woman not in the faith. He wasn't considered to be a strong Witness by any stretch of the imagination, but I didn't help matters either...

I remember one summer day when I was up in Flesherton hanging out with Richard and some other local youth. It was hot and we all went to the pond to swim. I didn't have my bathing suit, but I was wearing matching underwear and bra, which was no different than any bikini. It was bold, but I didn't care. I wasn't going to miss out on a chance to swim. I can say that Richard was impressed and it inspired some other people who were also without suits to just swim in their underwear too.

On one of our drives, Richard and I started talking about religion. I have always had an interest in religion and mythology. I knew from grade school that he identified as a Jehovah's Witness. He was always out in the hall with the other Witness kids during Oh Canada and the Lord's Prayer. During that drive, I flippantly challenged him about his religion. I asked him why he didn't just leave the faith and live like a normal person. He quickly pulled off to the side of the road and passionately explained his devotion to Jehovah and how important it was to live by the bible so that you could survive Armageddon. I was surprised by his dedication. That is when I decided to check it out because I had never heard someone speak so passionately about their faith before.

In March of 1990, I started studying the Witness material with a young Ministerial Servant and his wife and even attended an Assembly. I found it all very interesting. Things were starting to progress in my relationship with Richard. He asked if I would consider him as husband material. We would go out on dates, but every time I tried to make out with him, he would tell me to stop. It was obvious to me that he wanted to keep going, but he would not cross that line (though he did other things that would not be approved of by the elders in his congregation). This was the one thing we had to honour; we would not have sex or even mess around before marriage. This was very attractive to me. In my previous relationship, I was sexually active and there was infidelity by my partner. To know that Richard would stay so strong to his convictions felt like a guarantee that I would never get cheated on again. Slowly, I was being pulled in.

I found Richard's mother endearing as well. I came from a family which felt emotionally constipated with a vast divide between myself and my mother. I could never understand my friend's close relationships with their mothers. Don't get me wrong, I learned a lot from my mother. She is a walking encyclopedia and is always encouraging you to learn and do, but she was not what I considered cuddly or warm. Richard's mom Mary, on the other hand, was everything that I felt I was missing. She was concerned about her son seeing a "worldly" girl, but she always welcomed me with open arms and affection. She only had boys and always looked forward to her sons getting married so she could have girls around.

As I read back in my diary from that time, I am struck by how many warning signs I missed. The couple that I had been studying with must have let the elders in the congregation know how serious Richard and I were getting. They warned us to wait until I was a baptized witness before dating. Things were getting stressful at home for me too. I had decided to go to college in the fall for forestry rather than finishing off my final year of high school which was then grade 13 or OAC. I was missing the bus home to hang out with Richard and no one from either side was thrilled about that. In April Richard was sent off to stay with his grandfather in Florida. He was forbidden to see me again.

By May of that year, I was struggling with my beliefs. I wrote,

> *"I don't know what is it with me. Last week I felt very strongly towards the Truth, but now there is doubt. All religions claim that they are the one and that no others other than themselves will be saved. That seems to be a view of selfishness along with being cliquish and snobbish. They condemn things that the bible doesn't condemn... they gossip and slander others constantly along with cheating others. They are hypocrites with some of their teachings. Some are actually good and go by their teachings but others (the elders mostly) are sly, nitpicky and can be hypocrites. Richard's Grandfather will rip off family members on vehicles and other things. He doesn't live with his wife for half a year and won't share a room with her for the other half of the year. He says he cares for his grandsons yet he constantly puts them down or hurts them with words. He may not realize that verbal abuse can cut sharper than a razor.*
>
> *I get the feeling that Armageddon is coming soon but it won't be what they expect. The liars will be picked out and punished. I also get the feeling that I don't know if I want to live a thousand or more years.... I want to continue with fortune-telling and palmistry.... I feel a slave to two masters.. who do I follow? Do I want to live? What is Richard to me really? Why do I feel different?"*

Looking back on this now, I wish that I had stayed with that intuition and followed my clairvoyant spiritual path. Then again, there were lessons that I learned as a Jehovah's Witness that I would have missed.

Despite the efforts of Richard's family to keep us apart, where there is a will, there is a way. Richard came back from Florida when his grandfather found out I was going to college halfway across the province in the fall. I still studied and attended meetings. At the summer assembly in Hamilton, Ontario on July 13 of 1990, Richard formally proposed to me. In October I had quit college and by November we had eloped.

We wanted a real wedding but because we were not baptized, we could not have a wedding at the Hall. I remember the day clearly. My soon-to-be mother-in-law Mary was excited and woke up early to do my hair. Richard came to pick me up at his parent's house, where I had been living since quitting college a month before. He was living alone in a nearby apartment until we were 'safely married'. We drove up to Owen Sound to the Justice of the Peace.

When we arrived, the clerk had us sit down in the hallway to wait. We were a ball of nerves. You could see the judge and clerks peeking from the courtroom doors as we waited. I suspect they have you wait to see if you will bolt after a significant amount of time. Finally, we were invited into the courthouse. Our best friends were not able to stand up with us that day because they were travelling, so the clerks acted as witnesses. The judge was so serious when talking to us and the rest of the ceremony was a blur. The next thing I knew we were married. By the afternoon we were picking up pink champagne and Chinese food to celebrate our wedding at the apartment.

I felt like I was finally safe and guaranteed to be loved until the end of my days.

Mouse Emerges

I quickly fell into the role of wife and keeper of the house. Suddenly my diaries showed comments like,

> *"I've lost 20 lb. with working but with Richard so down it seems unimportant and irrelevant. He is down on himself and can't work as well as usual. How can I relieve this?"*

Gone is the powerful woman and in comes the mouse, whose only concern is her husband.

The next summer Richard and I were baptized together as one of Jehovah's Witnesses. We had the opportunity to be baptized together at the Lovers of Freedom convention. At this convention, I saw my youngest brother-in-law get brutally hit by my father-in-law for not shining his shoes. He was only 11 or 12 at the time. I tried to stand up for him. Richard was promptly told to "control your wife". That incident never sat well with me. I thought it was just in our family. Later I found out it was everywhere in the community.

There are gaps in my diaries and my memory through some of this time. I was going to meetings, to work, renovating the house and trying to spend some time with friends. There were a bunch of us that hung out. We met each other at the assemblies and would sit together. On long weekends we would hang out. The parties were crazy, with a tonne of over-drinking and messing around. I never really drank, and never felt the need since it wasn't a taboo thing when I was growing up. My Witness friends made it a sport. I was amazed looking back that no one died, but I remember calling the ambulance at least once.

It was not long before I was pregnant. I was the first of our friends to get pregnant and I remember being up at a friend's place and taking the pregnancy test. Richard was floored. I think he would have fallen if he hadn't been sat down by his best friend. At that time the direction for the Watchtower was to avoid having children. Armageddon was coming and running with a babe in arms would be difficult. I was 19 and I had failed yet again in the organization's eyes.

On a very cold day in February 1993, our daughter was born. I was 20 years old the day she was born. Suddenly my whole world changed with this small person. The first day Richard held her he was smitten. Our house was under renovation so we were living at my parent's farm. This was an anxious time because there was tension between Richard and my family. We had lived with his parents for a couple of months, but I didn't get along with his dad and I did not want to live there when the baby came. So, we moved in with my non-believing family. Richard spent long hours out playing computer games with friends and I tended to my daughter. I was also asked to manage the house when my mom took a vacation to Turkey with her sister, my brother and cousin.

Suddenly I had a colicky infant and a farmhouse to manage. I had no idea how to cope.

Once it was in a livable condition, we moved back into our small schoolhouse again. For the first few weeks, I had to carry water from our neighbour's place because the water was not yet hooked up to the well. It was not ideal but I felt like I could breathe again.

The pattern of my husband being out a lot did not change when we went home. The isolation and inability to get around were hugely challenging. Although we had two vehicles one was always in need of repair. With the baby, I was not working and Richard was only making $8.25 per hour. We were on social assistance so we could pay our bills. I saw this as the sign of the times and felt that things would only get worse. The joy in my day was watching my daughter eat orange jello and discovering her world.

I wrote,

> *"I have no one to talk to. I mean really talk to... I can't open up freely to anyone and Richard doesn't seem to listen anymore. He claims that when I tell him how I feel and my problems that I am just adding to his stress. Where else can I let out my feelings, my frustrations?"*

I remember sitting on the steps outside of our house so I could cry and not wake the baby. I would be alone, hoping Richard would come home early from visiting with his friends.

We did our best to make ends meet. The government offered an opportunity for Richard to go to get his GED and go to college as a stipulation to continue getting assistance. This meant student loans to pay for the schooling and extra gas to drive to Barrie for classes. I think he enjoyed most of the classes. As I found out later, it is challenging to study when your family is trying to get your attention. During his time at college, he made some friends. These were "worldly" friends. I had been trying my best to get to the hall with the baby. More often than not I went alone with my daughter because he had homework, or was too tired.

One evening we went to a worldly gathering, which ended up being a Christmas party. At that point, I was totally in as a Jehovah's Witness, and I made it clear that we should not be there. Richard insisted we stay so I waited until 10:30 pm. He had been drinking quite a bit. It was far past our daughter's bedtime and she also could feel the tension and impatience in me. I had a contract that was supposed to start the next day and we were in desperate need of money. I finally got him to leave. In my diary, I wrote,

> *"He screamed at the top of his lungs the whole way home about how much of a prude I was and (like) a 30-year-old dead person. He said he'd rather have a divorce than live like this (so unjustly confined to a reasonable request). He said in the next breath that the most important things in his life were Jehovah, his wife and his daughter."*

I went on to write that if that was true, he wouldn't be at a Christmas party, nor yelling at his wife while she tries to drive in wintery weather and he would make sure his two-year-old daughter was at home at least close to her bedtime.

There were so many incidents of verbal and emotional abuse. Richard has even said to me in the years after, that he felt he had to defend himself because he never felt good enough in my eyes; that I always wanted him to be more than who he was. He would punch out the wallboard on either side of my head, which always seemed to happen a couple of days before a family event. I learned to hide this evidence from everyone. My drywall skills are amazing because of this. I blamed myself for saying the wrong thing or demanding that I have time with my family too.

Although I tried to make our relationship look OK from the outside, it wasn't. My world came crashing down when I found out about the first affair. The guarantee from so long ago when he would not mess around before marriage ended up to be false. He said I changed; that I wasn't the gutsy girl who swims in her underwear but was a mousy woman like all the rest. My desire for 50th wedding anniversary was shattered and the devastation went to my core. Richard was also struggling with what he had done. He was depressed and I suspected he was suicidal. I remember following him to the lake in my bare feet to make sure he didn't jump in and let himself drown.

Turning Point

I can't remember how, but the elders found out about Richard's affair. He was pulled into meetings with them that I was not allowed to attend. I requested to speak with the elders as well, to let them know that he was suffering from depression and was potentially a risk to himself. I believed that disfellowshipping him would not just punish Richard, but would probably end him. Shortly after these meetings, Richard packed his duffle bag one morning and left without a word. His parents had moved to Michigan a few months after our daughter was born and he ended up moving in with them. I was left by myself again.

I had a younger elder come to my house alone one day to provide "counsel and comfort". I suggested he come with a second person and to please leave. I was outside in my garden and was grateful for my neighbour being across the road and working on their garden too. I had bells and whistle going off in my head that this was not right so I held my ground. I even waved at my neighbour to ensure she saw that he was there with me and that I was encouraging him to leave.

I was at a loss for what to do next. I was 25 with a 5-year-old child, with only a high school education. I had only been able to find seasonal work. My car was almost 10 years old.

In Richard's absence, the elders in my congregation met with me again. They said they would not disfellowship Richard. They believed he had wandered because I was not a submissive enough wife. I was floored. My decision to take my daughter to meetings alone without him was counted against me. They said I should not have usurped his authority by studying for the meetings by myself. More importantly, I should not have had the audacity to tell the elders what they should or should not do with their judgements.

I could not believe my ears. I had been fighting a war on all fronts and now I was being crucified for the actions of someone else. This was not what I wanted for my daughter and it was no longer what I wanted for myself.

Divorce Out – The Road to Roar

My first step required humility in large doses. I approached my parents to apologize for how I acted over the years. After some time had passed, I asked if I could still access funds for my continuing education. There was no way I would do student loans, so I would need another plan if school wasn't an option.

Thankfully they agreed. After applying as a mature student to a handful of universities I was accepted by the University of Windsor. My whole world changed now as a single parent. Now I was a psychology major at the University of Windsor and was taking courses in Women's Studies and Theology. I loved my courses and getting back into writing again.

The way back to myself was not a smooth one. Richard found his way back into my life again for two short years. I still wanted that dream of milestone anniversaries and just wanted to feel like somebody. We bought a house which was a huge step up from the apartment I had been renting. I wanted to believe his words of apology and promises for a better future. We celebrated our 10th wedding anniversary, but the relationship was strained. I remember having full-blown panic attacks before my family arrived for the anniversary party. I knew that everything I was showing my family and friends was a lie. The only truth was my little girl and the desire to make a difference in the world.

During my time at school, I decided to seek mental health support. I had been volunteering at a distress centre and had been taking on a lot of responsibilities there. My director asked me one day if I was hiding in my education and my volunteer work. I had to admit that I was. She suggested I scale back at the centre for a bit and take advantage of the free counselling at the university. I look back now after all these years and I thank her from the depths of my soul. She had so much compassion, even though she was desperate for regular volunteer coverage on the lines. She was my first mentor to my recovery.

I started therapy and I could tell my counsellor was concerned for me. Slowly we found the pieces and started to work on rebuilding ME. With her support, I applied for a transfer to another university. Because of my learning disabilities, I had never thought I had a chance to get into the University of Guelph, which had always been the university of my dreams. With her encouragement, I applied and was accepted to start in the fall semester. I had also been passively looking for summer work near where my parents lived and a full-time summer job came up that was perfect.

Things came to a head one day in the kitchen when Richard and I were arguing again. I can't remember what it was about, but I remember smashing my favourite dish on the edge of the counter and yelling, "ENOUGH!", which had always been a full stop word for us in our relationship. But this enough wasn't just enough to end the discussion; I told him I wanted a divorce.

Everything moved quickly after that. I wrote my letter to The Watchtower Society of Jehovah's Witnesses letting them know I was no longer to be considered one of Jehovah's Witnesses. This wasn't because I wanted to play by their rules, but as a proclamation to God that I was no longer going to be living that way. I knew that I would want to date again and wanted to be honest with God that I would not be rushing into marriage so that I could have sex.

I got my transfer to the University of Guelph and accepted the summer job. My daughter was transferred to my old elementary school and I got help to move back home. Soon after the Windsor house sold.

Part of me still longed for that happily ever after, in paradise. I wrote in my diary,

> *"It makes it more painful for longer if you think there is a chance.*
>
> *There is no chance.*
>
> *Make it legal. Let this part die. Move to heal. Then get up and see the world and all that it holds for you.*
>
> *Don't look for love too soon. Real love will be there waiting until you really love yourself. Without loyalty to yourself then no one can be loyal to you. You are precious and lovable. You have honour and will one day be honoured if you honour yourself. Love yourself and hold yourself up to the possibilities of the future."*

For years I never considered that I had left a cult or that it had shaped so much in my life. It took me just over a decade to untangle from the 10 years that I was a witness. I sought therapy for what I thought were unrelated issues and made my breakthroughs when I started my coaching training and uncovered the real me that had been hiding within the mouse.

During this healing, I realized too that Richard was just as caught up in this web as I was. He was always reaching for the things that fed his soul and then the frustration of never being the person expected by his religion or his wife. There was also the fear of not measuring up at Armageddon and never seeing his loved ones again.

Mouse No More

My divorce was finalized in Sept of 2002. I was 30 years old. In February of 2003, I received my Honours Degree in Psychology at the University of Guelph. To commemorate this, I got a tattoo of a unique tree of life to remind me that there is wisdom in my decisions.

Since then I have been in a 16-year relationship with my common-law spouse, who has never been a Jehovah's Witness. I built a strong and successful career as a trainer, facilitator and supervisor in crisis response for distress centres and victim services. For the past 5 years, I have focused my energy on becoming an internationally certified Life Coach. In February of 2018, I received my Associate Certified Coach (ACC) designation with the International Coach Federation, which allows me to practice all over the world. The summer before that I opened my private coaching practice near Fergus, Ontario, Canada. My practice specializes in supporting individuals who have emerged from highly controlling communities, religions, families and workplaces. Supporting them to move beyond the shame, guilt and isolation; to create their own lives so they can see the possibilities for their future!

That 17-year-old me believed that I could do great things.

The mouse in me could not see past her limitations.

I have built a new life from the broken pieces of my old world through vision and determination. Now I am an entrepreneur. I have spoken in front of hundreds of people. I have published my first book as well as this narrative. I am working on my second book called Finding My Clear Path, which should be out in 2021 if not before. I walk with people as they discover their new lives and new possibilities. And I have a voice. A voice that will never submit or grow silent. I stand for my authentic self and I advocate for others to find their authentic truth.

Even when I felt my world was crumbling around me, it was clearing the slate so I could create a new life and write in an entirely new book. The book of my authentic life.

Libby Pease HBA CVRM ECPC ACC
Clairvoyant Coach with Listening Tree Studio & Coaching
www.clairvoyantcoach.ca
226-838-9772

NOTE: Other than my name, all the names have been changed out of respect to their privacy.

Chapter 14

Finding Family Freedom and True Happiness

by Meandy Bishop

"Better is the end of a thing than the beginning."
~Ecclesiastes 7:8

As a Jehovah's Witness, I was taught 'better is the end of a thing than the beginning.' When I ponder over the proverb I just quoted, I must admit that I whole-heartedly agree with that statement--but not in the way that you might think.

Life is a fantastic journey, and I've learned to expect the unexpected. As someone who was born-and-raised as a devout Jehovah's Witness, I never thought I would be sharing a story of departure out of the religion. I remember reading about so many experiences in the WT and Awake magazines that were designed to 'encourage' us. My own story turned out to be quite different than those experiences that I read about in the magazines.

There's an idiom that says, 'things don't always turn out the way you plan.' I've come to love the motto I just quoted, because some of the best decisions in life can stem from unexpected events. After spending my entire life in a box, here I am: Sharing with you my adventure of exiting the only world I ever knew. My story is one of personal growth and overcoming obstacles in the face of tremendous adversity.

It was a Struggle!

My mom came in contact with the Jehovah's Witnesses at a vulnerable time in her life. She was pregnant with me and decided to dedicate her life to the organization. Despite my father's wishes, she raised me in her newfound faith.

The years of my youth were challenging for me. I felt the constant pressure of being pulled in 2 different directions. I felt a tremendous amount of mental anguish. My parent's endless arguments made me feel insecure. As they always argued why the other was biblically wrong, I questioned how I could earn their love. Mental and verbal abuse became the norm that left me with emotional scars that lasted into my adulthood life.

I felt that, somehow, my parent's divorce was my fault. My feelings of worthlessness were compounded by my father, who told me I was less than wanted. To this day, I don't know if he remembers all of the things he said to me. My father's behavior influenced me to reason on the other side of the spectrum. My mother held the better promises, and that way of life seemed to offer a better future for me.

Being raised in a high-controlled environment, such as the Jehovah's Witnesses, suppresses a big piece of your life. An oppressive religion affects you in so many ways! It prevents you from becoming a well-functioning, healthy, thriving adult. Repressing your goals and dreams results in such a meaningless way of life. I was so disconnected with my true self!

Growing up as Jehovah's Witness, there was no planned goals for a career or further education. I was encouraged to set spiritual goals that were void of personal goals. The lack of family goals, as well as preventing me from discovering my true self, made life very difficult for me.

Within three months of graduating from high school, I became a regular pioneer. I dedicated over 90 hours, voluntarily, every month in the field service. I had a goal to become a missionary. To 'do more for Jehovah,' I started learning Spanish. To jump-start my missionary career, I switched to the Spanish congregation. I was so sure this was the best way of life!

Within the Jehovah's Witness religion, there's a constant pressure to do more in the organization. Despite the fact of pioneering for over six years, I struggled daily with the lack of self-worth. I felt a lack of personal direction. I felt a void that you shouldn't associate with 'the best life ever.' No matter how much I did, I felt like it wasn't good enough. I never kept the house clean enough. I didn't have enough return visits or Bible Studies. My study habits needed improvement. I didn't comment enough, and the comments I did give weren't deep enough.

I was raised to believe it's a 'sin' to have personal goals. The only goals I was allowed to have were 'spiritual' goals. As a young adult, I yearned for direction in my life. Within my inward parts laid a burning desire that, as a Jehovah's Witness, was untapped and wanted to be awakened.

As a young woman, I wanted a family of my own. I wanted to get married. However, my desire for marriage came with the condition that every Jehovah's Witness woman knows all too well. I was told the man I looked for needed to be a man with only 'spiritual, theocratic' goals in his life. It didn't matter if he was a hard worker, honest, sincere, faithful, and loyal. If he didn't have an appointment within the congregation, then he wasn't suitable marriage material.

I took an interest in someone who didn't have an appointment in the congregation. Despite his outstanding qualities, none of that mattered to anyone. He didn't fit the description that others wanted for me. Many of the Jehovah's Witnesses, including close friends of mine, discouraged me from pursuing any kind of relationship with him. They went behind his back and told me he would treat me like a slave! Many times, the discouragement and negativity were mentally taxing to me. All's I wanted was to be happy! I'm delighted to say that we've been happily married for 23 years. We've been blessed with four beautiful children. My husband is my true soulmate!

My husband came into contact with the Jehovah's Witnesses through his sister at 19-years-old. She talked to him while she was studying with the JWs. Just like my mother, my husband came in contact with the JWs at a vulnerable time in his life. He got baptized at 21-years-old and went all in. After just one month after his baptism, he started to auxiliary pioneer. After six months of auxiliary pioneering, he became a regular pioneer. After one year of pioneering, he was accepted into Bethel. After the birth of our first son, he served as a Ministerial Servant for several years. He had many responsibilities in the congregation. He visited many congregations and gave public talks. He always had work to do at the conventions. He even auxiliary pioneered when our children were young. For my husband, being a Jehovah's Witness wasn't just part of his life; it was his life.

From a young age, I dreamed of having children. As a Jehovah's Witnesses, having children was frowned upon and highly discouraged. Because of our 'spiritual' goals, we initially decided not to have children. However, that decision changed when medications counteracted with pure chemistry, and I found myself pregnant with our first child — at first, realizing that I was pregnant devastated me-but that feeling was only momentary. The thought of becoming a mother excited me!

After the birth of our first child, we decided to have more children. In disbelief, we were told it's the wrong time to raise a family because the Great Tribulation and Armageddon is coming. I can't count how many times the Jehovah's Witness elders blatantly told my husband that we were 'burdened' and 'in a mess.' We could no longer pursue 'spiritual' goals. This type of phobia indoctrination played into a lack of enjoyment of my children's lives while they were small.

As a young mother, apathy from JW elders caused me to feel very discouraged. I was afraid my children would be snatched away by the authorities during the Great Tribulation-even though there was no sign of it starting. To add insult to injury, my Jehovah's Witness mother displayed the attitude that having kids was a chore instead of a blessing. She worried more and more with each pregnancy. She expressed her concern, both in word and deed, that I couldn't fulfill my role as a mother. She never was excited any of the times I told her I was pregnant. Her fear continued to grow with each additional child and unhappy to have more grandkids. It wasn't until our children were older did my Jehovah's Witness mother start to enjoy them.

As a mother, the pressure from the organization to do more carried over into my life. My kids didn't comment enough. Congregation elders told my husband and me that our kids didn't behave well enough. Being told my kids didn't behave well enough got me in the defensive mode--as I knew elder's children's behavior was way worse. I often wondered if other adults felt this way, but they all appeared to be so happy and content. I assumed something was truly wrong with me. I often wondered how I could be the only one feeling so down in the dumps. Aren't I supposed to be one of the happiest people on the planet?

Hitting Rock Bottom

At one point in my life, I remember having such low self-worth and self-esteem that I felt that life for others would be better without me. I remember sitting there one night, feeling so worthless, that I was trying to figure out which was the best and fastest way to end my life. Should I jump in front of a speeding truck or aggravate a wild predator to charge at me? At that time, we lived in the mountains, so bears and mountain lions were always a real threat.

I felt that my husband & kids would be better off without a mom who had no direction in life. I reasoned that they would be better without someone who wasn't depressed all the time. It seemed that I was only taking up the air on this planet and that the world would be a better place without me here. I didn't want my husband nor my kids to live with a depressed wife and parent anymore. At the time, my husband had no idea how I was feeling.

I had no clue that so many people loved me. I couldn't see it at the time because my self-esteem was so low and buried under so much pain. When I finally opened up to my husband about how I felt, he pleaded with me and told me how his world would turn upside down if I weren't here anymore. He showed me how he truly loved me and helped me see that ending my life would devastate him and the kids. I am forever grateful to his foresight in knowing what to share with me at the pivotal moments when I need it the most. Throughout our marriage, my husband has continued to be a strong pillar for me!

Coming to Light

At my place of employment, one of the men in a position of authority began to harass me as well as three other women sexually. One of the women whom he harrassed was pregnant. Many of the incidents was captured on the company's video cameras. The sexual harassment I experienced took a toll on my husband and me.

My perpetrator started attending the meetings at our local congregation. My skin crawled in disgust every time he walked into the Kingdom Hall. It angered my husband. I no longer felt safe in the congregation. To protect the others, we warned the elders of this man's conduct at work. My husband and I were about to obtain a restraining order against my perpetrator.

After few weeks, the elders called my husband and me to meet with them for a meeting on this matter. To our utter shock and disbelief, the elders told us this man was an 'inactive brother,' and they were going to 'help him. The elders assigned another Witness to study the Bible with him and related to us that he was making 'good progress.'

The elders said they made a call to the organization on this matter and gave us 'council' from a Watchtower article. We were told to drop all talk and never to mention the subject to anyone else in the congregation. They informed us if we pressed charges legally, we would face discipline in the congregation.

My husband and I left the meeting with a feeling of conflict. We felt confused by what we knew was right vs. and being told something completely different from men whom I knew well. After all, I believed the holy spirit appointed the elders.

In the search for answers, I prayed for guidance to help me make the right decision. After carefully considering the matter, I decided to speak with my lawyer on this matter. He told me to run as fast as I could to get away from these men and that they were breaking the law. Looking back now, I would give the same advice to myself and anyone else. At the time, I thought, 'but this is my life, how can I believe a "worldly man" over the elders?' After all, this "worldly man" does not have the backing and direction of our Heavenly Father. Yet, somehow it also felt strangely right.

To help our special needs child receive medical treatment, we moved across the country. Unknown to me, my husband continued to search for answers. My husband had many contacts with a variety of Jehovah's Witnesses from across the country. Some of the witnesses worked at Bethel, and others were Elders whom he learned were also conflicted. My husband discovered that this sort of thing was not a rare incident. Indeed, it was happening to Jehovah's Witnesses all over the world. Many of them were dealing with abuse that was far worse than our experience.

My husband saw, with his own eyes, just how conflicted the Jehovah's Witness elders are. As you can imagine, this also caused him to feel a great deal of conflict. For about three years, my husband simply didn't feel like his usual, happy self. At the time, I wasn't quite sure what it was. My husband managed to get his hands on a variety of letters and manuals that clearly showed how Jehovah's Witness elders are instructed to handle a wide variety of cases.

When he tried to show me the documents he received, I refused to read it. Even though the information came straight from the horse's mouth, I was obstinate and refused to listen. In my mind, this was nothing but false information and lies. He experienced an internal struggle. He desired to break away but torn because he didn't want to lose the kids or me. He struggled with separating himself from the evil of the organization and his love for me and the kids. He would often tell me, 'I'm a happier person when I'm not at the meetings.' At this time, he was also recovering from a life-threatening brain injury where he lost two years of his memory.

On one occasion, at a local assembly, he had told me he just couldn't stay and decided to go home. I refused to leave the 1-day convention. I remember telling him, 'this is who I am, this is who you married and you just have to live with it.' For the rest of that day, I was sitting in the audience. I remember thinking, 'well, this is what it feels like to have an unbelieving mate.' I proceeded to cry most of the afternoon. Looking back, I can't believe I was so blind. To me, it was normal behavior and thinking. Sometimes, I still look back and often ask myself, 'how could I be so blind not to see the simple truth?' My indoctrination prevented me from seeing or accepting anything else.

Soon afterward, my husband tried a different approach by asking me analytical questions. He was very methodical, patient, and skillful with his use of questions-questions, which I couldn't answer. At this time, he was attending college and was required to take two semesters of psychology.

My husband began to apply what he learned in his psychology classes with me. He was forcing me to do something I had never done before: to think and ask questions. This new way of thinking and reasoning awakened something within myself that I never knew existed.

As you know, Jehovah's Witnesses are told not to believe anything critical of the religion. However, my husband had no interest in showing me what others say about us. His goal was merely to show me what our organization says, and this was something new to me. I trusted the organization with my life, and I never had any reason to think deeply about anything. He asked me one question, which I'll always remember, "If it can't be tested, how can it be trusted?"

I then decided to look at the organization's documents, which he obtained..and it showed me what was happening behind closed doors. Just from my knowledge of the Bible, I could see how scriptures were being misapplied. I was in awe to see, with my own eyes, how the organization taught Jehovah's Witness Elders to keep cases of murder confidential. In many cases, the Governing Body was lying, even in the court of law.

My Turning Point

During this time, I desired to start a home-based business. Initially, I just wanted to make some extra money working from home. Like many of Jehovah's Witnesses, we struggled with not having enough money because of "living a simple life." I had no idea the impact that small decision would have on me.

I began to connect with amazing people who were so positive. They had a strong passion for personal development. Within the world of Jehovah's Witnesses, self-improvement is discouraged. For the first time in my life, I was shown how to set goals. It took time for me to learn how to master the skills I learned.

I was shown a genuine, personal interest that I had never experienced as a Jehovah's Witness. My coaches showed me what real friendship is and that it's possible to have a genuine friendship that's not based on a mere handshake. I was soaking in this new feeling. I met people who were truly interested in me as a person. For the first time in my life, I now had real friends. Initially, I was still apprehensive. I asked myself, 'should I get close to these people? I mean, they are worldly.' Their continued support, along with their patience, really encouraged me to continue learning more. My new gurus had no clue of how they were impacting my life. At first, I didn't even notice the change that was happening within myself.

My coaches encouraged me to read personal development books such as Tony Robbins' "Awaken the Giant Within" and "Unlimited Power." Starting to read these kinds of books unlocked a person within me that I never even knew existed. Reading "The Big Leap," by Gay Hendricks helped me see the mental barriers that were blocking me from attaining my goals. I began to see that I had a power that was deep within myself, which I could harness to create amazing changes in my life. I was now starting to desire something more than just a hope for Paradise. I never told any Jehovah's Witnesses that I was reading these books. Within Jehovah's Witnesses, any material that teaches you how to think or reason is highly discouraged. Our reading and relationships revolved around the Jehovah's Witnesses publications. However, my husband was of great encouragement to me to continue reading my personal development books. To this day, he tells me he knew what the end result would be.

Starting to Use Analytical Thinking

As I continued my personal development training, my husband continued to ask me analytical questions. My new, emerging thinking abilities forced me to reason on matters. I remember telling my mom that I couldn't support how the Governing body instructs elders to keep murder and child abuse 'confidential.' In her earnest effort to keep me under the radar, she told me, "things happen for a reason, and we have to let Jehovah handle it. He will take care of it in his time." However, I reasoned, 'by allowing the lawsuits and authorities to see what was being hidden, maybe Jehovah is taking care of it.'

Being the spiritual person that I am, I was afraid to let go. Having experienced the other side of religion, I feared there was no other 'truth.' I was scared to leave the Jehovah's Witnesses!

I felt stuck and unsure where the future would lead me to. I was feeling anger towards myself for giving so many years of my life to something fake, untrue, and deceptive. How could I allow myself to be deceived for so many years? How could I be so dumb? Why couldn't I see the deception when my husband tried to talk to me about it? Here I was: a grown adult. I'm supposed to know right from wrong. I'm a mother of 4 children whom I guide through this world and help them become healthy adults. However, I had no idea how the world worked. I had no clue how to teach my children about setting realistic, attainable goals. I was barely learning personal development myself, and I had years of catching up to do.

With no clear direction in life, it was almost worse than just having a spiritual goal only. Now, I realized I was truly lost. We knew we could no longer remain Jehovah's Witnesses. However, we continued to attend meetings and participate in the ministry. I felt torn between leaving the Jehovah's Witnesses and going into a world of unanswered questions. I was fearful of the unknown.

What Should We Do?

My husband and I had a discussion that stuck with me. I asked him, "If we leave all of this, where will we go?" He responded, "That is not what Peter asked. Peter asked, ``To whom shall we go?'" That question put me in my tracks. It opened my eyes and my mind. It allowed me to see this religion held no ultimate value over anything else other than the number of people attending.

As the weeks melted into months, we noticed we weren't getting any value from staying in the religion. The structure of the meetings seems to model more of a business now. During this time, I began to attend network marketing meetings, and I could see the similarities in the meetings of Jehovah's Witnesses. On one occasion, we walked through a shopping mall. As we exited the mall, we noticed two shoe salespeople who were standing next to their display of shoes. The similarities between the shoe salesman's display and the Jehovah's Witness cart display was surprising! The only difference between the two booths was the products. I was volunteering my time to a business that was operating in the name of religion.

We decided to leave as a family-all 6 of us. I was not going to allow an institution that had no real interest in me to destroy our family. From that time forward, we began to plan our exodus out of the Jehovah's Witnesses. To everyone who knew us, we were a 'spiritual' family that attended meetings and participated in the door-to-door work. However, behind the scenes, we researched everything we could on how to leave a high-controlled environment. The two semesters of psychology training my husband at college were of tremendous help.

Our family had phone conversations with therapists who dealt with people leaving tough situations. We studied everything we could on emotional control and how to break free from an abusive institution. My husband did a great deal of study on dealing with narcissists. We researched how to let go of the anger and hurt we had inside and how to create a positive environment around us. Our goal was to make the transition so that, when we did leave, we wouldn't sink into a depressed state. As a family, we realized we had outgrown the people who were in our lives, and it was time to let them go. Bear in mind, all of this took place while still attending meetings regularly, so no one knew what we were planning on doing.

We begin developing close relationships and friendships with people outside the organization.

Becoming close to someone and learning how to make real relationships with someone not in the organization went against every ounce of my being. It was a new skill I had to learn. On many occasions, I felt like a fraud because I was supposed to know already how to have just a regular conversation with other people. In reality, I had no clue how to converse with everyday, normal people. Taking the time to learn that it's ok to spend lunch or dinner with other people was utterly foreign to me. I had to learn how to talk about every day, regular life in general. I had to learn how to make real conversation with real people. At first, making changes was hard. Thankfully, I had one friend that I was able to get close enough to. When I told her what we as a family was doing, she became even closer to me. Ever since then, she's been my go-to friend!

We also obtained legal advice on what we could do if the Jehovah's Witnesses began to stalk us. We learned that we had every right to legally protect ourselves by requesting a cease and desist letter from a lawyer. We also knew that since they are all about control, we had the power to take that control away from them by refusing to meet with them in their "committee." We put up 'no trespassing' signs up on the house, and this prevented them from coming to visit us. We installed security cameras on our property to monitor any illegal activity from the Elders.

When we finally stopped going to the meetings, it took about four weeks for the elders to start calling us. I refused to answer the phone or text back to them. Then one day, because I was at work, I was unable to look to see who was calling and I answered the phone. During this conversation, I found out that they had been profoundly stalking me on social media. They wanted to meet in a committee with me over a comment I had put, tagging someone on a different Bible app. (Yea, huge disfellowshipping offense, right?) I told him that I was at work and since it was the busy season, I couldn't meet. The elder refused to take that as an answer. I said that, because I was at work, I would go home and talk it over with my husband. The elder wasn't expecting the conversation that hence ensued.

We called the elder back from my phone. Before leaving, we changed the home phone number, so they didn't have our new home number. The elder answered the phone; only this time, it was my husband who talked to him. When my husband inquired why they wanted to meet with me, they refused to tell him. My husband's reply was, 'unless you tell me why you need to meet with my wife, she will not meet with you.'

During the conversation, my husband quoted from the elder's manual... you could have heard a pin drop. He shed light on how an elder can commit adultery and never receive discipline for his immoral behavior. After all, my husband wasn't supposed to know the information he quoted! Jehovah's Witnesses love to control every aspect of your life. They don't want their members having access to information. The control of information is one of the signs of a high-controlled group.

The time had come to show that, as a family, we have boundaries. No longer would we allow a narcissistic religion to disrespect our boundaries. My husband told the elders they were not allowed to call, visit, or send us certified letters. He informed the elder that we wanted no further contact with them. Failure to honor our wishes would result in a criminal prosecution against the elders.

The following Monday, we contacted our lawyer and had him send a 'cease-and-desist' letter to the congregation, informing them to cease-and-desist in contacting us. We have not heard from them since. That was over a year ago. However, it was recently brought to our attention that our names were announced at a meeting that we are no longer Jehovah's Witnesses. On occasion, we see different JWs slowly drive by the house to "check in on us.' We've also received some 'highly suspicious' Facebook messages from people who seem to be 'out of place.' We laugh at the drama!

You have the Power to Proclaim Your Life

To prevent people from harassing us, my husband blocked every single Jehovah's Witness that he knows on social media. At first, I wanted to let them see I haven't changed one bit by allowing them to see me on social media. I wanted to show them I have nothing to hide. However, I quickly realized that it was a useless endeavor. So, I took their power away by blocking them too.

We decided not to meet with the JW elders. After all, what good would it do? In the world of Jehovah's Witnesses, you always feel like you have to explain yourself. As a JW, nothing is private in your life. However, we are no longer under the power of a man-made institution. We no longer play by their rules. The only book we need is the Bible.

When you set personal boundaries with JW elders, it confuses them. When you set boundaries and take power away from any Jehovah's Witnesses, it puts them in their tracks. You can make a conscious decision to reclaim your life. When you set boundaries, they have no clue what to do other than to stalk you. Within the world of narcissism, the goal of the narcissist is compliance. You no longer have any need to conform to their rules. These men don't own you. Never feel guilty for setting your own standards. Apart from the religion, JW elders have no clue who they are as a person. We view this whole process as one big chess game. As a family, we had the pleasure of telling the Jehovah's Witnesses 'checkmate.'

One of the first steps to reclaiming your life is to realize that you don't need to answer to other people's demands. Please don't confuse this with the need to respond to people, such as your employer or your spouse. There are times that we need to report to others. However, when it comes to personal matters, these are decisions that you make. There's no need to ask permission or explain to anyone who's not involved.

Like many religions, Jehovah's Witnesses provide a need... but that doesn't mean they set you free. For example, in the world of Islam, they offer men who join the movement with a wide variety of things--such as a wife. However, what happens to a person who decides they want to leave Islam? The penalty for leaving Islam is the death penalty. Jehovah's Witnesses don't try to behead anyone as Islam does, but they will still do everything in their power to cut you off at the knees.

One thing we've noticed with many former JWs is that they don't prepare themselves to leave the organization. They haven't prepared themselves for a world that's completely different from the world they know. For many years, they've lived inside of a box. They have no clue how to continue daily life without someone telling them what to think, feel, or how to reason. You can compare this to a person who moves to a different country, and suddenly, there's no electricity or running water. You have no idea how to operate without the personal electronics you've used for your entire life. You've never learned how to purify water. You're in the dark, and you feel disconnected from the world around you. This is the essence of being institutionalized, and it's one of the many reasons why you need to make preparations before leaving the religion. Before leaving the JWs, our family created new friendships. We had a new support system in place. As a family, we even knew where we would go to worship. All of this was planned before our departure. As a family, we remained united. We defeated a multi-million dollar corporation called 'Jehovah's Witnesses' in every way imaginable, and it's a very empowering feeling.

My Past Does Not Define Me, and Neither Does It Define You.

As I reflect on my life as a witness, I realize that all things happen for a reason. The departure from the religion comes with great sacrifice. To this day, my mother shuns me and wants nothing to do with our family anymore. On one occasion, our car broke down on the side of the road. The hour was late, and the weather was cold. Unbelievably, my mother was upset that our beloved friends in our newfound faith came to our aid and provided money, as well as a warm place to stay until our car got fixed. Even though her grandchildren were rescued from the cold, it didn't phase her at all. Our family doesn't need that type of psychological abuse in our lives. We can say, without hesitation, that our entire family is far happier now than we've ever been as Jehovah's Witnesses.

The experience of leaving the JWs has made me into the person who I am today. If I hadn't left the JWs, I wouldn't have the focus to be so in-depth with personal growth, nor would I have the desire to help others so profoundly. I've become relentless with my personal growth. I genuinely enjoy helping others who are in need. These are some of the many things that I would never have learned without leaving the

JWs. It has shaped me for who I am today, but it doesn't control me. My departure from the JWs awakened a person inside of me that I didn't even know existed.

Learn to overcome and outgrow what you have lived in the past. You are who you are today because of your history. Your past doesn't control you, nor does it define what you are capable of accomplishing in life. You have something to offer that no one else possesses. You are strong and unique! What you've gone through hasn't killed you–it made you stronger! You are a fighter! You are a survivor! You have continued to make each day better than before. Believe me when I tell you: some days are hard. However, you took action and decided to leave the control of a narcissistic institution. You are becoming stronger every day than those who know simple truths but won't leave. It takes a special person to go against the grain. In fact, studies show there's a danger with following the crowd–and that makes you a special person!

If you are someone who's thinking about leaving the JWs, start by developing relationships with people outside the box. Connect with those who live the kind of life you want to live. Become close to them. Learn from them. Study their habits. Learn how they think and take action to duplicate their work. Study their skills and their life. Let them in on your goal of leaving and let them help you make the transition. You would be surprised at how many people around you are willing to help. If you don't know anyone close enough in your area, find someone that you respect. Read their books and listen to their videos. Get to know their thought processes. Study how they have created a life worth living.

Before leaving the religion, you need to prepare yourself to let people go. During my mom's last visit, my husband told me, 'this is the last time I'll ever see your mother alive.' My husband prepared us for the backlash that was to come--and it did come. Thank goodness for his two semesters of psychology training in college! When the backlash did arrive, it didn't bother us as much as it would have if we didn't plan before leaving. Our kids had already formed new friends, and they weren't affected by the losses. Looking back now, our kids comment that the JWs were never their friends, to begin with, so letting them go worked towards their benefit. If we stayed in the religion, would our children have the friends that now have?

Take control of your life from the start. Put up no trespassing signs on your property and block everyone on social media. Set healthy boundaries, and don't give in to the elder's misguided direction to control your life. You are in charge, not them. Read personal growth books like the ones I mentioned. Watch the documentaries of people who have created success in their life. All these things will help you progress from feeling hurt and angry to building a beautiful, full, and happy life. Get a life coach that will teach you how to develop in the areas in life you lack. For any former JW, a coach who I highly recommend is Rodney Allgood. He has an incredible amount of experience in helping former JWs make the successful transition out of the religion. He offers courses to help you make the transition into everyday life. His classes are available at a very modest price. Realize you can only grow so far on your own, so take advantage of the resources that are available to you.

Make connections with people you know. Develop a real relationship with someone. Let them know where you are coming from, and you need help to heal. There are people out there who genuinely care and want to help you. The worst thing to do is to try to repair the damage on your own. A sick person can't get better without a doctor. No matter how much you think you know, you can't fully heal all by yourself. Despite my husband's medical background, and the knowledge that he had that helped us to leave successfully, some things trigger him. He wisely reached out and received the proper help. Realize what you're feeling is perfectly normal. After all, we're only human!

My husband tells me his life-threatening brain injury changed his perspective on many things. Do you think he woke up that morning, expecting to fall and hit the back of his head on ice? He states the recuperation process taught him we can spend too much time worrying about things that aren't as important as we think. He's grateful to be alive, and he counts his blessings. Life is too precious to allow JW drama to have control over your life.

Begin reading experiences about people who have overcome similar situations. Personal development and self-improvement books, like the ones I mentioned, will help you with your mindset shift. Also, take classes (whether online or at the community college) on managing your finances. This will help with improving the areas you lack in with money. Learn from people, like Dave Ramsey, on how to build and grow your finances. The knowledge he offers can help you to find the best way to improve your financial future. And don't expect your life to improve overnight. This is something that takes time. Rather than thinking short-term, keep your focus on long-term commitments. The Roman Empire wasn't built in one day!

An essential aspect you need to address (whether your just beginning to leave or are entirely out of the religion) is your spiritual needs. Leaving the religion feels like someone just pulled the rug from underneath your feet! We can say, in all honesty, that our biblical knowledge is 100 fold beyond what it ever was as a Jehovah's Witness. My mother hated it when I began using Yahweh's name! It's incredible to see a religion, who puts so much emphasis on using the name, bash my family for using the correct name! If anything, her behavior only fortified my convictions.

Whatever you decide to fill your spiritual needs, make sure the decision is coming from you. Don't allow anyone to manipulate you into believing something. Do your research, and never allow anyone to 'spoon-feed' you. As previously stated, if a teaching can't be tested, then how can it be trusted?

Believe me when I tell you: there will be plenty of bad days that await you. Putting things in perspective will help you to take one day at a time. You aren't the villain--you're a victim of a high-controlled group who did everything in its power to control your B.I.T.E model. During those times when I did have a bad day, I remembered the old country way of dancing. It's called the 2-step method: 2 steps forward and one step back. Learn, grow, and take a step back to have the time to digest what you learn.

Overcoming what we've all experienced isn't easy, and there's no quick answer. As my husband says, you have to be prepared to leave the religion the same way you came in. When he became a JW, he experienced fierce family opposition. Isn't it ironic that he experienced the same backlash on his way out? The funny thing is he's very close now with the same family members who at one time opposed him! He experienced the previous backlash in the past from the immediate family. Therefore, the cold treatment from the JWs didn't bother him as much. Growing up, my husband played a lot of sports, and he says the mindset that came with the competition helped him to withstand the backlash.

Remember, you're on a journey, so give it some time. Trust in the process. Be patient with yourself. In our modern world of instant gratification, having patience is one of the hardest things for former JWs to have. Realize that personal development takes time to develop. There are no shortcuts. And when you feel yourself slipping, do not stay down on yourself. Acknowledge what you feel and look for the positive in your situation. Each small step taken builds on another small step!

The rich get richer due to the power of compounding interest! Let the recovery process compound until you have a mountain under you. Initially, you won't feel like your making any progress. However, with time, your new foundation will become visible--especially to those from the outside. Jehovah's Witnesses who are no longer in your life won't listen to anything you say, but you can bet your bottom dollar they watch what you do! Make a conscious decision to change your mindset, and I can assure you that you will change your life. History is full of examples of courageous people who overcame unbelievable challenges in life. You are capable of so much in this life! Out of 10,000 sperm cells, you beat the odds! You are here, alive, and reading this because you have a purpose.

Where are We Today?

As a family, we took something back that every high-controlled group seeks to take from their members. We reclaimed the power of decision. The power of making decisions is something that lies within all of us. May I remind you that our journey began with one decision!

Today, our family is happy, healthy, and thriving. This year, I'll complete my Health & Life Coach Certification. Upon completing my certification, my husband and I are opening a private membership school that focuses on personal development. Currently, we're in the early stages of creating additional courses and audiobooks for our Health & Wellness blog. At this exact time, public schools and places of employment are requesting that I speak to their employees and students on personal development.

My husband operates a full-time Health & Wellness blog that receives over 60,000 views every month. Readers from countries such as New Zealand, Australia, the United Kingdom consume his content, and many are listening weekly to our podcast.

Also, my husband is an avid bicyclist who has a passion for riding, plyometrics, and psychology. As I speak, he's training to make his appearance on the national BMX racing circuit. His love for bicycles has helped him to create amazing friendships. Now, our kids want to join the BMX racing fun too!

As parents, my husband and I have empowered our children with the same power that we have: the power of decision. Our kids are no longer under the umbrella of a corporate empire. Through much pain and sacrifice, we've provided our children with the tools to ensure they'll never get sucked into another high-controlled group ever again.

I have a genuine smile and a deep sparkle of satisfaction and fulfillment in my eyes. My sense of self-worth is secure, and I'm passionate about helping others learn how to overcome their limitations. After living forty-two years under the thumb of an organization that had no personal interest in me, it took a while to gather myself up and find out who I truly am.

For the first time in my life, I am truly happy. Looking at my life now, I have real value and a reason for living. We have the purpose of making a difference in the world. Eight years ago, I would have said that unless Armageddon came, that feeling of self-worth and confidence would not be possible. Even as an adult, I had no clue who I was. I believed attaining true happiness wasn't possible unless Armageddon happened. Today, I know what my purpose is. As a Jehovah's Witness, my smile was superficial. Today, my satisfaction and joy stem from deep within myself.

Yes, the Jehovah's Witnesses are right: Better is the end of a thing than the beginning!

For additional information on how to improve your mindset, visit us at: www.KoolKatHealth.com

Chapter 15

Escaping My Cocoon

How I Found My Wings

by Rose Smith

"Feel the Fear and Do It Anyway"
-Susan Jeffers

I slap my face to stay awake. My daughter and brother are fast asleep. I crank up the music, nodding in and out, struggling to keep my eyes open. *If only I can make it to the next exit… if I can get a drink, I can stay awake…* Relieved... I see an exit sign.

The sudden impact of my car hitting tough metal wakes me. Praying, *please let my daughter and brother be alive!*

My car was totaled, the cruise set on 75, crossing the median and four lanes of highway before colliding with a guard rail. What started out as an enjoyable trip to the science museum turned into a disaster. Miraculously no other vehicles were on the road, and none of us were seriously injured. A few weeks before, desperate I checked myself into a Crisis unit; I wanted the mental & physical anguish to go away. The medicine left me numb and in a fog. What happened for my life to be in such turmoil? Would I ever escape this nightmare and have a happy life?

Building My Cocoon

If only I had the strength to get out of bed.

Leading up to my breakdown, my bedroom had become my safe zone. In my twenties, the chatter in my head was relentless; blame, guilt and unworthiness. My hair was falling out. Itchy, red rashes covered my scalp, causing bald spots, only prescription shampoo could calm. Being on one antibiotic after another, starting as asthma, then bronchitis and pneumonia. I developed malignant melanoma. DCIS Breast cancer came later. Almost bleeding to death twice, once with toxemia while giving birth, and once during an ectopic pregnancy. I passed out from blood loss and was rushed into surgery. I feared an accident, and bleeding to death, leaving my daughter without a mother. Jehovah's Witnesses don't take blood, even in an emergency. I seemed to attract near death experiences. I was in an unhealthy place mentally and physically, but I was no stranger to hardship, as this all started early in my life.

Generations of GOO

My three siblings and I were raised in a family of dysfunction. Our parents were a product of their dysfunctional upbringing. Mom walked miles in Jehovah's Witness missionary work with her mom and siblings. Her dad died at an early age, so food came from the people, whose homes they knocked on. Mom, obsessed with religion, put her family last. My dad's father was an alcoholic, so dad was left to scavenge in garbage dumpsters. Leaving home at an early age, with the dream of becoming rich, my father became a workaholic. He would burn mom's religious literature for spite. Incompatible, they divorced when I was five. Bitter custody battles followed.

At a young age, I had hospital stays with pneumonia. When I reached 12, I was prescribed depression drugs that basically kept me comatose.

Mom was in and out of mental institutions, so I suffered in silence, as to not upset her. Being dissatisfied, she moved a lot, to the projects, in with relatives, and even people we just met. I was forced to take on the caregiver role due to her panic attacks, depression, anxiety, bipolar and multiple back surgeries. Mom also suffered unexplained body convulsions, but tests would show nothing wrong. She cried behind closed doors, putting on a happy face at the Kingdom Hall. Many Witnesses are plagued with unexplained physical and emotional conditions. My uncle, a devout member, appeared happy; he hung himself following treatment for depression. His condition hidden due to shame; we were supposed to be a happy people. The suicide rate is five to ten times above average. The effects of a stressful childhood cause structural, maladaptive changes in the brain, in the functioning of the immune system, and in the ability to respond to stress, leading to disease.

After school, I prepared for three Kingdom Hall meetings a week and for field service. I had to help make ends meet with cleaning and babysitting jobs. We were always encouraged to do more to gain God's approval. I put in 60 hours a month knocking on doors during school breaks to spread the good news. Putting on my happy face, I hid the pain of my broken family. I longed to watch cartoons on Saturday, instead of fearing a classmate answering my knock. Our only goals were advancing in the preaching work as a pioneer or free labor at Bethel. The end of the world was always right around the corner. Being reminded we all fall short many times in the eyes of Jehovah, I never felt good enough to survive Armageddon. I feared being unfaithful during persecution with my nightmares of torture with spiders. I felt extreme sadness my worldly friends would be destroyed.

I craved to fit in and be normal, but had to sit in the hallway or library by myself during holiday parties. I felt like a traitor, all eyes on me, sitting during the Pledge of Allegiance every day. I wanted to play in the band, participate in sports, to dress up pretty for the prom, and go to college. I wanted anything but to be cleaning toilets. Once, a teacher saved me a bag of Valentines after missing a party. The decorated Valentines, with my name on them, made me feel special like I fit in. I hid them and looked at them daily. Feeling guilty I was being watched by Jehovah or that someone would find out, reluctantly I threw them away.

Giving My Family a Voice

Mother obsessed with reading her bible, did whatever the elders asked her to do, even not protecting her children. My 14-year-old sister was raped by a married member with children. The elders disfellowshipped both, without reporting to police. Seeing him at the meetings was continual trauma. I wasn't allowed to eat or talk with my sister, excommunication with disfellowshipped family members being an unfortunate reality in the religion. The abuser was accepted back with open arms (literally) from the congregation and my own mother. He attempted to molest me, I reported it, but it went ignored. The ignorance sickened me. I couldn't protect my sister, and later in life wasn't allowed to meet my nephews. As a Juvenile Detention investigator, my sister gets confessions from high profile sex offenders but is too traumatized to face her **own** abuser to find her **own** justice, despite fighting for other victims. If only she had someone to stand up for her. Where were the morals to protect the innocence of a child?

Waking Up

After I married, my loyalty to the religion faded. The injustice for my sister haunted me. The world predicted to end on five different occasions didn't make sense. Having children was considered selfish, with the end right around the corner. If I had obeyed, I wouldn't have my 26-year-old daughter, who also suffered trauma from childhood. She wrote a memoir reflecting on the gory illustrations of people dying in the *My Book of Bible Stories*. Not wanting my daughter to miss out on holidays, I threw parties but did not call them birthday parties. I wrapped "Christmas" gifts in snowman paper (nothing too worldly, like Santa Claus) and hid them around the house for a scavenger hunt, rather than under a tree. My life was a façade.

My husband was a homebody, not liking travel. Adventure was my passion. Marrying young, we didn't even know who we were or that we were incompatible. Not allowed to leave my unhappy marriage, due to the religious beliefs, short trips to the beach were an escape. A childhood friend, Shawnna and I began taking our daughters during school breaks. Creating a pathway to freedom. Openly questioning our beliefs without fear of judgement or worry of being told on. In our rebellion, we decided to get hidden tattoos to symbolize our freedom; she got a palm tree and I got a sun. We felt energized and at peace by the ocean. It was like we met God there every trip. A true spiritual rebirth.

Shunned-2005

Suddenly, my whole world came crumbling down. The business I worked hard to build with my husband was failing and we struggled financially. My father in law was dying and my marriage was ending. I felt the predictions of failure by the religion had come true. Stress became too heavy, and I checked myself into the Crisis Facility. Hearing my father call my mom crazy, I avoided treatment until I couldn't function. I didn't want to carry that crazy label but ended up with a list of diagnoses; clinical depression, panic disorder, ADD, social and generalized anxiety and PTSD. As part of treatment, I was given affirmations to say while looking in mirror to build my confidence, because I was told this was one of my biggest problems. I didn't even like myself. I begrudgingly did the affirmations one time.

Then the horrific accident took place. The elders never checked on us, despite knowing our marriage was suffering, and my mental health was weak. Shortly following my breakdown, my fifteen-year marriage came to an end. My husband's family, the closest I knew to a real support system, was now gone. Suddenly, the elders wanted to meet to discuss rekindling my marriage. I had been jaded for twenty years, where were they when I desperately needed them? They ignored previous cries for help my entire life, only getting involved whenever it pertained to someone else's suffering. Angry at all the wrongdoing, I declined. The announcement that I was disfellowshipped was made in front of the entire congregation. It was as if I was wearing a huge red stamp that said "BAD ASSOCIATION" across my forehead.

My mom no longer could talk to me, unless about business. This destroyed me. The congregation expected me to continue to care for her, but not connect with her. I did it out love, not obligation. She took down pictures of me, which completely broke my heart. Even though I saw witness friends in public, we couldn't even acknowledge one another. It felt ruthless, and unnatural. Shunning is one of the emotional and mental tactics used to scare members into remaining loyal. In the first five minutes of ostracism, basic human needs are threatened, separating children from their parents. Many young people can't deal with the existential grief of loss and sadly take their own life.

My heart was aching with rejection and abandonment like I suffered from my father. I was lost. Nobody was there to tell me what to do next, making my own decisions alone seemed overwhelming. At the age of forty, I began to live my teenage years that I had never experienced. I found myself in codependent, unhealthy relationships. I was afraid to be alone and rejected again, drinking to numb my pain. I'm grateful to be alive after my drunken stupors; alcohol had contributed in the deaths of two of my cousins, who were also shunned.

Awakened-June 2013

I was leaving on a two week backpack trip to Costa Rica for my sister's birthday. Tears of fear for all the unknown ahead of us streamed down my face. On the trip, I tried things that scared me like ziplining, class five white water rapids, and propelling. It was invigorating in a way that I had never felt before. I reflected how happy I was, content with only limited possessions in my backpack, some used, and some ignored. Then, a miraculous event occurred while standing in the waters of Isla del Coco, where *Jurassic Park* was filmed. I was embraced by a warm light and feelings of unconditional love and peace. It was as if time stood still, and I felt like a different person in the same body. I could breathe easier. I saw more vibrant color. There was a sense of calm that I had never felt before. Not knowing this was my great spiritual awakening.

I not only arrived home from my adventure ten pounds physically lighter, but there was an internal weight that had been lifted. There was an urgent need to declutter my mind and space, to live without what was unnecessary. I surrendered my struggle to find my truth and inner light. I researched online, finding comfort and clarity to help with the aftereffects of child sexual abuse, domestic violence, suicide, and emotional damage from extreme shunning. AAWA.co (Advocates for Awareness of Watchtower Abuses), silentlambs.org, and stories by former witnesses were my gateway to a new world. I shook while I typed, reverting back to old belief systems and patterns that had to be broken. I wasn't prepared for the release of tears from years of suppression that held me prisoner. What were my spiritual beliefs now? I had the freedom to make that decision.

I am Loved –April 2014

My daughter had been my world. When she left to college, I felt alone. The brainwashing chatter stuck in my head. *I deserve this. Nothing will go right.* Paralyzed in fear, not wanting anyone to know the shame, guilt, and deep depression I felt. I wouldn't leave the house fearing seeing friends who wouldn't speak. I closed the curtains of my dark cocoon and gasped for air. I was screaming to speak, but there was only silence. I feared living and dying. I wanted to feel alive and loved, but how could anyone love me, if God even disowned me? Why was I stuck after leaving everything behind to live the life I wanted? Why try to succeed, if failure was inevitable? Did I have a purpose?

I was a total mess, standing in my dark bedroom. I was taught God would no longer hear my prayers after I left my religion, desperately I began to plead, *"If you can hear my prayers God, give me a sign or do something great in my life as proof."*

That week I was led to *Feel the Fear and Do It Anyway* by Susan Jeffers. This book would completely change my reality. Susan spoke directly to my situation, ways to cope with fear, and to silence the programming chatter echoing in my brain. Words of love and positivity. I could love myself and not be haughty or conceited. It was a brand-new concept, thought of as selfish as a Witness. Using affirmations and exercises, slowly my thoughts changed from pain and self-doubt to empowered and excited about life. My heart opened and a light shined in the darkness. I threw out my old journals with the trash from a road trip, in a nearly full McDonalds Drive thru in the middle of nowhere Texas. Replacing the doom and gloom with a new gratitude diary. Wanting to share what I learned from Susan Jeffers, I bought 10 used, yellow paged, copies for friends and gifted them. This was starting over.

> *"God loves me and listens to my prayers. I'm helping others and it feels good that my life has true meaning."*
> - An excerpt from my journal

Angels

Planning my move to Florida, I canceled a paid for cruise that I was to go on that week. I contacted Susan's company, to reach out how her book had changed my life, and I wanted to help domestic violence survivors. Susan passed away a year before, but her husband directed me to Dora Carpenter. There was an instant soul connection over the phone. She encouraged me to write a book and be one of the five to keep Susan's work alive, I started a two month *Feel the Fear and Do it Anyway,* mentorship program. It was divine timing as my move was in two months, and I needed all the help I could get.

As a group, we began carrying on conference calls, homework assignments, and sharing our challenges and wins. Even being put on the spot on my birthday to visualize speaking to an audience at my book signing. I was nervous, but Dora gave me confidence. This had been a stranger who believed in me, when I couldn't believe in myself. She loved me for who I was, not conditionally due to religion. No strings attached, with no expectations in return. Dora continued to walk beside me in my most difficult days ahead. *When the student is ready, the teacher will appear.* One event or one person can change your life forever. It was as if she was put in my path to help me find my truth.

And the Truth Shall Set You Free

Lori Morgan stood in front of us to sign the guest book. Accompanying a friend to a funeral, instead of being excited over a celebrity, my mind raced with guilt. Guilt because attending a service with a worldly preacher was supposed to be of the Devil. Pre-conditioned thoughts filled my mind, but surprisingly I heard happy, inspiring words. Confused and overcome with mixed emotions, I couldn't control the waterfall of tears. A week later, a friend lost her sister in law and eight nieces and nephews in a tragic house fire. The father of the children, a preacher, did his own tribute to his family. The sermon, music, and overall feeling of the service was of love and acceptance. I felt guilt but was moved more by the love in the room, tears flowing down my face.

I left feeling peaceful like I was floating. I don't remember ever feeling this at the Kingdom Hall. Feeling the Holy Spirit was considered bad. How could this, like my experience in Costa Rica, be bad? How could two sad occasions make me feel so good? As I walked into a church for the first-time, with my childhood friend, fear burdened me. Again, the love and spirit were undeniable. My first hands on healing was like nothing I had ever experienced; release of buried pain and hurt. *Break Every Chain* played, feeling it was created just for me. I used to fear ridicule and betrayal for leaving my beliefs, but now I wanted to help others free their pain. I wanted to come out of hiding and to break my silence. I no longer felt oppression but felt genuinely free.

Finding My Truth–August 2014

Before hitting the road, Dora surprised me with a gifted copy of her new book *Staging Your Life,* cowritten with her daughter, Christina. Another moment of divine timing, as it served as a roadmap of inspiration to illuminate my new path starting over. Becoming a mentor, I gained the courage and confidence to act on the callings of my soul. I set out on a journey to Florida, the place I had originally began my spiritual awakening all those years ago. I was finding my authentic truth to offer my gifts to the world. I left behind my familiar life, most of my belongings. I didn't know where I would work, live, or who I would meet. Little did I know then how much of a struggle this would be, and the strength I would gain.

At one point, I was in paradise sobbing at random times. I expected sadness when shedding old beliefs, but I was supposed to be happy now. I questioned if I made the right decision and felt like a failure. Dora explained this was perfectly normal when letting go, and she gifted me her online grief course. I had left behind more than I realized: a relationship, friends, a daughter, home, comfort zone, and my past. Even 2% of unresolved grief can affect every area of your life. I let my grief wash out to sea.

Spiritual teachers came one after another. I gained inspiration listening to Wayne Dyer and Louise Hay, who suffered traumatic childhoods, and used what they learned to help others. Susan, Wayne, and Louise were my Hay House tribe, each discovered at the perfect time. Opening my mind, I visualized what I wanted my life to look like, as if it was already happening. I discovered a high school friend lived in the same area, working in the domestic violence field. I started to manifest what I needed and desired. Angels appeared to lead the way. While attending a victim advocacy meeting, I met Allie, who wept hearing me say I arrived on faith with my car packed down. She had been released from the hospital an hour before, but she had to make it to that night's meeting no matter what. She said I was the person she was supposed to meet. Allie was a childhood abuse survivor, who started *Be the Voice,* to help others speak their truth. Perfect timing. That same night I was invited to her church, the only Caucasian, and I stood up to give my testimony. Trembling due to my fear of speaking, but I was free.

I received my Domestic Violence Rape & Victim Advocate Certification. As Witnesses, we weren't allowed to volunteer for causes we believed in, so going to court helping victims with restraining orders and helping at the shelter was beyond rewarding. I could relate with my lack of self-confidence, due to the religion and my parent's violence. Hanging posters for a Domestic Violence event, I saw myself in the poster. I had been hiding behind my mask of my past, and I pictured taking my mask off to be my authentic self.

Miracles happened before my eyes. Renting a room, the renter and her young daughter both resembled my daughter, and I became an adopted parent. More divine timing. While looking for a job at the Children's Advocacy Center, I met Gail, who I bonded instantly with. She asked if I needed a room to rent, someone was moving out. I had slept in my car the night before in 100-degree temperature. I rented until I wanted my own place, I put a prayer request in a tackle box at Sharkey's church service on the ocean. I visualized a view with a palm tree and a beach. Turning off the last street by St Andrews Park, I saw a U-shaped building with eight numbered doors, someone had just moved out the day before. My apt had a view of a palm out each window and beach view. I even had a soul connection with my landlord, also wanting to write a book, and gave me a job cleaning condos.

With my prayers and positive beliefs, I was manifesting. My neighbor, a hurricane Katrina survivor, recognized Gail from the newspaper and started crying. She once had a nonprofit and delivered furniture to him, he never got to thank her. Everything was truly coming full circle. Ten minutes after giving cupcakes to my neighbor, I thought I would love to have a wind chime. That same neighbor came with a tangled wind-chime, offering if I would want it. A homeless lady asked if I had been to the Catholic Charities. I thought it odd and dismissed it, until I was at the Career Center working on my resume, when staff asked if I've spoken to Robin at Catholic Charities. Meeting her, I found out she had also wanted to write a book and we became friends. She gave me odd and end furniture I needed, including a desk. My landlord also helped fill in the rest of the items I needed. My air mattress sprung a leak, after sleeping on the floor for a month, my sister blessed me with a bed.

I attended a church I had an attraction to on previous trips as a Witness. I experienced a hands-on healing and began to participate in miracles. The preacher and his wife were from a town only an hour from mine. At my first meetup group, I met a Laura who had just moved an hour from my hometown. Both newbies, we went on a sailboat wine cruise and became instant friends. *Just what we both needed.* I attracted what I wanted and realized I had attracted unwanted experiences in my past with focus on worry and fear. If I continued to think positively, the relationships and material items I needed would slowly start to take care of themselves.

To be able to make my own decisions, without judgement, seemed unreal. I started marking off my bucket list, exploring new cultural concepts and keeping what resonated. I attended many churches and a baptism in the ocean, attended hobby groups and classes. I obtained my reiki certification, attended a prantic and crystal healing course, Buddhist meditation, and even a new moon meditation circle on the beach. These would have been considered spiritism to the Witnesses, especially since Smurfs and Scooby Doo were considered Demonized.

Without having internet or TV, and poor cell phone reception, I spent a lot of time outdoors. I slowed down to notice the little things. I went on a canoe and camping trip, road my bike along the coast, took photos, listened to bands, beach yoga, and paddle boarding. I worked on my book and read a new testament bible a friend gave me. My 3 am nightly walks on the beach were my favorite, as I connected with God. The star filled night sky brought me peace and grounding. I was in awe, seeing five shooting stars one night, deer jumping from the park onto the white sand beach, and enjoyed hanging out in the water with a crane I named Ted. Nature healed me.

Don't Stop Believing -Dec 2015

After four months, I returned to Kentucky renewed. Certified in reiki and aroma touch, I started a business, only to find out I had DCIS breast cancer. The doctor said it was an act of God it was found. A mastectomy, bronchitis, and medicines made me lethargic and numb. My relationship ended, my business was put on hold, and I grieved. My rapid healing bewildered doctors. I attribute this to God, natural healing remedies, and an outpouring of love. My ex-husband's wife even supported me, making breast cancer pillows to donate to the hospital. A gift of unconditional love. A week following my mastectomy, my doctor allowed me to drive to meet Dora and Christina in person. A very emotional event. I even shared my breast cancer story in *Roots of Holiday Grief*, a collaborated book with Dora, Christina, and other grief coaches.

My mom said she would die if she had to have her breasts removed. Little did she know she too had a cancerous spot she wouldn't have checked. Two years later she passed away from breast cancer, not knowing until a week before she died that it spread through her body. I have had my share of sorrow, but nothing prepared me for this. The day she found out the diagnosis, I heard fear in her voice when she said 'I love you' twice. Her voice was also filled with real love. I waited my whole life to hear those words mean something.

Before becoming so ill, my mom lived in a personal care home. Bingo became an event she wouldn't miss, which was something the Witnesses would have scolded her for. Her childlike joy with her rebellious new passion. She didn't like our visits to end, saying I was the only positive thing in her life despite having the support of Witnesses. I was able to forgive, she done the best she could with the knowledge she was taught. She was seeing a different world from the love of the staff and the residents.

Don't give up on your loved ones. You never know when love will break through their hard shell.

In her last moments, it was touching seeing my daughter feed her, like she had once fed my daughter. I was also triggered seeing Witness family who had disowned me. My elder cousin came with his suit and bible to pray with Mom while looking straight at me and not speaking. After, I held her in my arms, seeing her true spirit and love in her eyes. My sister, who was shunned, had the final words 'I love you' before she took her last breath. Forgiveness and unconditional love, something Mom was never taught. I felt sad and angry losing out on the years we couldn't connect. I journeyed out west for four months, to heal in nature the lingering pieces of grief. My sister and I converted my Astro Van, complete with a bed, sink and solar panel. Finding myself most comfortable with misfits, lost souls, and crossing paths with ex-witnesses trying to find their way and heal. Realizing we are all connected and aren't alone.

Set Free

I was at one of the darkest times of my life when a prayer was answered, and I found Susan and Dora. When feeling all alone, be open to your life changing drastically. It's never too late to start over. Don't be afraid to investigate your talents and unique gifts to offer the world. During my first painting class, I thought *I'm not artsy like my daughter.* In two hours, I had created one of my most prized possessions. I continued getting outside my comfort zone, with journeys across the country, running a 5K, scuba diving, going on cruises, seeing unexpected sights like whales migrating in California, meeting life-changing people, and learning so much about myself all the while.

I'm continually discovering who I am and what I enjoy. I feel so free having the choice to create the life I want. I could never return to a fear-based religion. My life altering choices has been worth the sacrifices to create a life I love. One of my greatest challenges was learning to love and believe in myself, and that I'm worthy of being happy. Grief has grown me to help others like Dora helped me. I felt the fear and did it anyway, escaping my cocoon. What is your story and hidden purpose that is waiting to be fulfilled?

Chapter 16

Rebuilding from the Rubble

Building a new life after my foundation in Mormonism crumbled.

by Terina Maldonado

*"Owning our story can be hard but not nearly as difficult
as spending our lives running from it. Embracing our
vulnerabilities is risky but not nearly as dangerous
as giving up on love and belonging and joy—the
experiences that make us the most vulnerable. Only
when we are brave enough to explore the darkness
will we discover the infinite power of our light."*
~ Brene Brown

It's a beautiful winter morning; the sun is warm in the Arizona desert. As I sit down to write this chapter I'm watching my children play, and I'm overwhelmed at the peace of this moment. I sip on a hot chai tea, a delicious cup of freedom that was once forbidden from my life. My children will never be bound down by such arbitrary man-made rules proclaimed to be from God. I envy the life that lies before them, free of religion. I reflect on my life in comparison to what they have experienced in their brief travels on earth. I had lived through so much trauma by the age of 18 as a survivor of child abuse and sexual assault, I never imagined experiencing another trauma that could meet or even exceed the impact those had on my life. Yet, as I found my belief in the Mormon religion unraveling, my faith crisis and loss of my community turned out to be just that. Having the spiritual foundation for my entire life crumble beneath me was absolutely devastating, leaving me with the all-too-familiar aftershocks. Every trauma I've survived hit me so hard, it took the breath out of my life. Each time, I lost the desire to fight to get that breath back. The task of healing and rebuilding would seem overwhelming; the thoughts of life being too hard, the pain being too great, and family being better off without me would enter uninvited into my mind. At this point, you might be wondering why I would say the shift in my belief system has been more difficult to heal from than child abuse and sexual assault. I promise you will not be left wondering for long.

Just as I am a survivor of child abuse and sexual assault I am a survivor of a high demand religion. As a survivor I am breaking cycles of abuse and trauma for my children. That is what I held onto as I traversed this journey out of Mormonism.

My Mormon Foundation

I was born and raised a member of the Church of Jesus Christ of Latter Day Saints. I have ancestors who crossed to the West Coast of the United States with the early members of the church on my Dad's side of the family. My Mom was a convert, the first in her family to join the church. Growing up, I was proud of my mom and my pioneer ancestors, and thankful for their courage and strength.

As a child growing up in an abusive home, I assumed my life was normal. But we weren't normal. Not only were we different because we were Mormon, but we were different from our fellow Mormons as well. Not until adulthood was I even able to identify and label what I endured as a child as abuse. I spent a lifetime feeling like I didn't quite belong, either in my birth family or church family.

Nevertheless, I followed the rules and path laid out for me by my Mormon Faith with diligence. I desperately wanted love and acceptance from my parents. I wanted Heavenly Father to be pleased with my decisions. What I wanted above all was happiness, the everlasting joy that was promised to me if I was obedient to the laws and commandments I had been blessed with. I cherished being one of Heavenly Father's most faithful and noble spirits. It was amazing to me that of all the people in the world, I was lucky enough to be part of God's one true church. Sure, everyone had portions of the truth, but we, WE had it all, his whole plan, the fullness of truth. I felt truly blessed, and was determined to do my best to show my gratitude by earning the greatest blessings God had to offer.

My journey on the straight and narrow path leading to eternal exaltation inevitably led me to the temple doors. The temple, a place I had been taught about since I was a toddler. I had sung songs about going there someday. I was promised keys to entering the highest degree of heaven in those hallowed halls. It was there that I was sealed to my husband for time and all eternity. Because we had stayed strong and remained worthy to enter those holy doors, we were promised our children would also be with us eternally in the presence of God. After growing up in a home full of turmoil and fear I was looking forward to starting my own family that would be full of love that would last for eternity. It was in that sacred building I found so much peace in the stillness it provided. However alongside the spiritual highs and insights I experienced while at the temple, I also had a front row seat to the sexism that permeates the LDS church in general. I was left to wonder why it was necessary for me to promise to obey my husband but no such requirement existed for him to obey me? Why did I have to put a veil over my face? Why was it only men who prayed and led the temple sessions? Why could a woman use the priesthood within the temple walls, but in everyday life, that special gift and power was exclusively used by men? Why is the priesthood practically synonymous with leadership? Is a woman not capable of communicating with God and leading, helping, and serving others in the same way a man is?

As the years passed and I continued to go to the temple, I was provided with peace, yes, but also questions. I wondered— is a secret handshake really required to be in the presence of God? I understood the purpose of symbolism, but why does Heavenly Father require us to wear such weird garb here? Do my sacred garments really offer protection to me? Is it really possible for underwear to channel divine protection? Why is paying 10% of your income such a hard line requirement to be admitted to the temple? I knew good people who were denied temple recommends because they chose to feed their family rather than pay their tithing. Sure, many of these outward expressions are supposed to demonstrate an inward faith, but couldn't Heavenly Father see inside, know the commitment and intentions of these peoples' hearts? Yes the temple provided peace, but it also provided questions. I was proficient at letting these questions leave as quickly as they came. I did not dwell on them; they could not help me. They were probably from Satan. I chose to have faith.

All in all, I managed to fit into the box of Mormonism fairly well. But I noticed not everyone did. When a recent acquaintance of mine left the church, I felt drawn to ask her why she did so. Perhaps it was the fact that our relationship was not intimate that made me feel comfortable asking her, knowing there was not as much risk involved. She mentioned the church's stance on homosexuality and then shared the shelf analogy with me. "You know the questions you don't have answers to? The ones you tell yourself you'll I'll ask Heavenly Father about later, or that you'll find the answers in the next life because not everything's meant to be understood in this life? You put those on a shelf and forget about them. Well, my shelf got too heavy and it broke," she explained. After our conversation, I thought about my "shelf." At first, I thought I didn't have one. Then I realized what she'd said about how the church treats people who are LGBTQ and its teachings about homosexuality were actually items weighing heavily on my shelf. My next thought though was, "but that's it! That's the only thing on my shelf!" I decided from this woman's response that she just didn't have enough faith and was just not strong enough to trust in God.

It pains me now to think how easily I swallowed all the lies I was told. If I'm honest with myself, I had lots of doubts. I saw many things that I thought were wrong. Despite that, I did what I was taught. I had faith. But eventually, I had to decide between what is faith and what is blindly following?

The Truth That Showed Me It Was Not True

I had spent much of my life serving in various church leadership positions, also known as callings, starting at age 12 as a Beehive class president. I loved serving and connecting with people in my ward family. I loved the feeling of being needed that those callings provided. I felt a sense of honor knowing my Heavenly Father trusted me in positions of influence. While I was serving in a leadership calling as the secretary for the Relief Society in my ward, I had a life altering conversation. The presidency was meeting together on a Sunday after church. With my family left at home I went to discuss the women in our ward and how we could help them. After our meeting one of the other women in the presidency asked, "have you guys read the new book *Saints*? It has some interesting stuff in it." I had not read it, but I knew about it and wanted to. The way she said "it has interesting stuff in it," piqued my interest. So, I moved *Saints* to the top of my reading list. Boy, did it *ever* have some interesting stuff. This book produced by my own church had things in it I'd never heard before, or if I had heard about them, I had assumed they were anti-Mormon lies. As I read about Joseph Smith's treasure digging, illegal banks, a seer stone in a hat, and polygamy, I felt very unsettled. All of this information was presented in a very faith promoting manner, but it did not increase my faith. As I read, I knew there had to be more information that would explain these things better; there *had* to be more information with good explanations, because what I read did not feel right. It did not bring the spirit into my heart— it brought confusion and doubt.

After I finished *Saints*, I knew I had to talk to my husband about the things I had read. I was nervous to tell him. In our marriage, I had always been the strong one, the faithful one. I was scared if I expressed doubts, he would feed them instead of reinforcing my faith. Or what if the opposite happened? What if I told him and he told me I was misinterpreting things and needed to have faith and not question? What if this information led one of us out of the church, but not the other? Despite these fears, I knew there was no way I could carry on as normal with so many questions. I told him about the book and how it had not exactly been a faith-promoting experience for me. I let him know how sure I was that there were good explanations, and I just needed to do some more research. I made it clear I was looking for answers to support my faith. He was supportive and encouraging, and even mentioned something someone had told him about called the CES Letter that he had wanted to research himself. So together, we decided to dig a little deeper into our lifelong religion.

I began a faithful search for answers, only interested in church-approved materials. From somewhere in the back of my memory, I remembered hearing about the Gospel Topic Essays. After some searching, I found them on the church's website. The first two were easy reads, nothing new or controversial was mentioned as I read about how Mormons are Christians and that we believe we can become like God. I started out reading on my phone but quickly realized that was not going to work. The essays had many footnotes, I wanted *all* the information, so I intended to follow every one. But on my phone, many of them were broken links or not available and had to be read on a desktop. I ended up reading all of them obsessively. I had never before spent as much time in my Gospel Library App and lds.org studying church history. I followed every footnote reading before and after what was actually referenced to try and get as much context as possible. For the next week, I was tethered to my computer. Reading all of the essays was completely consuming. As I read, I was shocked. The history presented in these essays was not what I had been taught my entire life. I began to pray harder than ever before to know the truth. My everyday life as a mother of three kids derailed as I spent hour after hour reading. My house went to shambles, and my kids spent a lot of time watching TV as everything not essential to our survival was forgotten. With each word I read, my heart broke a little more. Not only was the information in the essays disheartening I noticed that a lot of the most troubling information was in the footnotes as if it was being hidden in plain sight.

Every night, my husband and I would stay up sharing the things we had learned about our church. Some of them were weird, some unbelievable, some awful, all of it heartbreaking. I prayed to find something, anything, that would make these things okay. With each essay I read, and each new truth revealed to me by the church's own website, I began feeling more and more uneasy. I finally found the courage to say to my husband the thought I had been avoiding. With a trembling voice, I asked, "What if the church isn't true?" Oh, how those words made my heart ache. He seemed to conclude the church was not true, I was not ready to accept that. Even with all this new information, I continued to pray, "Please let it be true." I still held out hope for anything to hold onto, as literally everything I had been taught was crumbling and disappearing. I kept reading, sure that I would find something that would make everything ok. Surely, there was something that explained it all.

I asked our family to please pray for us. My husband and I attended the temple, but it only added to the confusion, increased our doubts, and with new information added yet more questions. I left not having found the solace and comfort I was seeking. I didn't have the peaceful feeling I had always felt before.

With every new bit of information, I clung to my faith. I remembered the moments I had felt the spirit confirming the truthfulness of the gospel to me. When my husband asked me what I thought about all we were learning, I replied, "We've been told to doubt our doubts." By that time, it felt like much more than doubts. I had evidence staring me in the face. My heart begged me to find a way to take that evidence and white wash it with faith, but my mind knew this was not right. There were so many things I could accept not understanding, because

God works in mysterious ways, and Joseph Smith was just a man who was flawed and human. These spiritual coping mechanisms somewhat calmed my mind for a moment, until I read the story of Hellen Mar Kimball. Not only is her story heartbreaking to me, it was triggering. As I read of how Helen, a young teen bride of Joseph's, was manipulated and taken advantage of, I saw myself as a child, trusting my parents despite the fact they did not protect me. I saw a sexual predator taking advantage of his prophetic power to manipulate and abuse people. *Sexual predator.* Once I saw that the tactics and behavioral patterns of Joseph Smith matched those of all predators, namely grooming and manipulation, I knew he was not a prophet. Yes, all God has to work with on this earth is imperfect people, but God would not choose a sexual predator. My husband is a better man than Joseph Smith was, even though he is just a man with imperfections. He does not prey on women, children, and those whom he has power over. He is a good man. God would choose a good man. The more I read about Joseph Smith, the more I realized he was not a good man, let alone a man of God. He was not the person God would have chosen to supposedly do more for the world that any one save Jesus himself.

Oh, how I had respected, revered, and loved Joseph Smith! To learn his true nature was catastrophic for my life. I had been so sure just a week prior to discovering Joseph's seduction scandals that I was a member of Heavenly Father's one true church. Just one week! How could everything completely unravel so quickly? In one week, I went from having a burning testimony and so much faith, to knowing it was all a fraud.

During this time of personal anguish, we were anticipating General Authority and Church Historian Steven E. Snow (the perfect person to discuss these things with) coming to our stake conference. With every tattered thread of faith and hope I had left, I reached out to the stake president to see if my husband and I might be able to meet with him. I prayed so hard and pled with the Lord, "please let us be able to meet him so he can answer our questions and calm my troubled heart." I also enlisted a few family members to pray for us to be able to meet with him. Despite our earnest efforts, we were not granted a meeting to discuss our concerns with Elder Snow. We did, however, get to chat with him for a few minutes after the meeting where he spoke. In our conversation, he said exactly what I had prayed and hoped he wouldn't: "We have to remember Joseph Smith was an imperfect man and have faith." Those words broke. my. heart. I began to cry, slowly accepting I had received the answer to my prayers and it was not the one I had pled for. He left us with his card to reach out to him in an email, which I did. His response did not provide any answers or comfort. My last hope had officially been shattered. Where was God? If this was his one true church, why didn't he give me the answers I needed? The answer was finally clear— it was not God's one true church.

I felt like my most intimate friend had died, although I have never had a friend as intertwined in my life as the church was. In the mornings, I would wake up and a tidal wave of grief would hit me as everything I had learned would come flooding back, leaving me devastated. I was in denial, hoping that the new truth I knew could somehow disappear, but it remained and still remains, forever documented in history and in my mind.

Devastated and heartbroken, I was left knowing only that God loved me and that my husband and I would be ok. I thank God every day that he and I have gone through this transition together. I'm thankful we both chose each other over a religion, and were brave enough to look at the facts and information honestly together and together walk away from the only life we'd known. His love and support helped me make it through one of the hardest thing I've experienced thus far in my life. Recovering from child abuse and sexual assault were incredibly difficult, but as I navigated through those I trusted myself, I still had a foundation to stand on. This was like I was standing in the rubble of my life, not trusting myself to know where to begin the task of rebuilding it.

In order to move on we felt we had to do it officially, and went as a couple to meet with our good and kind Bishop. I poured out my aching soul to him. I sobbed in his office as we shared what we had learned. I told him I didn't go looking for this information, in fact, the opposite—I was looking to strengthen my testimony. I wasn't tired of all the rules and looking for an easy out; I wasn't committing major sins and too lazy to repent. The thought of not wearing my garments made me heartsick. Thinking about drinking coffee or alcohol made me incredibly ill. I was not excited to not have to pay tithing. I was **devastated**!!! I was absolutely crushed. This poor, good man also had no response beyond, "Just have faith." With tears streaming down my face, I asked to be released from my calling. This was a clear message: "we are done, and will no longer be involved in the church. We have seen it for what it is and are walking away." In two weeks, I had gone from a position of leadership, respect and admiration, a woman in good standing and full faith in the church, to an apostate.

Owning My Truth

The next day, I felt so much lighter. My soul had been in complete turmoil as I desperately searched for anything to hold onto, anything to make what I had learned ok. After so much prayer, fasting, scripture reading, and attending the temple, we decided to leave the church and had conveyed that to our Bishop. After that, my heartfelt peace. It was still broken; I was still saddened to my core, but I found peace.

After we left the church, I realized how completely ignorant I had been of the pain and devastation of a faith transition. I had no clue how hard it would be to leave the church. I joined a support group on Facebook called Mormon Enlightenment for those who have left the Mormon religion. There I read story after story of those who had decided to leave. Not one of those stories was absent of pain, grief, and tremendous loss. I decided to write a blog post about our family's decision to leave. My main intent was to help true believing members understand in some small measure what those of us who had left the church were going through in a non-threatening way.

I do not regret the decision to share our story publicly, and I never have, though I'll admit that sharing it in such a vulnerable way certainly added a layer of difficulty to an already impossible situation, a situation I was unprepared for. I was even less prepared for what came next.

I had heard about people being treated badly when they left the church, but I didn't think it would be an issue for me. I knew my friends. They were good, they were kind, and they would surely treat me with love. That is what I thought, what I hoped, and for the most part, I was right. But those who were less than kind and loving cut me to the core with their words. Many of the people who commented, and reached out to me were doing so with good hearts, without knowing their words stung. I was surprised to have to defend myself. Not only did I have to explain my decision to leave, I also had to try to explain my new beliefs before I even knew what they were. "If you don't believe in the church any more, what do you believe now?" people asked. Did they not realize my entire foundation had just crumbled?! I didn't know anything!

Some people made it clear that my leaving the church meant I was also leaving them. I was told I had completely insulted people by sharing my new truth. I was even told I was only a beautiful person who brings light to the world *because* of the church. How dare I defame the organization that once brought me such joy and happiness? I was asked, "How could someone as smart as you fall for this?" My husband was told, "If Terina can leave the church so easily, what makes you think she'll stay with you?" I was told I had been deceived by Satan. People told me, "Even God's most noble, great, and elect will be led astray in the last days; don't let yourself be led astray!" I was told I was wrong, making a mistake, and would come to regret my decision to leave. I was told multiple times I was breaking someone's heart with my decision. I was begged to reconsider, to stay in the boat, hold on a little longer, and just have faith. Even harder to accept than the hurtful words was the silence. With the exception of only a couple friends, all my church-based relationships have silently disappeared. The loss of community was profound. Not only was I navigating one of the most challenging and confusing times of my life, I was doing it without the support system that had always been there for me and with me, regardless of what I was going through or where I was in the world.

Rebuilding

I remember one day of my post-Mormon life being particularly hard. The task of rebuilding the foundation for my life, my marriage, my parenting, and my beliefs was overwhelming. I started to pray, "Dear Heavenly Father..." then stopped. The words were caught in my throat behind a dam of tears. The pain was too great, and the tears broke through the dam. I sobbed, ugly crying at its ugliest. One question kept swirling around in my brain, — how, *how*, HOW? How do I do this? How do I make it through one of the hardest times of my life without the things that have gotten me through the hardest times in my life?

While healing from child abuse and sexual assault, the comfort of prayer, the stillness of the temple, and the ability to turn my pain over to Jesus had always been the main bandages I'd used to bind my broken heart back together. I had relied heavily on the concept of Jesus' grace as I found acceptance and peace in my life. Not only did I no longer believe there was a heavenly power to turn my pain over to, but so many of the questions and pain from past trauma came rushing back. If what made those life-altering experiences bearable before was no longer there, could I still be okay, and if so, how?

How? The continuous, burning question that caused an ache that burned down into my soul. How would I survive when I didn't have a Heavenly Father to comfort me? How would I make it through without a Savior to take away my pain?

In the midst of all the sorrow and sobbing, a thought came to me—, if it isn't true now, it wasn't true before. If a loving, intervening Heavenly Father doesn't exist now, he didn't exist then. If there is no miracle balm for my sorrows now, there wasn't before. This means I've always had the power to navigate the biggest, hardest moments of life on my own. The power to overcome has always been within me. The ability to forgive and release the pain and hurt was and is within me. It has always been inside me. I have always possessed the ability, but never recognized it because I believed I was not strong enough on my own, being told I required divine intervention. Perhaps I do require divine intervention, but it is my own divine power. I slowly began to once again trust myself.

This realization was a major turning point for me as I navigated my faith transition. I started to analyze, meditate, and ponder. The question "how?" was no longer overwhelming; it became intriguing and exciting.

Just as I had found a safe place to grieve and heal from previous traumas, I found spaces to process all that I had lost and was rebuilding outside of Mormonism. I found people who had been through the same experience and knew what I was going through; I found a couple of amazing support groups for those who had chosen to leave Mormonism. They provided community, wisdom, and hope.

In my support groups, I saw so much trauma. I know trauma, know what it feels like, what it looks like. Trauma and I are all too well acquainted. It is easy to see reflected in others what you have experienced and are so familiar with yourself. I could hear it in their words and I saw the pain I felt on their faces. Part of what makes trauma so damaging is the secrecy shrouding it. Trauma carries a blanket of shame that makes you believe if you wrap yourself up in it, you will be safe and protected. The truth is, that blanket traps you, suffocates you, and will kill your soul. When we share our stories, we release the shame they hold over us. I took baby steps in sharing my story of child abuse, only doing so with safe people. The more I shared it, the more I healed. Sharing the story of my assault with safe people also greatly aided in my healing process. I then found safe people to share the trauma of leaving Mormonism. As we sat, belly to belly, heart to heart, and shared our stories of discovery and leaving the church, together we healed. As we shared our stories we unwrapped the blanket of shame and wrapped each other in love and acceptance. This shedding of shame and embracing of love brought life to my healing.

It was in those groups that I was able to express the stages of grief I was going through without the fear of judgment. I could rant and spew my anger, allowing myself to rage when I learned about things like how many instances of sexual abuse there are within the church, and how it shocked and disgusted me. Even more outrageous was the cover-up of the abuse that was orchestrated by leaders of the church. I discovered that the hotline provided to bishops for guidance when they learn about the sexual abuse of one of their congregants connects directly to the church's attorneys. It doesn't go to a counseling service or to other trained professionals to help guide a victim to resources for healing; it goes to a law office with the interest of protecting the church's image. I read about so many women being sexually abused and assaulted, and just like I had done, they repented for what happened to them. This brought up so many new emotions in regard to my sexual assault. I once again felt victimized and was staggering beneath the weight of my pain. I realized that the purity culture of the church had a profound influence on my life. Because of the church's teachings and my lack of understanding on the matter, I didn't even realize I had been assaulted until years after it happened. The same church that had guided my decisions since I was old enough to make them had betrayed not only me, but so many others. As hard as it was to accept and process all of this, it did fit with what I had learned from the uncensored version of church history. I couldn't help but wonder how a church founded by a sexual predator could even pretend to be a safe place for vulnerable women and children?

Maybe none of the church's many abuses of power should have been all that surprising, considering the patriarchy of the church is, above all, a breeding ground for narcissistic men. I had seen how many Mormon men were abusive to their families. The church sees men as the head of the household and the leader of the family, specifically the one who holds the priesthood and communicates God's will to everyone within his stewardship, which can leave a family in a very vulnerable position. The control and manipulation justified as means to make it to the celestial kingdom as an eternal family became clear. It wasn't just men who were part of the problem either; people who loved their religion more than their families were a dime a dozen. All of the mind games disguised as love only confirmed for me how toxic a place the church can be.

While I wouldn't wish abuse of any kind on anyone, I am grateful for the coping skills for healing from trauma and learning to thrive that I acquired as a result of mine. I began to implement those skills consciously in my life, while also realizing I had to allow myself space to grieve. Our society often limits expressions of grief for the death of someone close to us. The truth is, we experience loss in many areas of our lives. The loss of my religion, my foundation, was definitely something I needed to mourn. I gave myself permission to feel all my emotions as I visited all the stages of grief multiple times. Grief more often feels like spinning in a hamster wheel than it does a one-time climb up a set of stairs. Around we go, from anger, to denial, to bargaining, to depression, and then, once we think we've found acceptance, we step off the wheel, only to learn something new and be thrown right back on it. After running on the wheel of grief for a time, I knew I had to get off. I had to remember the tools and skills I had developed. I had to become less involved in the post-Mormon world and work on embracing the outside world and all it has to offer without the cloud of Mormonism hanging over it all the time.

Tools for Healing

For me, gaining an understanding and educating myself on the psychology of my offenders and my own lived experience has been very helpful. I had researched abusive parents, toxic families, overcoming child abuse, sexual assault wounds, and healing from trauma. That information helped me to heal, so I decided my next step would be to study religious trauma. Just as with previous traumas I had endured, once I was able to see and identify my experiences as trauma, I was then able to begin healing from them. When people would try to minimize what I had been through, I could go back to the research and point out that not only were my experiences and emotions valid, but had also been experienced by enough people to have been given a name: Religious Trauma Syndrome. There have been many people who have healed and are thriving after religious trauma such as Dan Reynolds of Imagine Dragons. I knew I would be one of them.

One of the most confusing things for me to process was the spiritual witnesses I had received of the truthfulness of the church and the spiritual experiences I'd had. If those were not from God, where were they from? If I had been so sure of Mormonism's truth claims because of my experiences and feelings, how could I trust myself ever again? I felt so alone and lost. No longer did I have the comfort of prayer or the companionship of the Holy Ghost, not to mention how my religious community had completely abandoned me. I had relied on the spirit to guide my decisions throughout my life, and as a result, had lost trust in my own inner voice. The "spirit" I had followed for all of my life up until that point had betrayed me and kept me on a path full of lies and toxic doctrine.

While perusing YouTube one day, I found a video called *Spiritual Witnesses*. It showed person after person bearing the same testimony of the truthfulness of their religion. Each expressed their beliefs with the same conviction I had once possessed. Such surety, without any doubt, all given to them through divine means. God had spoken to each of them, giving them a sense of peace and a sure knowledge that they were on the right path. I was not completely ignorant of other faiths while still active in the church; I knew there were people who were deeply converted to their religion and intensely faithful. I had always written them off because I knew I had the *full* truth. There is truth in all things, so of course they felt the spirit; it was bearing witness to truth, but only a small portion of the truth.

Now, here I was, knowing what I had thought was the fullness of the gospel, the whole truth, was in fact, lies. So, why had I felt so strongly my church was the truest one, and why did others experience the same thing? I found information on what is called elevation emotion. I read about the brain's ability to manufacture emotions, especially when they are strongly desired. Let's be honest, no one wants to be the only one in church who doesn't *know* that it is true. As a child, I was instructed on how to receive such a witness for myself; that is where the foundation of my testimony started, with those experiences as a child. Looking back, I had to ask myself, "Would I expect my own children to be able to discern truth at such an impressionable age, with so much pressure on them to conform?" With objective reflection, the answer was no. I knew I should not judge my own childhood experiences and how they influenced my adult decision making any more harshly than I would judge my own children. The same goes for decisions I made or continue to make that have been influenced by the abuse I endured as a child. I have found forgiveness and acceptance for my ignorance. I've acknowledged it was my damaged parts that made decisions that were not in my best interest. I've accepted that just because I trusted my feelings and they led me astray did not mean they were completely untrustworthy. I knew as I healed, the damaged parts of me would no longer influence my decisions and life. I knew I could overcome the trauma and damage I had sustained in a life of religious abuse. Just as I had overcome and healed before, I knew I would be whole once again.

I also acknowledged there were many times my soul, my own divine intuition, had tried to tell me the truth about my former beliefs. I experienced this as cognitive dissonance, a term I had never heard of prior to leaving the church. As I read and learned about how a person may feel unsettled and confused when presented with facts and information that contradict their beliefs, I knew I had felt that way myself many times. I had chosen to ignore my own instincts and listened to "the Lord's anointed" because I'd believed that God knew better than me. After all, that was part of faith—putting aside doubts and desires and following the path God had laid out for me. I realized I was following others who were leading me down a path littered with lies and harmful teachings when what I needed to do was learn to trust and listen to my own intuition. This has turned out to be much easier to do than I had originally thought it would be. Learning to trust myself has been liberating. Finding the ability to turn inward with questions has led to great spiritual growth. I have found if I listen to my higher self, the God within me, I have the answers. When the answers are unclear, I now know how to discern them, by looking to those I trust and asking for their opinions and advice. Rather than blindly accepting *their* insights, wisdom, and intuition, though, I look at and examine them, and use that information to make my own decisions. It has been powerful to let go of so-called holy voices and trust my own.

The experience of leaving a high demand religion can be encompassed with fear. It has been said that one of the greatest human fears is that of the unknown. When my life was interwoven with the religion I was born into, the picture of what living without it would look like was a completely blank slate. In addition to the fear of the unknown, I also had to face the fear associated with Religious Trauma Syndrome. My entire life, I had been taught the only way to find true happiness and joy was to live the gospel and follow the prophet. I had been taught the best foundation for a marriage was on the principles of the church. I had been taught being a good parent was keeping my children on the straight and narrow path. By leaving the church, I was not just leading my children off that path, but telling them the path we'd all been taking was wrong. I knew all about fear; it had been steadily ingrained into me.

I have found mindfulness to be my antidote to fear. As I've shifted my focus from commandments and obedience to spirituality and love, I've found great value in savoring the moment. With honest reflection, I have come to realize faithful members of the church have about the same divorce rate as everyone else. Those who raised their children following the counsel of the Lord's anointed still found themselves navigating teen pregnancies, addiction, and criminal behavior. As I looked at the lives of everyone around me, there was no denying they had happiness and joy, and mine had not been greater than theirs because I'd worn sacred underwear. Hard times and challenges are not a punishment from God, and they are not because we are doing anything wrong. They happen because we are living, and it comes with the territory. I felt a great sense of serenity as I learned to let go of yesterday, leave tomorrow for when it comes, and be present in the now.

As I began to look objectively at the organization I had dedicated my life to, it became easier to overcome feelings of shame and self-hatred. I realized it truly is a corporation, and not a church led by God. Not only is it a corporation, it is a corrupt one that is hurtful and damaging to so many. Once I accepted that, I wondered if all religious organizations were corrupt. I wanted to place a pantopic judgment on all religious organizations, to label all believers as blind and unenlightened. However, I was also aware of what a hypocrite that would make me. As I left the church, I pleaded for people to continue to hold space for me, to love me. How could I dare to not offer the same for my family, friends, and fellow humans walking this earth alongside me? As much as my heart broke during my transition out of Mormonism, since then, it has grown even more. I've let go of the elitism I didn't realize I was carrying. Although I've always been a non-judgmental person, I've learned to extend respect and genuine love to those with varying views and lifestyles than my own without thoughts that I can respect them but their decisions are wrong. To this day, it can still be difficult for me to hold space and offer love to those who remain in the religion I once called my own. I am practicing and improving in this practice daily. When leaving organized religion behind, I also wanted to distance myself from the toxic ideology that came with it. This has meant embracing love and letting it lead me.

As I have embarked on the journey of rebuilding my life from the rubble left after my research into Mormonism, I was determined to find the Truth, with a capital T. It turns out, truth is relative. So now, my search is for *my* truth. I search for goodness, love and light, wherever it may be.

Initially, it was so difficult letting go of the security that comes with having all the answers. From a young age, I could tell you why we're here on earth, where we came from, and where we're going after this life ends. As I grew up, I could even give advice about what to do in times of trouble—how to overcome and endure hardship, the best way to ensure familial happiness, everyone's proper role within a family and society, and the superior stance on moral questions. With all of these "right" answers gone, I've learned to embrace uncertainty, and the fact that some questions don't have answers. Just as I previously explored the question "how?" with wonder, curiosity, and excitement, I've learned to ask life's big questions in the same way, letting go of the fear and resistance to the unknown and embracing it with reckless abandon.

True Freedom and Joy

The majority of my fears about how post-Mormon life would be have turned out to be unfounded. Our family is happy! My children are still full of joy, and have morals, a sense of right and wrong, and a desire to do good in our community. My husband and I have seen our relationship grow and have become stronger as we've navigated this transition together.

There has not been a moment of regret. I have found life to be so much more beautiful and fulfilling outside of Mormonism. I remember how others used to often say that following the rules and commandments bring true happiness and freedom. I now see how that statement was utterly inaccurate. True freedom is making your own choices free of fear and shame. I would never choose to go back or unlearn the things that lead me out of Mormonism and into true freedom.

Without leaving, I may have never learned to embrace my own potential, the strength I have within my own soul. I would never have had the audacity to claim to know what is best for me, or recognize that my spirit is whole on its own, without a need for repentance and redemption. Without leaving, there would be so many questions I never would have been compelled to ask.

Do not be afraid to ask the hard questions. Don't let fear keep you from searching for and studying the available information that provides unprejudiced facts. Having the religious foundation of my life crumble beneath me was completely devastating and heartbreaking, and I am so thankful! After clearing away the broken, toxic rubble, I have built a life that is even better than I could have imagined. I clung to the hope offered by those farther along the post-Mormon path than me that it would get better, and I'm so glad I trusted their experiences and knowledge. Now that I'm on the other side, I can truly testify that when you shed the guilt, shame, and toxic teachings of the church, you can more fully embrace the possibilities of a life filled with freedom, curiosity and love.

"Our job is not to deny the story, but to defy the ending—
to rise strong, recognize our story, and rumble with the
truth until we get to a place where we think, yes. This is
what happened. And I will choose how the story ends."
~ Brene Brown

Chapter 17

The Stories from The Same Planet

by Nesly Ann Brulee

"Keep the flight in mind, the bird may die."
~Ferruhzad

here are days when problems seem to be overwhelming. Challenges, too big to overcome. Stress, anxiety, sadness we all experience them don't we? When that happens sometimes I reflect on stories of people who would love to have my problems. Story of a lady who buried her child with her own hands. Another one who in order to save her 5 children end up killing them. Stories of refugees who lost everything and everyone. As they were overcoming traumas from war, their life had to start over. I'm sharing with you these stories to help you appreciate every day of your life as we all need a reminder of how lucky we really are with the problems we have.

Leyla

The First Travel of a Newborn Baby

A woman whom I assumed was my age, but later found out was twenty-eight when I read the news, a Syrian refugee, was seated in a wooden chair. The embroidered white cheesecloth covering her head made her face look plump and round. Her pale eyes looked almost nowhere. To the right of the photo frame was an x-ray device and a cardboard case which apparently came out of it. There was the image of the checkpoint at the entrance gate of Gaziantep State Hospital. My story, which sent me thousands of kilometres away from my homeland, started when this photo shattered the relationship I had with the truth.

No reality could be personal. I was the culprit.

As for the content of the news, I could not fully concentrate on anything again after reading it. The menus of the following days began to move away from satisfying my French, American and local customers who were accustomed to my sensibility. I devoted myself to putting together the missing pieces in the woman's story. It was not happening. I just couldn't get out of it.

Let's forget about the name. The Syrian woman, which I'll call Leyla, entered Turkey from Gaziantep Carchemish Border Gate while she was already two months pregnant. Her husband and three children died during a bombing, or that was what Leyla thought. She was also injured in this attack. Her right-hand little finger was broken and unjointed in such a way as to make an inverted V. As such, she had somehow walked alone. She had reached the border gate from her village which was 80 kilometres away from Turkey.

I even thought of adding a note to the menu board held by the chef's trinket that greeted the visitors at the entrance door of the restaurant: "Ladies and gentlemen, think about what Leyla has eaten on her journey which I can name a kind of death march. God damn you all complainers." They complain about food being too cold or served too slow. What about people like Leyla? She had no food at all.

She entered my country, and then went to Adana to work as a day labourer in cotton fields. When the time came and her pains started, she was taken to a hospital in Adana. You can just imagine how she must have felt when she realized her new born baby was not breathing.

Authorities said that she had to register the dead baby. The birth was to be reported. The problem was that the incident was to be reported to the relevant authorities in the province where the woman entered Turkey. This was the procedure to be followed. Thus, only two hours after bringing out a three kilo and seven-hundred gram creature, Leyla, my age, was discharged from the hospital with a dead baby in her arms.

In a shock about where to go and how to go without knowing a single word in Turkish or Kurdish, she arrived at the Adana bus terminal with the half-cleaned baby still covered with a fluid, no heartbeat, not breathing.

First, she put her baby in a bag that she found from the garbage and cleaned, and then put it in a bottle. A five gallon water bottle. She then settled in her seat numbered thirty-seven. She had only seventy-four liras and two hundred and fifty pennies. When the bus arrived in Gaziantep, it was very difficult for her to get out of the seat. Her bleeding did not stop, and the possibility of staining her seat with blood was the last thing she wanted right now. Life was in its usual flow, so, in order to tell the bus attendant who was also responsible for the cleaning what happened, she needed to know all the gestures and facial expressions in his mother tongue and to add some psychological intonation to her voice to arouse compassion. Her head leaned against the trembling window and indifferent to the scenic nature flowing extraordinarily, she rehearsed what to say for miles. Thank God, there was no blood on her seat.

On the other hand, Leyla was a smart enough woman to be aware of how the bus attendant looked at Syrian immigrants like herself. Perhaps, he was someone who had enough life experience to know that it would be unfair to expect a woman with a dead baby to be ashamed and to ask her clean the seat that she stained.

I don't know how much I messed it all up. I was also in the post-truth phase of my life, where reality lost its importance. The problem was that I could not help turning the incident into an inevitable tragedy, as the details I didn't know put pressure on me. The more I found pain in it, the more I was torturing myself. What Leyla was going through was one of the abuses that were always everywhere. Drama was all around. What was the point of worrying about someone new? As far as I know, things have not changed a bit in human history in the past ten thousand years. I could talk about Colombia, not Syria. She could be Gabriella, not Leyla. I could go back three or five hundred years and find dystopic elements that describe a hundred years later, but it was always the same. I had to tell something new, shed light on an unknown layer of human beings.

Just imagine those two pictures in your mind. First, people in a baby shower party celebrating the arrival of a baby, a mother complaining that the cookies were not baked enough and the name of the baby printed in blue instead of pink. There is another picture; Leyla with her just arrived baby.

The Mystery of a Survivor

Stop complaining about how hard you work or how your life is difficult...

In September 2015, I went to the United States at the invitation of the United States Department of Foreign Affairs. It was an intensive one-month program, starting in Washington DC and covering a total of 5 states.

The International Visitor Leadership Program (IVLP) is a professional exchange program funded by the U.S. Department of State's Bureau of

<u>Educational and Cultural Affairs</u>. The program is nomination only by staff at U.S. Embassies.

An official from the American Embassy contacted me and said that they examined my voluntary works on Child and Women's Rights and Refugees at the Bar in addition to my business life, and wanted to invite me to this program. They had given me a visa issued to diplomats, and I had arrived in Washington, D.C. with my suitcase carrying an autumn creation suitable for all seasons.

All 15 participants of the IVLP were exploring both America and our micro group with a bunch of great people from 15 countries in Europe, involving successful lawyers, journalists, activists and academicians. The biggest gift that the program brought to me was three gorgeous friends, Agusti, Hanna and Karin.

We had a meeting with the conservative Senator David Vitter in Washington DC. While Vitter's secretary was explaining that the Senator's "concrete wall on the border" project developed to prevent the forbidden transition from the Mexican border.

Pope John Paul II, who was in Washington DC at the same time with us, traveled to New York City on the same day with us. As a result we could not leave the hotel for hours for security reasons due to the religious ceremony held at the cathedral opposite our hotel at Rockefeller Center. What could this representative of earth under the auspices of God have to do with this wall of protection?

Finally, we met someone who knew Leyla's husband in an NGO in Lincoln Nevada. In fact, the man, whom I will call Ferid from now on, survived the bombardment.

While Leyla thought her husband and three children had died, Ferid also thought that Leyla and his children had died. However, the truth about the family was that three children died and the parents survived. Neither knew what actually happened. After the bombing, the town they lived in was captured by the opponents of the regime and the survivors could not return to the town again.

One does not lose his wife every day.

Being a Syrian in the two millennia more or less meant to be born from a mother and a father, live in peace for a while and wake up to the heart of a meaningless civil war.

To collect the remaining parts of the bodies of your loved ones here and there, to flee to Turkey if not killed, to fall into the hands of human traffickers or to be drowned in the dark waters of the Aegean Sea. Many who tried to cross the sea ended up completely losing the sense of direction in any coordinate point of the world and to die in agony.

Buying ticket to freedom

The milestones of the small and worthless story of Ferid and countless other people like him were laid precisely in this way. Ferid met a Syrian smuggler like himself in Istanbul. He worked in a polishing job in an aluminum workshop for six months.

Let me tell you what polishing job means. I had to know their personal adventures in order to write the expected report about the refugees. So, I did some detailed research on each refugee I spoke to. Ferid's story was one of the most painful.

Like its neighbour Iran, Turkey had rich mineral deposits in terms of aluminum. Therefore aluminum industry was quite developed. Many industrial sectors used aluminum as raw material. One of them was the construction sector and the carrier of the Turkish government's development model was the construction sector. Thus, immigrant cheap labor was mostly employed in the construction sector. Ferid worked as a polishing worker in the basement of a workshop in the organized industrial zone in Istanbul Dudullu, which made handrails of stairs to the residences.

His job was to rub the handrail pieces that came to him in crates against sandpaper strips rotated by a drum. He sanded joints, slotted plugs and coigns for hours. He disrupted the gridded structure of metal per square millimetre, thus making the metal shine. He wrapped his shattered palms with dirty shoddy pieces. Meanwhile, he breathed the metal particles leaping from the strips into the air. His teeth fell and he suffered partial permanent paralysis on his left leg caused by sitting.

In the circular issued by the professional organizations about the polishers' health, it was regulated that every polishing worker should drink a minimum of one litre of fresh milk daily. Ferid, of course, did not know about it. He had no value for anyone in this beautiful sphere.

A polishing worker would not be saved during fire.

He worked an average of fifteen hours a day, seven days a week, without taking a day off. He was sleeping in the shed on the roof of the building where the workshop was located. He had to economize. It was an obligation because there was no other way to save 4,000 euros that he had to pay to the human smuggler in order to move ahead to a more bearable life. His earnings increased according to the amount of the work he did.

This was called "piecework" there.

The need for money triggered the saving algorithm in his mind and put Ferid at a heavy pace where he would die of fatigue. I had a hard time understanding how someone who had lost his whole family and witnessed it could struggle to hold on to life so much. Finally, when his saving amounted to four-thousand and six-hundred euros, he turned off the counter.

That night he smoked his last marijuana with his ward mates. The next morning, a cold October day, he came to Turkey-Greece border. I report below what he went through afterwards, as taken from a news site. I leave it to your imagination what Ferid could have experienced with seventeen other refugees in a closed ISUZU truck safe in his last days.

"The corpses of 18 people who were thought to be refugees and died from lack of air in a truck. Only bodies abandoned on the A4 highway between Neusidl and Pandorf towns near Vienna, Austria were reached. Austrian Interior Minister Johanna Mitl-Leitner announced that 18 corpses found in an abandoned truck on the Austrian A4 Highway were estimated to be refugees. "Today is a black day for Austria," Leitner said in his statement. The bodies of the immigrants who died from lack of air in the cold storage of the two and a half-ton truck were said to have been waiting on the highway for five days.

Burgenland police chief and Interior Minister held a joint press conference. It was estimated that immigrants were taken from Serbia and brought to Austria via Hungary. Minister Leitner: "We think that immigrants come from Afghanistan and Syria. There are at least 10 children among them, and all of these children probably died due to lack of air. The tragedy that took place during the conference on the issue of the immigrant problem in the Northern Balkan Countries in Vienna shocked the participating leaders and the country."

As a speaker, I would present a paper at the conference.

I went to where Isuzu truck was. I was speechless. I can swear he smelled the terrible stench of corpse.

Decayed corpse instead of menthol. Smell from a group of people left to die on a highway in the heart of Europe."

Her Beloved Ones

A mother trying to save her children.

I suppose I was in primary school at that time. When Saddam Hussein invaded Kuwait, the rest of the world wanted to teach this Middle

Eastern dictator a lesson. The forces with considerable weapon stocks, especially the USA, joined hands and dropped 85,500 tons of bombs on Iraqi people. They shamelessly called the operation Desert Storm.

Oh, these American joker guys.

We had heard that Saddam had a guided missile called Scut. The whole Diyarbakır, a city in south east, talked about the range and influence of Saddam's missiles and, of course, Saddam Hussein's insanity that would set the world on fire. Missiles would fall into our city and we would all die from gas poisoning. Those who had the opportunity fled to their relatives in the west of the country, out of the reach of the Scut missile. Those who remained took whatever measures they could take. Almost everyone was drawn to their homes with sacks of bulgur, sugar, flour and a few cans of oil. Back then, tap water from the city's water supply network could be drunk.

Those taking extra caution insulated their windows thoroughly against radiation with box sealing tapes.

After a day or two, our city was shaken with the news of a widow. A poor woman living with her five young children. She'd fed her children, put them to sleep, and taped them in a way that they wouldn't get air from their throats after putting each of their heads in a plastic bag to protect them from a possible gas attack.

The children died, no missiles were launched in Diyarbakır, and Iraq is still burning as far as I know. I don't really know who's guilty here. Is it the mothers' ignorance? Saddam? America or Scut? The people of Iraq who elected him, or the Iraqi people who elevated him to a state of being the almighty?

Or is it me?

I don't know whom I'm going to blame for murders committed so smoothly, thanks to the airtight structure of nylon bag. I think if there is a crime, it must be God. Of course, if there is a God at all.

My mother must have been in her thirties, the same age with that woman at the time and surprisingly, she also had five children. It is again 2 different women close to each other with very different lives, one survived the other killed her children. Why this thing happens to some people? Why God does not prevent this? I was probably at the same age with one of the children who died. If they lived, one of them would be my peer. How meaningful it is to put myself in his or her shoes.

I don't know if mankind is a family, if everyone lives their own individual life. Is the truth independent of me? Is it an ontological process as such? As in that famous story, if a tree is knocked over in a forest that nobody knows, will the tree make any sound or not? Truth could not be created independent of the observer. I was the culprit.

I'm writing these lines, having just turned thirty eight far from my homeland and my mother tongue. Looking back, it seems that it is not possible to understand the whole story of humanity without feeling airless in that nylon bag, which was placed in the neck of five children, as a precaution.

Our Story

> *"No man is an island entire of itself; every man is*
> *a piece of the continent, a part of the main"*

I tried to tell you the stories of Leyla, Ferid and the five children who gave their last breath in a bag.

I had a happy childhood. I was coddled enough. I was loved much more than enough and I am still loved a lot, I feel it from thousands of miles away! I had the opportunity to create a comfortable cognitive space for myself.

My family had created an emotional safety zone that I could take shelter in no matter what happened to me.

Yes, it is a safe harbour where I can be protected against storms. I am thirty-eight years old, and I realize that the essence I have distilled from life, while I am so far from the culture and geography where I have begun to know myself, is to live in somewhere you feel in peace.

I had a good education and I had the chance to do what I wanted, which very few women would have in the Middle East. I've seen many countries in the world. I lived in Paris and London for a year or two. I learned how to make dessert from the most talented chefs of the planet. I taught how to make panna cotta to our middle eastern chefs who smoked with one hand while sticking kebab on skewers with the other. Thanks to my legal education, I worked with criminals, which is a rare chance. I had loving, devoted friends, which is also rare.

I am one of those who believe that foreigners are reliable.

I was an ordinary person, still I am. An ordinary person who has aesthetic concerns, having her nose broken in two places and fixed again as she didn't like it, persuading everyone of this operation while enduring the pain and spending thousands of liras for it. Life dragged me here. The story of life and losers.

I'm here in Canada because I don't want to act as the lead actress anymore. I want to have more options than life and death, like a worm does. Maybe this is possible here. This country gave me a new start in life that allowed me to grow and experiance life I would never have growing up in Turkey. I also discovered how I could grow my self-consciousness. I discovered different layers and now I want to feel them.

I used to whistle in the school toilet and recited bismillah, which means "in the name of God".

My mother used to say that if I whistled, I would gather the demons around. Music, of course, was a secular act that disrupted the divine timbre. And the only way to get rid of that devil was to mention the name of God. I used to play a 'call and dismiss' game with demons with my child mind. I am now here to explain that both the devil and the God are within us.

I started having problems planning my daily routine. I was planning my work for the day at every opportunity I had, and I was making the same list hundreds of times a day over and over again.

My best friend enlightened me by pointing to this act as an expression of excessive anxiety. This tension was partly due to the fact that I was a lawyer and partly because of the problems I had with the workers in my workplace, and I preferred to escape. As far as possible, that is to Canada. Just before I made this decision, I terminated my marriage. I left the city where I lived and moved to Istanbul, which is one of the most challenging city in the world. I enrolled in a master's program in international human rights law there and, unfortunately, after a semester, I quitted the program in the hope of getting at least a part of the annual tuition I paid. Of course, I couldn't get my money back. I was dragged here to Canada. And, as you can imagine, like every little girl whose father died, I felt all alone in the infinite coldness of the universe.

I immigrated to Canada, the country of my un-lived memories, my beloved one's land...

I was not a baby, I was not a teenager, I knew what was right and what was wrong. Before my father passed away, he thought me as much as possible. One of which was, how to be a good and honest business women. He never smoked and drunk but he got liver cancer. He was a great man and a lot people's hero. And mine too. I learned that we must cherish each moment with the loved ones we have. We don't know how many more we might get.

Never stop love and dreams

I have no idea what kind of surprises life has prepared for Leyla. Nor I know whether her pale gaze brightened later. She is probably trying to give birth as the second wife of a local man above seventy who has gone on pilgrimage seven times, has a dozen children and runs a grocery store under his house. What life offers her as a woman of outstanding beauty must be a routine consisting of washing a baby in the basin. I do not underestimate their regime of life, instead, I can even argue that they specifically form a line of resistance to the technological paradigm, and that this protects our planet. At least, carbon footprint values will confirm me. They are not my concern. I'm in the grip of more personal things.

I live here in Canada as my choice. Like all my other choices, this action is also a kind of combination of partly my preferences, partly the preferences of other people, and partly the consequences of the flow of nature or destiny and the most remarkable part is love. On a track where there are countless parameters, we are all dancers who fight for life and death as well as trying to show our skills if we have the opportunity. We have somehow got a choreography without a centre that controls us.

Like a flock of thousands of starlings dancing in the sky. Finally, we can display a rhythmic integrity.

We can install ultra-complex systems. We build cities. We destroy the masses.

We are all unique birds, and the lives of each of us are as valuable as the sum of the lives of other birds. If you ask me what I have achieved, let me say that I try not to disturb the flight of another bird with my wing.

I have learnt to never stop to love and dream. Someone always fed the love inside of me which I believe that connects me to the universe. This connection is linked to something infinite, we are coming from the same source and going to the same destination. Being human is a unique experience and we are all same no matter what we believe in or what we don't.

I know it will sound a bit cliché, but I feel like a poet who says,

"when the sea breaks off a piece of land,
something will be lost in me."
~ unknown

We look at others who have a better life than us. We might envy them. In a world where we constantly see a perfect life on social media, sometimes it's hard to remind ourselves of how great our life is. Our problems are someone else's dreams. There are countless of people who are risking their lives just to get to the country most people take for granted. We need those reminders. We need to hear of other stories that can help us see our life in a different perspective.

Life is not fair. But it doesn't mean it has to be in order to be magnificent.

I understand now that I also have to listen to your story in order to complete mine.

Conclusion

by Jack Grey

I spoke with hundreds of people who left their oppressive religion, relationship or organization they were part of. Many of them lost everything they had, including their own children, and as a result never fully recovered from it. Due to the enormous injustices they experienced, anger and resentment set in, taking away their happiness.

I often asked them this one question that changed it all: "If you believe your life was destroyed by your exit from the religion, why don't you just go back?"

None of them would. No matter what they've lost, no matter how high of a price they paid, not one would ever go back. Why? There is something about living authentically with freedom of thought and personal expression that is more precious than anything else. Going back and pretending we believe in something that we don't would equate to volunteering to live in prison. Just the thought made some people feel like they would have to sell their soul in order to go back. Others said they would rather live one day free than spend the rest of their life in a high-controlling religion.

One of the biggest challenges for people who walk out from oppression is to become comfortable with not knowing. We don't have all the answers. No one does. But we do know this:

We would rather have questions we cannot answer than have answers we cannot question.